SALFORD IN 50 BUILDINGS

CAROLE O'REILLY & PAUL RABBITTS

AMBERLEY

To everyone who loves the city of Salford and its wonderful buildings

First published 2019

Amberley Publishing, The Hill, Stroud
Gloucestershire GL5 4EP

www.amberley-books.com

British Library Cataloguing in Publication Data.
A catalogue record for this book is available from the British Library.

ISBN 978 1 4456 9422 1 (print)
ISBN 978 1 4456 9423 8 (ebook)

Typesetting by Aura Technology and Software Services, India.
Printed in Great Britain.

Contents

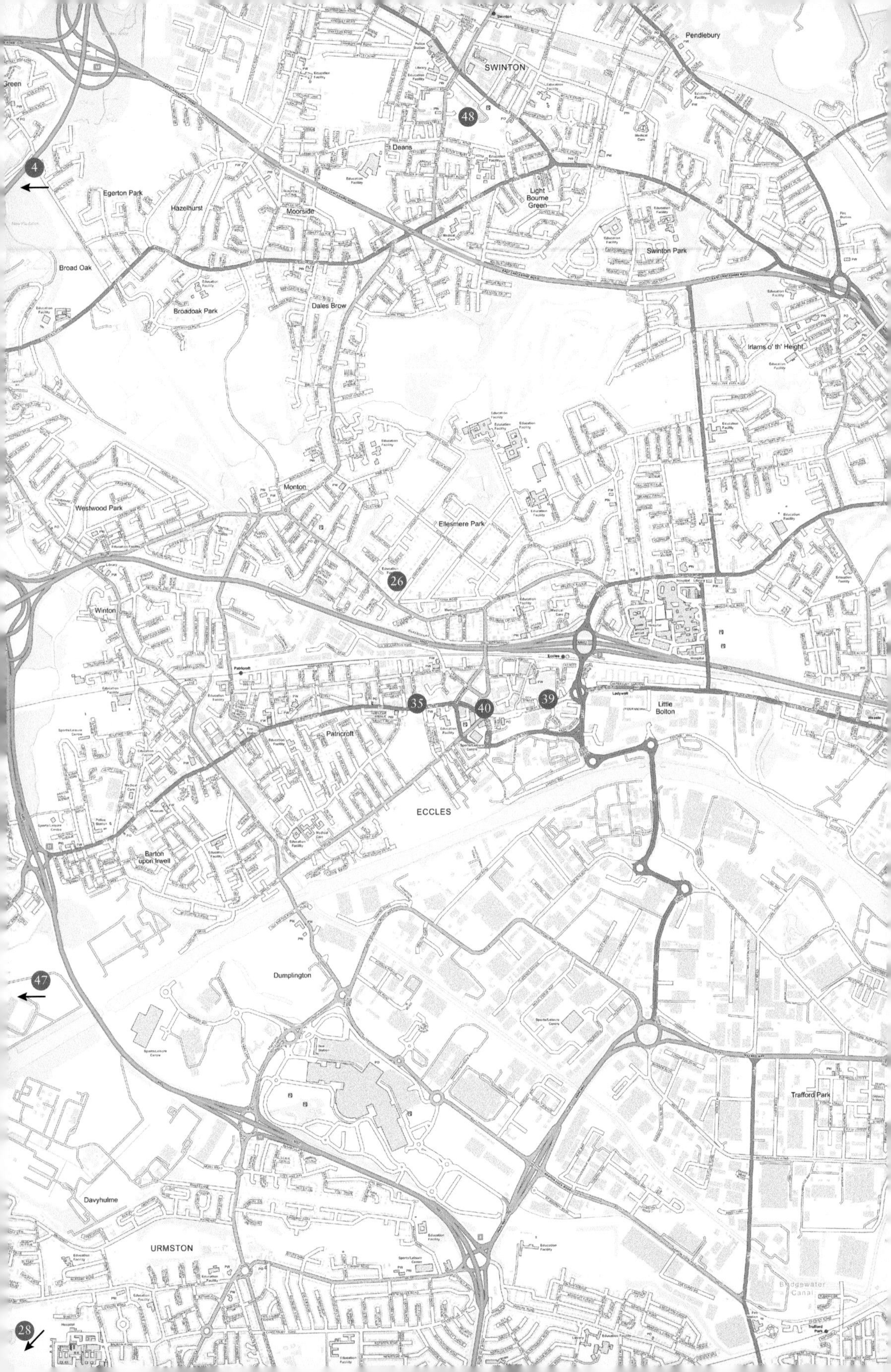

Swinton
Pendlebury
SWINTON
48
Green
4
Deans
Egerton Park
Hazelhurst
Moorside
Light Bourne Green
Swinton Park
Broad Oak
Dales Brow
Broadoak Park
Irlams o' th' Height
Monton
Westwood Park
Ellesmere Park
26
Winton
Eccles
Patricroft
35
40
39
Ladywell
Little Bolton
ECCLES
Barton upon Irwell
47
Dumplington
Trafford Park
Davyhulme
URMSTON
Bridgewater Canal
28

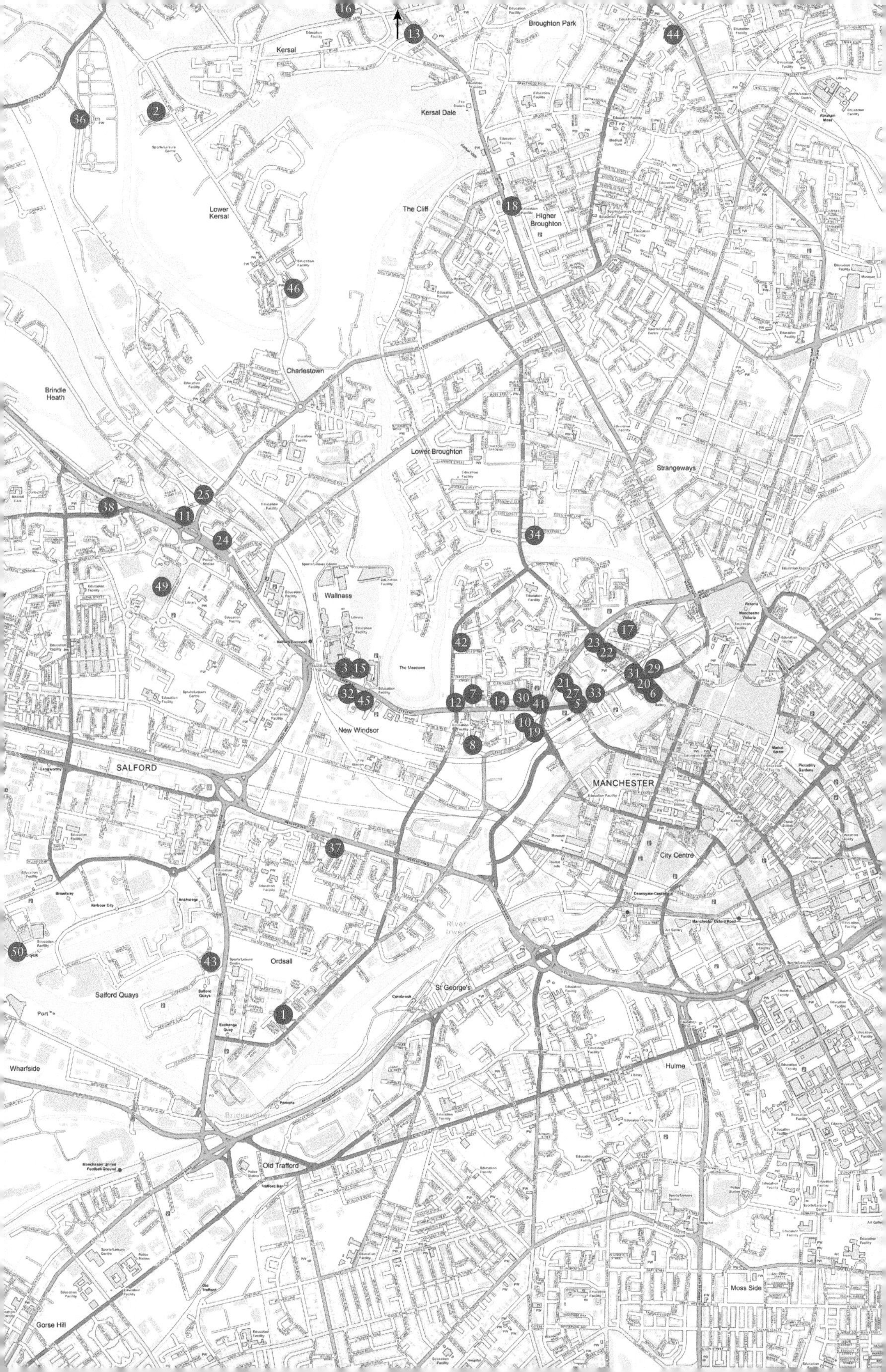
Broughton Park
Kersal
Kersal Dale
Lower Kersal
The Cliff
Higher Broughton
Charlestown
Brindle Heath
Lower Broughton
Strangeways
Wallness
The Meadows
New Windsor
SALFORD
MANCHESTER
City Centre
River Irwell
Ordsall
Salford Quays
St George's
Wharfside
Hulme
Old Trafford
Manchester United Football Ground
Gorse Hill
Moss Side
Piccadilly Gardens
Manchester Victoria
Manchester Oxford Road
Deansgate-Castlefield
1
2
3
5
6
7
8
10
11
12
13
14
15
16
17
18
19
20
21
22
23
24
25
27
29
30
31
32
33
34
36
37
38
41
42
43
44
45
46
49
50

Key

1. Ordsall Hall
2. Kersal Cell
3. Sacred Trinity Church, Chapel Street
4. Worsley Old Hall
5. Chapel Street and Hope United Reformed Church
6. Crown Tavern, Blackfriars Street
7. St Philip's Church, Chapel Street
8. Islington Mill
9. Buile Hill House
10. Salford Magistrates' Court
11. St Thomas's Church, Pendleton
12. Salford Royal Hospital
13. Kersal Bar Tollhouse
14. Salford Cathedral
15. Salford Museum and Art Gallery
16. St Paul's Church, Kersal Moor
17. Greengate Baths
18. Greek Orthodox Church of the Annunciation, Bury New Road
19. Ainscow Hotel (formerly Watson & Woodhead Brewery)
20. Baerlin's Warehouse, No. 10 Blackfriars Street
21. Arlington House (former Gas Board Offices), Bloom Street
22. Manchester Tennis and Racquet Club
23. The Black Friar
24. Brunswick Wesleyan Schools, Broad Street, Pendleton
25. Pendleton Co-op, Broughton Road
26. Monton Memorial Schools, Monton
27. Men's Model Lodging House, Bloom Street
28. Irlam Railway Station
29. No. 62 Chapel Street (former Police Station)
30. Salford Education Office
31. Peel Building, Salford University
32. Working Class Movement Library (former Queen's Jubilee Nurses' Home), Acton Square
33. Chester's Brewery, Cook Street
34. Victoria Theatre, Great Clowes Street, Lower Broughton
35. Crown Theatre, Eccles
36. Agecroft Cemetery Chapel
37. Salford Lads' Club
38. Halton Bank School, Broad Street
39. Lamb Hotel, Eccles
40. Eccles Central Library
41. Salford Cinema, Chapel Street
42. Adelphi and Centenary Buildings, Salford University
43. Dock Office, Salford Quays
44. Higher Crumpsall and Higher Broughton Synagogue
45. Hemsley House, Salford Masonic Hall, Chapel Street
46. The Racecourse Hotel, Littleton Road
47. Barton Aerodrome, Eccles
48. Swinton Civic Centre, Swinton
49. Salford Precinct, Hankinson Way
50. The Lowry Theatre and MediaCity complex, Salford Quays

Introduction

The city of Salford has an enduring and proud history. It has strongly protected its distinctiveness from its near neighbour Manchester and has created its own architectural legacy, celebrated in this book.

The River Irwell has long formed the boundary between Salford and Manchester. The Domesday Book survey of England for William the Conqueror, completed in 1086, already listed Salford as a separate manor. It had a total population of sixty-three households and the main landlord was Roger de Poitou. It was de Poitou who divided Manchester from Salford for administrative purposes, the city having been part of the extensive Salford hundred. Salford had been included in Cheshire, although it was not part of that county. In 1182, Salford became part of the newly created county of Lancashire.

It was granted a market in 1228 and its charter as a city in 1230. Historically, the city developed in the area around Greengate and the Sacred Trinity Church on Chapel Street. Indeed, Chapel Street was known as Salford Street in the eighteenth century. By the late 1700s, the city's population was 18,000 compared to Manchester's 70,000. However, it was not going to allow a smaller population from preventing its development. Salford was very much in the vanguard of Victorian social reform – one of the area's (and England's) first public parks was opened as Peel Park in 1846 with the public library following in 1850. The latter was the first public library in Britain, established under the Museums Act as the Public Libraries Act of 1850 was not yet in force. This provides another example of the forward-thinking and progressive civic culture of the city of Salford.

Queen Victoria made several visits to Salford, with her 1857 visit being marked by the addition of the Victoria Arch to Peel Park to commemorate the occasion. Lord Ducie presented the gates from Strangeways Hall and these were incorporated into the arch. The city's wealthy merchants established themselves in areas such as Monton, Eccles and Broughton Park and some of their handsome mansions remain today. An uninterrupted line of Georgian housing on the Crescent is a tantalising glimpse of the riches that once flowed into the city from local industries.

Much of the city's industry was centred on factories and mills, brewers and engineering works and these took advantage of the proximity of the railway and the city's docks. There were eight railway stations within the city boundary to facilitate the transport of raw materials and of finished goods. Flemish weavers introduced the manufacture of wool and fustian to the city and Irish cows were bought and sold at the Cattle Market on Cross Lane.

The rubber trade was very important to Salford, especially as an employer of women and girls. Rubber goods included pipes, tubes, tyres, balloons and overshoes. Notable Salford factories were Mandelbergs (Frederick Road) and Frankenburgs (Greengate), both of whom made waterproof fabrics and garments. Sir James Farmer Norton made machinery for textile mills at his Adelphi Ironworks. The iron and brass foundries of Sir W. H. Bailey's Albion Works was responsible for over 100 patents and innovations. Ancillary industries for textiles also sprang up such as Cusson's and Colgate-Palmolive, which supplied soap and starch needed for finishing the cloth.

Many have complained of the lack of a definable centre to the city, but it is clear from examining the architectural heritage that the Crescent and Chapel Street, taken together, form the hub of it. Many of the city's oldest and most impressive buildings are clustered around this street as it winds its way through Salford – from one of Salford's oldest buildings, Sacred Trinity Church (1635), to the flowering of great nineteenth-century architecture in the former Salford Magistrates' Court (1825), Salford Cathedral (1844), St Philip's Church (1822) and Salford Royal Hospital (1830).

Salford has always been a city that is flexible enough to accommodate all who wished to live there. Despite being a predominantly Catholic city, the Bible Christian Society were made welcome – they were responsible for the first vegetarian cookbook to be published in Britain. Salford MP Joseph Brotherton was a member of this church. Other faiths represented in the city were the Wesleyan Methodists, Welsh Calvinists, Congregationalists (of whom James Joule, the physicist, was a member) and the Swedenborgians. Similarly, the Freemasons established an important base in Salford and the Jewish community has been prominent since the nineteenth century. Alderman Isidor Frankenberg became the first Jewish Lord Mayor of Salford in 1905.

Like most cities, Salford architecture has been a combination of the stately and the substandard. Attempts were made to address Salford's nineteenth-century slums with a large-scale programme of social housing construction in places such as Ordsall in the later nineteenth and early twentieth centuries. Post-war tower blocks have survived in Pendleton and the city has resisted attempts to break up these neighbourhoods. Much of this newer housing was terraced, with ginnels (laneways) separating the backyards and creating the intimate communities so well reflected in Tony Warren's Coronation Street. A native Salfordian, Warren was a keen observer of human nature in these streets.

Coronation Street aside, Salford's contribution to the arts goes considerably beyond its size and it counts among its natives such luminaries as singers Ewan MacColl and Elkie Brooks, painters L. S. Lowry and Harold Riley, writers Shelagh Delaney and Mike Leigh and actors such as Albert Finney, Robert Powell and Ayub Khan Din. The city remains a focal point for the arts and the opening of the Lowry Theatre complex in 2000 began a new chapter in the history of Salford's docklands.

This was the beginning of the regeneration of Salford Quays, which has proved to be a successful and attractive destination for shoppers and diners. The arrival of the BBC to MediaCity on the quays in 2011 was derided by some, but has been important in bringing not just jobs but a definable increase in northern commentary and opinion on news and current affairs programming. The influx of new residents has stimulated the addition of apartment buildings across the city, many with swimming pools and in-house gyms that will ensure that the city continues to change, as it always has.

The character of the city of Salford and its people will continue to develop as the built environment changes around them. Books such as this one take advantage of the opportunity to celebrate and preserve that heritage for the future.

The 50 Buildings

1. Ordsall Hall

Ordsall Hall is the most important timber-framed building in Greater Manchester. The south portion of the hall dates from the fifteenth century. As with many buildings of this vintage, it was added to and altered over the centuries. Many prominent local families have been associated with the hall – the Radclyffes, the Egertons of Tatton and philanthropist Humphrey Chetham. The Radclyffe family owned the house and the land for 300 years, from around 1335 until they sold it in 1662. It is believed that there was a house on this site from the thirteenth century, which was then owned by David de Hulton.

The hall is one of the largest of its kind in England and originally had a moat. Unusually, it lacks a wall fireplace, which was common in these kinds of buildings. The distinctive quatrefoil panels all over the central hall began a fashion for this type of ornamentation, which can also be seen on other buildings such as Speke Hall near Liverpool and Rufford Hall in north Lancashire.

Ordsall Hall, much altered and added to over many centuries, but dates from the fifteenth century. (© Ben Abel)

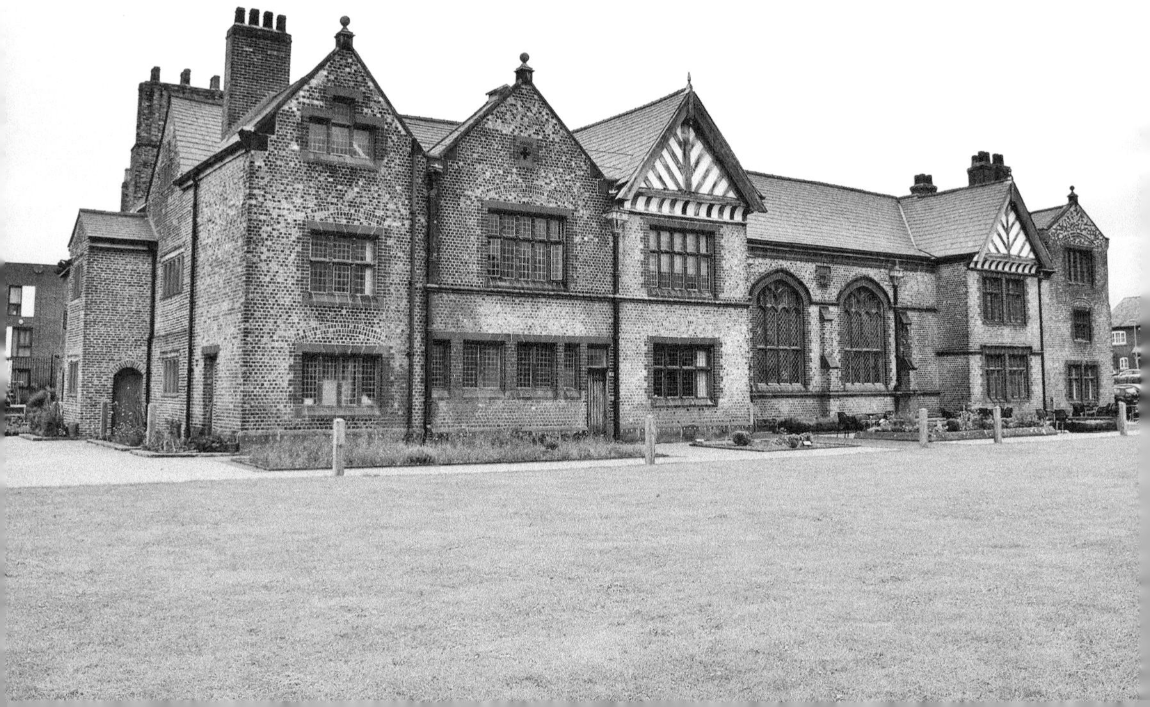

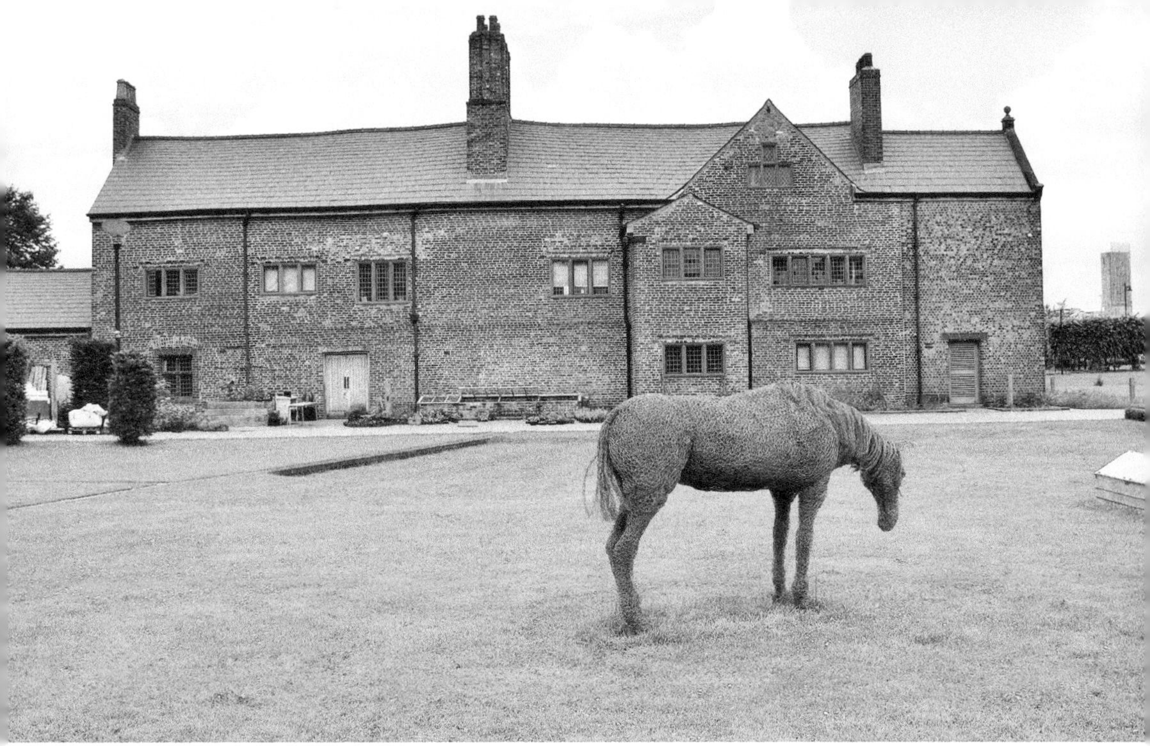

Above: Restored by the Heritage Lottery Fund, the hall remains popular with local people. (© Ben Abel)

Below: The timber-framed building of Ordsall Hall, one of the most important buildings in the area. (© Ben Abel)

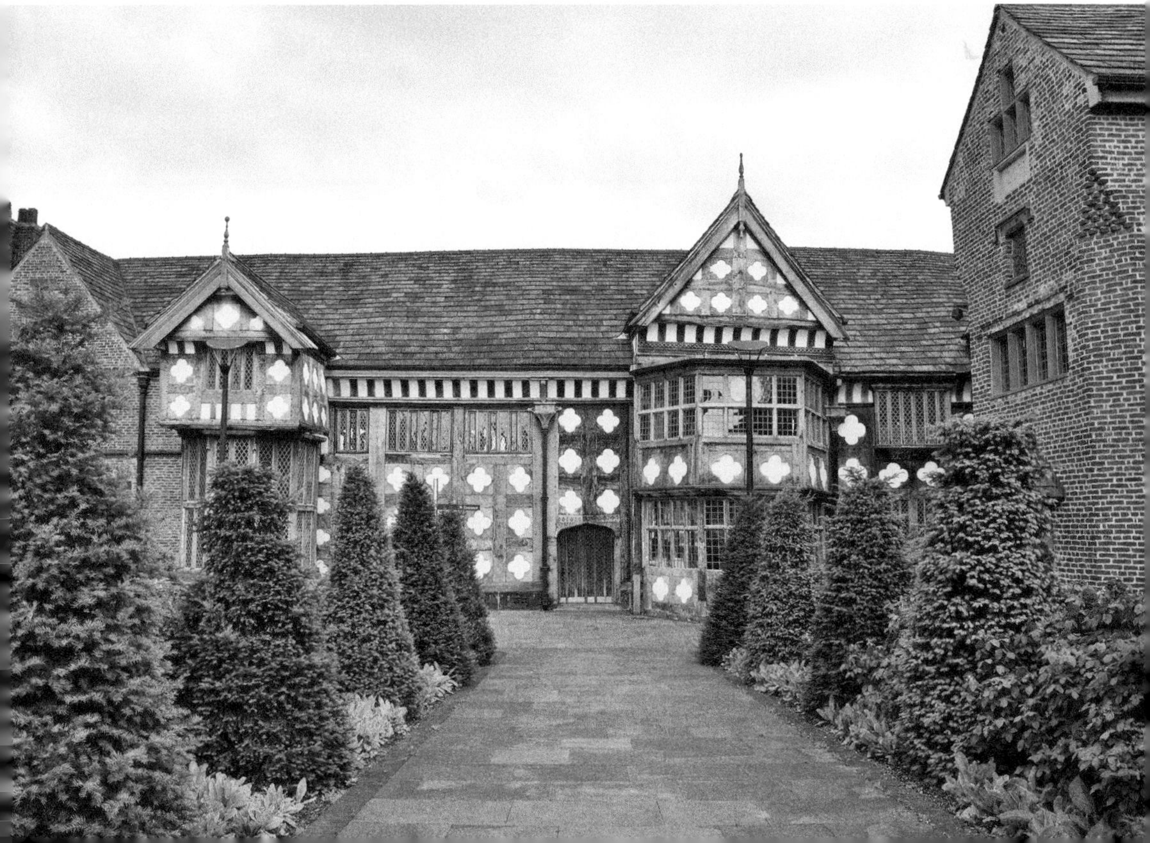

A brick house to the west of the main hall was added in the seventeenth century (1639), possibly for the estate bailiff as the Radclyffes were no longer permanently resident there. The family supported the Crown during the English Civil War and suffered financial hardship thereafter, forcing the sale of the estate in 1662. The Oldfields of Northwich bought the property and then sold it to the Stocks family who lived in the main hall and rented the two wings to tenants. The last permanent residents moved out of the hall in 1871 as the site was being encroached upon by industry and housing. Haworth's Mill used the hall as a social club from 1875, the Great Hall being used as a gymnasium during this period. In 1883, Lord Egerton of Tatton bought the hall and undertook some major reconstruction of the house, supervised by architect, Alfred Darbishire. Egerton established a school for clergy there. This formed the basis for Manchester Theological College, which was later established at Egerton Hall. The hall continued to be used as a social club until 1940 and the building was used as a radio station during the Second World War.

Salford Corporation bought the estate from the Egertons in 1959 and it was opened to the public in 1972. The hall underwent major restoration in the early twenty-first century (2009–11), funded by the Heritage Lottery Fund and by donations from the public. This work has helped to secure the hall for the future. It remains in the midst of a very built-up area and its presence there is an excellent reminder of the history of Salford.

2. Kersal Cell

The name Kersal originated as 'Keres-hel', derived from the word 'carr', which meant a wood situated on a boggy grassland, and 'hale', from the Anglo-Saxon Mercian 'healh', which means a piece of land at the bend of a river. Kersal Cell is the second oldest building in Salford and the current building was built in 1563 and was originally a monastic cell built for Benedictine monks, near the ford at Agecroft and was dedicated to St Leonard. It was originally a single-storey 'crucked' building, intended for just one monk – hence the name Cell. The monks themselves were given permission to 'enlarge to themselves the assarts [woodland clearings] and the fisheries and all other things whatsoever which they can enlarge or give ease to themselves'. Hugh de Buron was the first inhabitant of the cell and was a hermit monk who 'could pace the oak woods which lay in front [of the cell] ... there were fine pastures and meadows in the rich alluvial land for the milk kine [domesticated cattle] and the goats and the lambs, and situations for apiaries in the forest for the wax candles of the altar... the river abounded them in trout, grayling, perch, carp, dace, bream, and eels'. The Cell's grant was reaffirmed in 1182 by Henry II and between 1298 and 1405 the cell was recorded as having one prior and one monk in residence at a time. More monks eventually joined. A mill was built to grind corn with orchards planted, a kiln for pottery making as the monastic community became self-supporting.

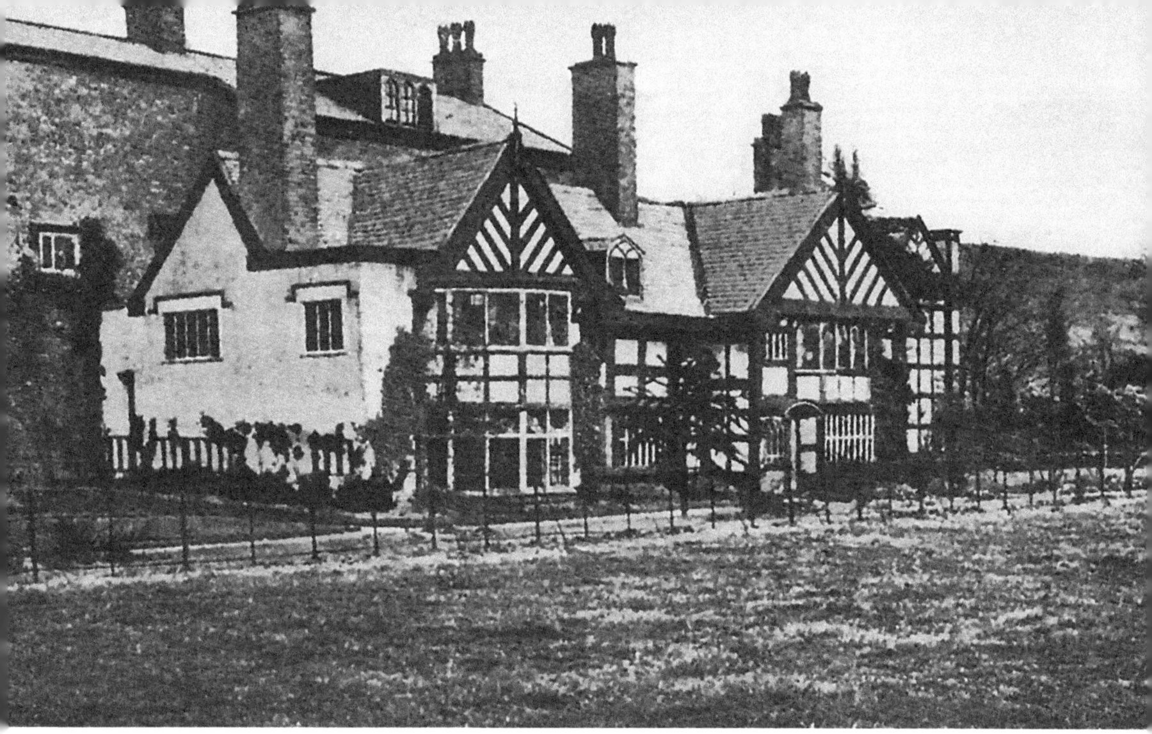

Above: Kersal Cell, an early Edwardian view.

Below: Kersal Cell, once again a residential property.

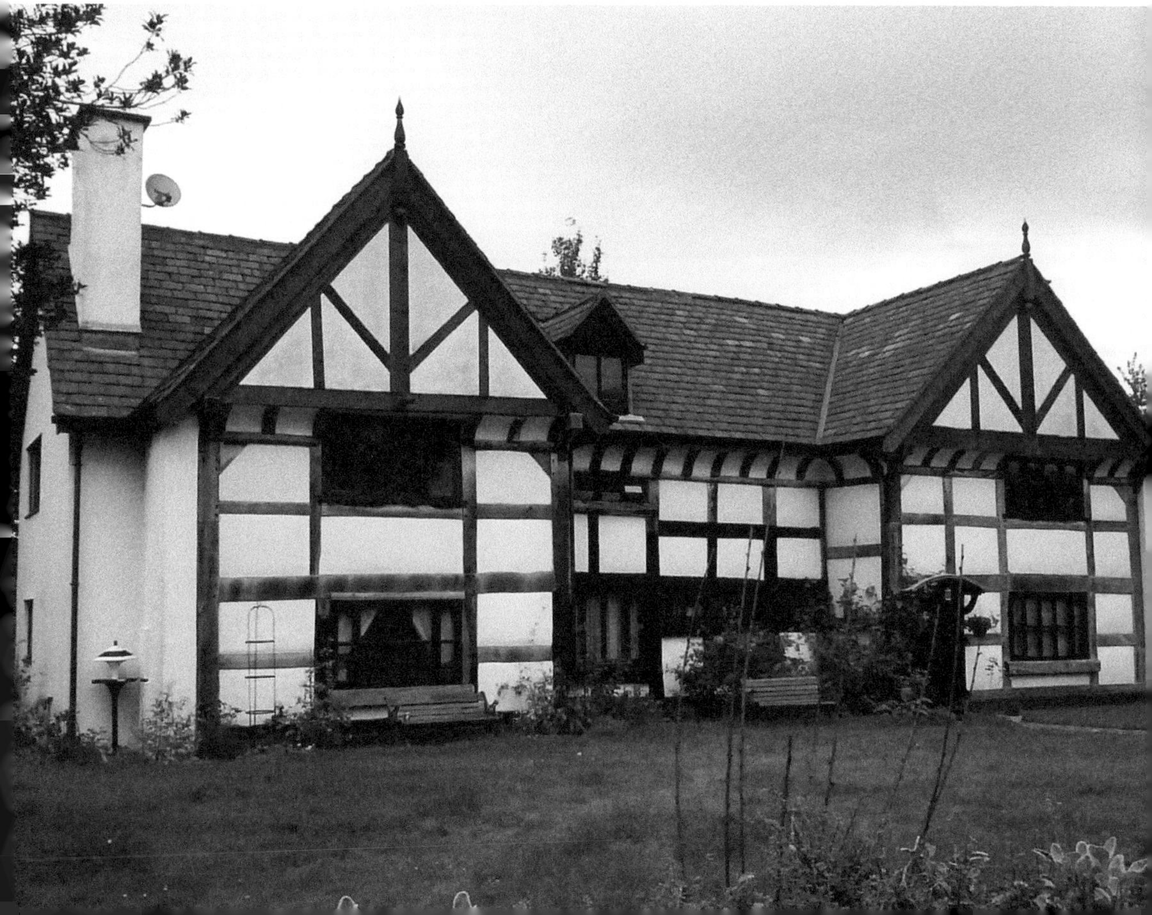

Kersal Cell fell victim to the Dissolution of the Monasteries by Henry VIII in 1536 and was sold to Baldwin Willoughby in 1540, along with the manor. It was enlarged further and was bought by the Byrom family around 1613. John Byrom (1692–1763) lived here and was a local landowner, poet as well as a hymn writer, most famous for the hymn 'Christians, Awake', which he allegedly sang to his wife Dorothy at Christmas in 1751. He also invented a system of phonetic shorthand, a forerunner to what became Pitman's shorthand. By 1870, it was a girls' boarding school, and reverted to a private house thirty years later. The building, like many in Salford over the decades, was threatened with demolition, but in this instance was bought by a Salford councillor in 1949 when it was opened as a restaurant and nightclub. Once again, it is now residential.

3. Sacred Trinity Church, Chapel Street

The need for a church in Salford itself became a matter of urgency in the early seventeenth century as the town continued to grow and this was of particular concern to Sir Humphrey Booth, a merchant clothier and woollen cloth manufacturer and a key figure who rose to prominence at the time. His name appears in the Salford Portmote Records in 1611 and, until his death in 1635, he appears both as a purchaser of further burgages and in various official positions ranging from the 'Overseer of the Pump' to the most important office of Boroughreeve, which he held on six occasions.

It was in 1630 when Booth set up a trust to administer property that he had purchased in Manchester over preceding years. His aim was to provide for the poor of Salford. It was not until 1634, however, that he at last succeeded in obtaining a faculty from the Bishop of Chester to build and endow a chapel of ease in Salford. Sir Alexander Radclyffe of Ordsall and other notable townspeople also subscribed to the building costs.

Founded as a place of worship in 1635, and believed to be the first church in Salford, the church occupies a key position at the junction of Chapel Street and Blackfriars Street. The church was consecrated on 20 May 1635 by the Bishop of Chester. Sadly, Booth died after only just taking his first Communion there in 1635. As intended, it began as a chapel of ease (a place of worship for those who could not reach the parish church) until the parish was created in 1650. After the church was built, fire equipment was stored here for many years and the bell used to sound the alarm up until 1835. By the mid-eighteenth century, Salford eventually gained its first fire engine. John Wesley also preached here before his final break with the Anglican Church, and when he returned here in 1747 he preached in the open at Salford Cross, from where he had to flee to a nearby yard when some of his more unruly audience threatened to bring out the fire engine.

William Webb Ellis, the founder of the sport of rugby was christened there. The west tower of the church is original and is of Gothic and Classical motifs.

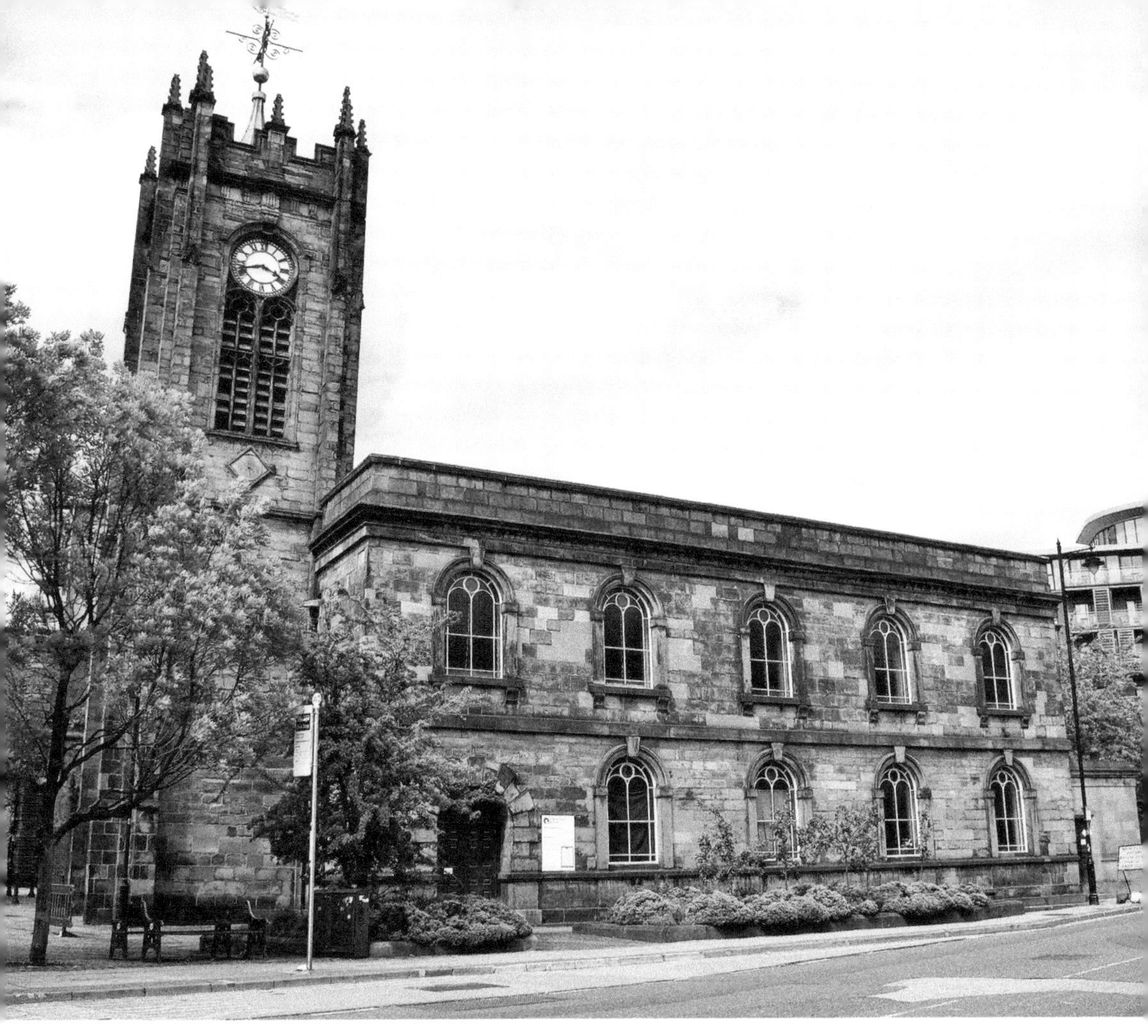

Sacred Trinity Church, with Gothic tower. (© Ben Abel)

Most of the rest of the building dates from 1752 with a considerable programme of restoration in 1874. The chancel is short and the roof is of Victorian timber. J. P. Holden, who also worked on Manchester Cathedral, completed most of the Victorian restoration of the church.

4. Worsley Old Hall

The earliest building on the site was a hall built for Sir Geoffrey de Worsley and is believed to date from 1376. The hall itself has been subject to many additions and extensions in its long history. It dates from the early seventeenth century (one of the upstairs rooms has the date 1639) and was originally a timber-framed building. Much of the rebuilding is in brick, with some timber-framed extensions. Most of the extensions were built in the nineteenth century – 1855 and 1891, with more work being done in 1906. Thus, it is challenging to identify the provenance

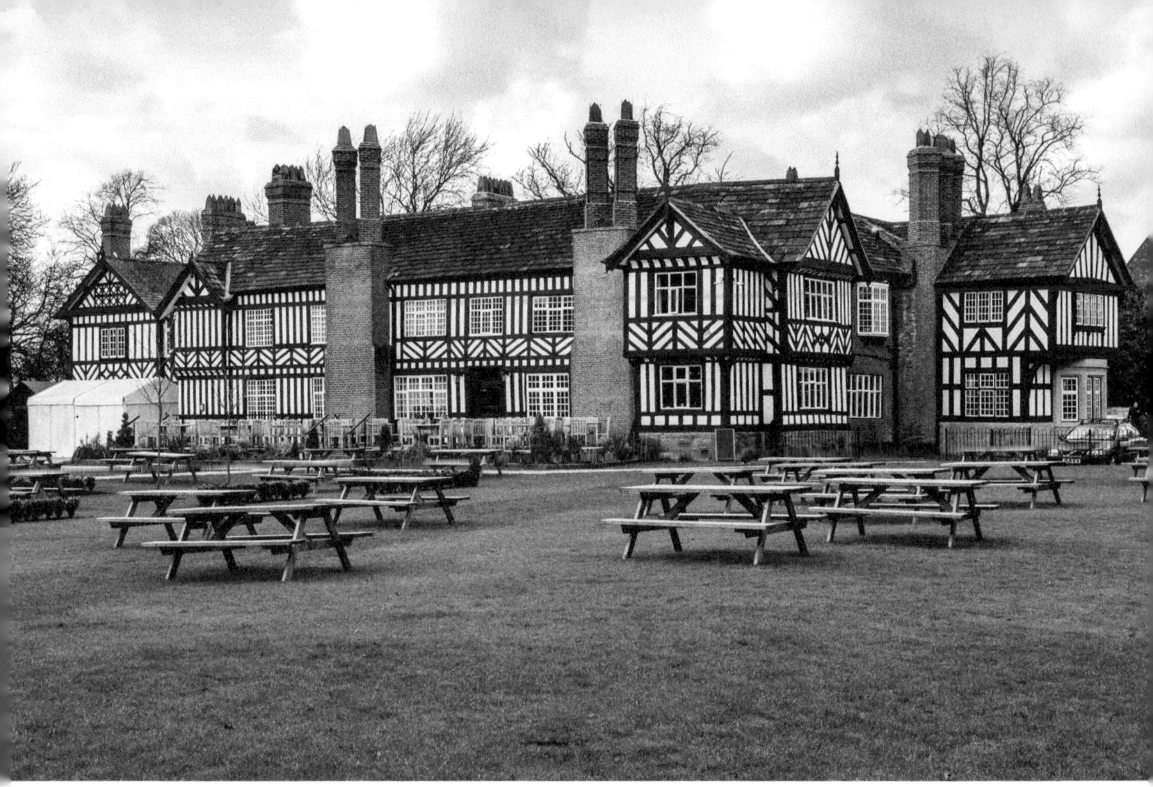

Worsley Old Hall, once the seat of the Egerton family, a prominent local family of the time. (© Steven Robertson)

of much of the building with the naked eye. The main range has six bays and two storeys, which was augmented by additional wings to the left and rear of the original building. The roofs are made of stone and slate. The mixture of building materials makes for a pleasing contrast of colours – red brick, black-and-white timberwork and grey roofs.

The building was the seat of the Egerton family, one of Worsley's most prominent families, and it was used in the planning of the Bridgewater Canal by the 3rd Duke of Bridgewater and engineer James Brindley. The canal was needed to transport coal from the duke's mines in Worsley to Manchester. Brindley stayed at the hall while the canal was being built in order to survey the route (which took forty-six days) and to supervise the construction until the canal opened in 1761.

The duke died in 1803 and his heir, Francis Leveson-Gower, inherited the title of Earl of Ellesmere and the Bridgewater estates. He moved to Worsley New Hall and built himself a new house there while one of the Bridgewater trustees lived at the Old Hall and managed the estates from there. The family did not live at the Old Hall again and the estate was eventually sold in 1923. The Old Hall became offices for the Manchester Collieries and then for the National Coal Board. It was subsequently used by the firm of W. S. Atkins, consultants to South East Lancashire North East Cheshire Transport (SELNEC).

The hall was converted into a bar and restaurant in the early 1970s and still operates today as part of the Marriott Hotel and Country Club.

5. Chapel Street and Hope United Reformed Church

As the population of Salford grew, many churches in the town proliferated, along with chapels and mission halls. By 1851, 42 per cent of believers were Church of England, a similar number were Nonconformist, and around 15 per cent were Roman Catholic. Religious and moral convictions were a powerful influence over local affairs, with the first temperance society founded in Salford and self-help friendly societies established, often connected to churches and chapels and offered assistance in times of sickness or bereavement, but only to those who could afford weekly subscriptions.

One such church on Chapel Street was built in 1819 and is of simple design, made of brick with a hipped Welsh slate roof. It was originally known as Chapel Street Independent and is set back from the street line. It consists of a single storey over a basement. Two main doors are approached up a flight of stone steps. Each door is crowned by a fanlight as are the three main windows. An engraved tablet above one of the doors states 'Independent Chapel'; another over the other door, gives the date of the building as 1819. Chapel Street was one of the first areas in the town to become built up, and later the first slum area of Salford. It was very near to the centre of Salford and therefore contained many public houses and inns.

Built in 1819, the chapel is still very active locally. (© Ben Abel)

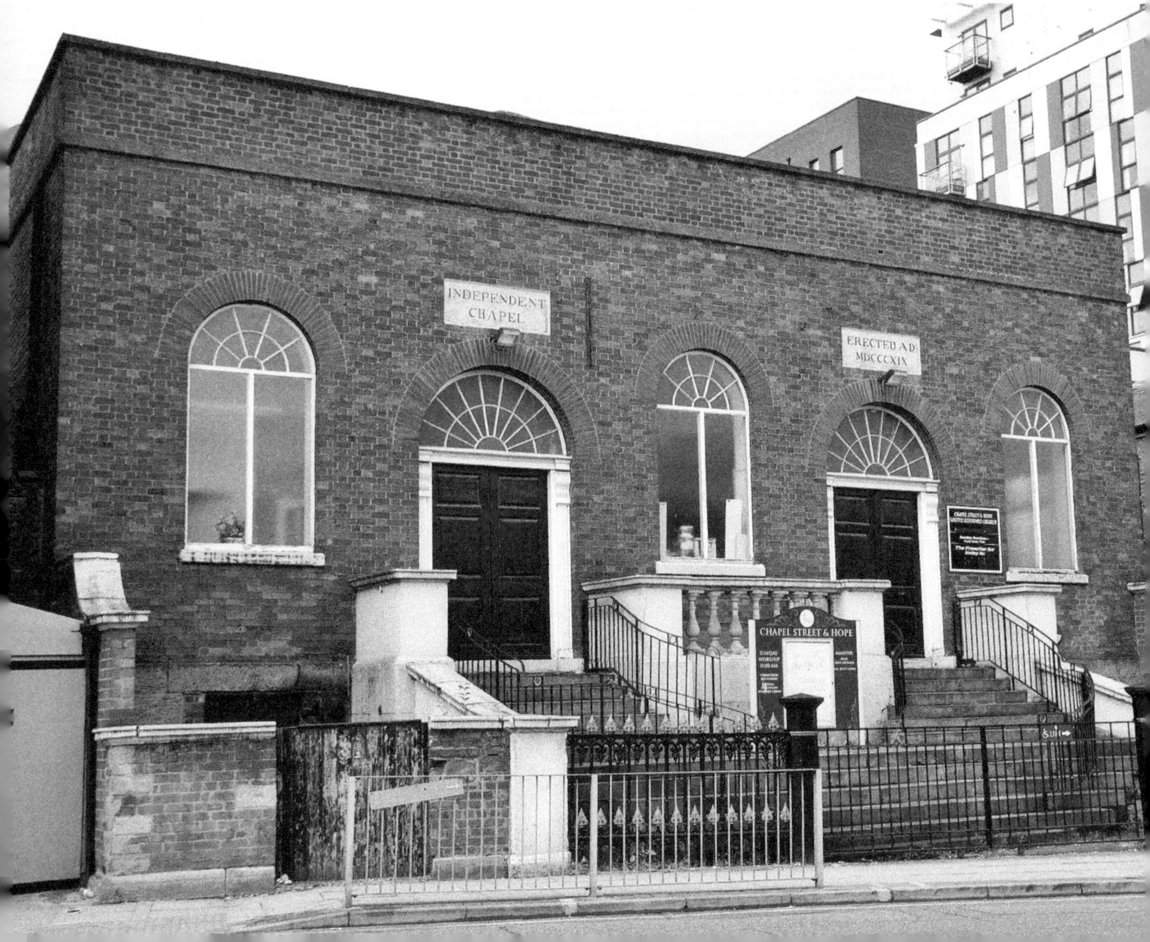

Today, a number of the church rooms are hired out to the general public and the church is involved with local ecumenical ventures with the other Anglican churches in the area.

6. Crown Tavern, Blackfriars Street

The Flat Iron conservation area in Salford is centred around the Grade II * listed Sacred Trinity Church and is bounded by Blackfriars Road and Blackfriars Street on the east, the River Irwell to the south, Booth Street and Bury Street to the west and the railway line to the north. The Flat Iron conservation area derives its name from the triangular-shaped plot of land that contained both Trinity Church and the market itself, resembling the shape of a flat hot-coal-heated iron once used for ironing clothes. The original town of Salford was contained within the triangle of land bounded by the River Irwell, Chapel Street, Gravel Lane and Greengate.

One building that remains on Blackfriars Street is a handsome, three-storey building with three sets of sixteen-pane sash windows on the first floor and

The former Crown Tavern, with inappropriate introductions contrasting with its coloured tiles.

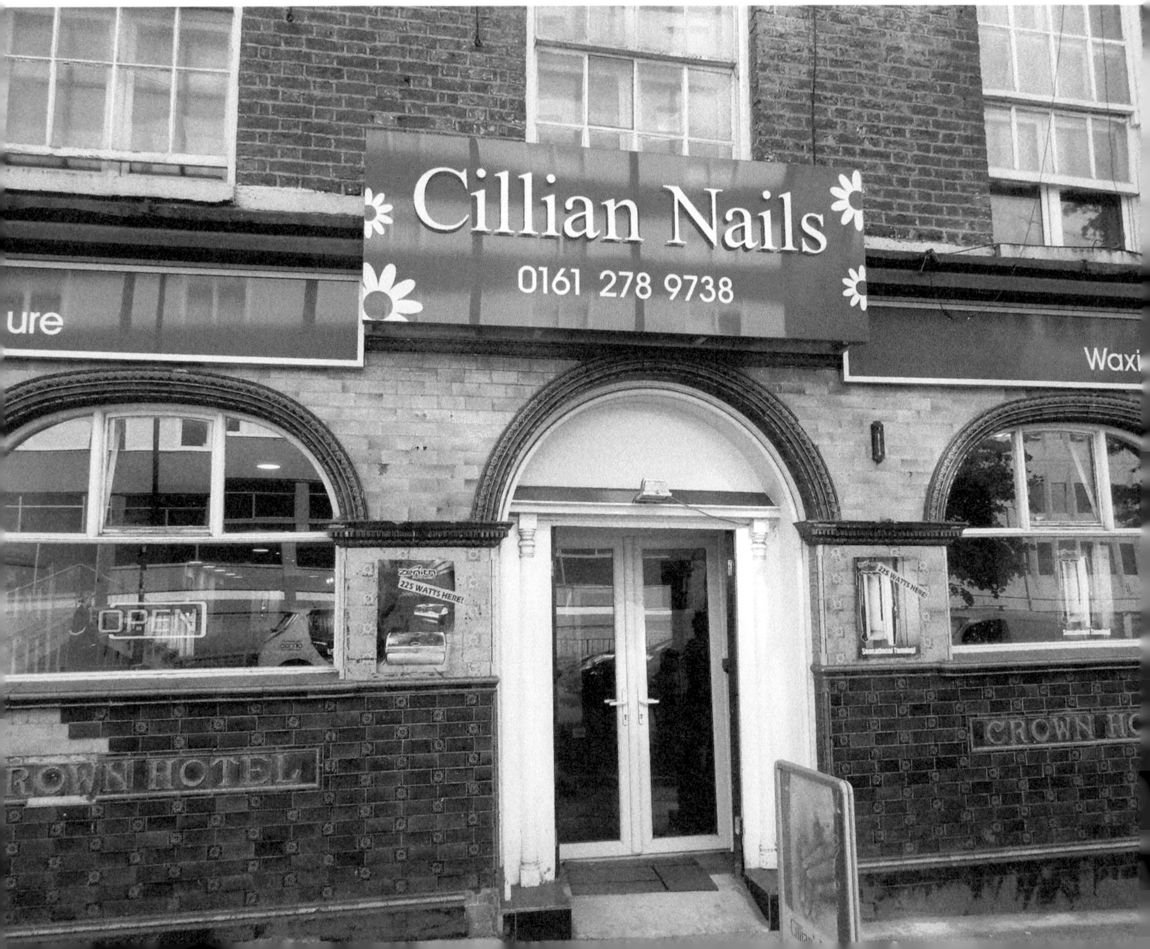

three sets of twelve panes on the second floor – the former Crown Tavern, one of many lost inns and public houses of Salford. The ground floor consists of two arched doorways (one main entrance door and one smaller door, offset to the side), complemented by two arched windows and is covered by coloured tiles. This floor dates from the later nineteenth century. 'Crown Hotel' is written in tiles underneath the windows. The roof is of Welsh slate.

The building is currently in use as a nail bar with its former use still visible to those passing by daily.

7. St Philip's Church, Chapel Street

St Philip's Church was designed by renowned architect Robert Smirke (1822–24). The church cost £14,670 and is in Greek Revival style using ashlar stone. The use of this style makes the church unusual for this city. It was a Commissioners' church, for which a grant was received from the Church Commissioners. The church is very similar in style to others by Smirke, such as St Anne's Church, Wandsworth and St Mary's in Bryanston Square, London. The semicircular portico is very distinctive and is capped by the bell tower. The bell was made by the Derby-based Whitehurst and Company. The portico sits on top of an Ionic colonnade.

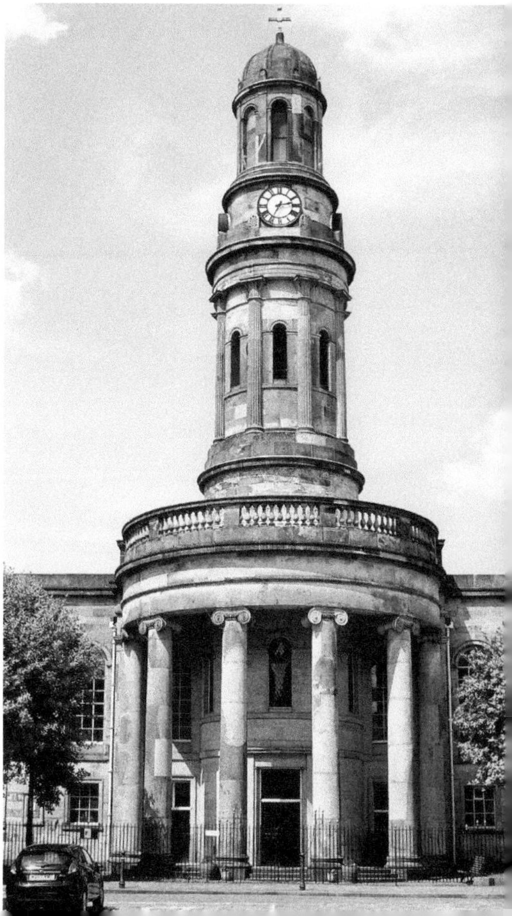

St Philip's Church, designed in the Gothic Revival style by Robert Smirke. (© Ben Abel)

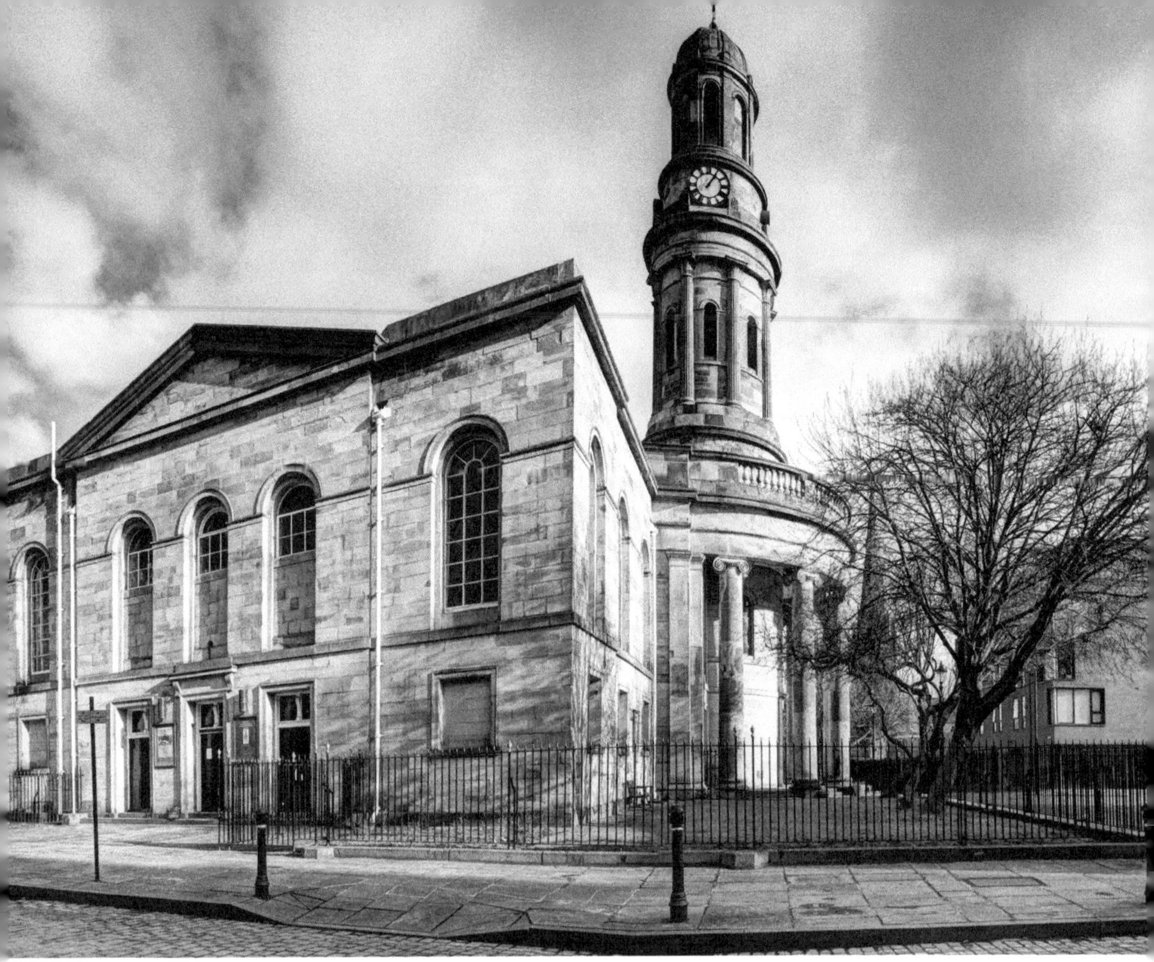

St Philip's Church, an unusual design for Salford, but a magnificent building nonetheless. (© www.spirituallandmarks.com)

The south-east chapel contains a First World War memorial by Humphries, Jackson and Ambler of Manchester. The organ was made by Renn and Boston and is a good example of its type. The interior was remodelled in 1895 by J. Medland Taylor. Underneath the church is a crypt containing eight coffins, although it was designed to hold many more. Most of the burials are anonymous except for that of General Sir Thomas Arbuthnot, a distinguished local British Army officer who died in 1879. The crypt was used for shelter during the Second World War.

In the present day, the church is very involved in community activities and has been used regularly for popular music concerts.

8. Islington Mill

The mill was constructed for Nathan Gough and Company in 1823 by David Bellhouse, a well-known builder of cotton mills from Leeds. It is a six-storey cast-iron frame fireproof building. Bellhouse was also involved in the building of the Manchester Portico Library and the original Manchester Town Hall on King

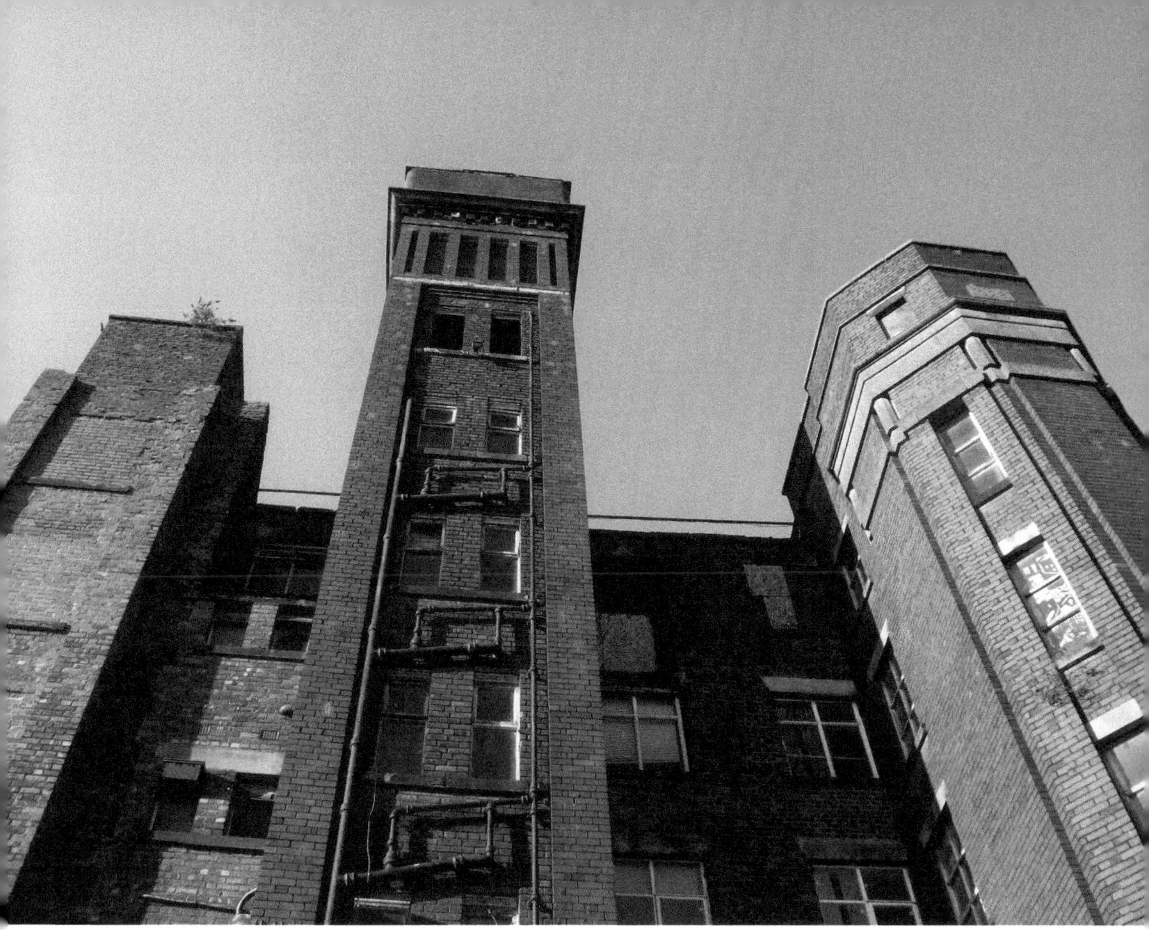

Above: Islington Mill, a former cotton mill.

Right: The former Islington Mill.
(© Carole O'Reilly)

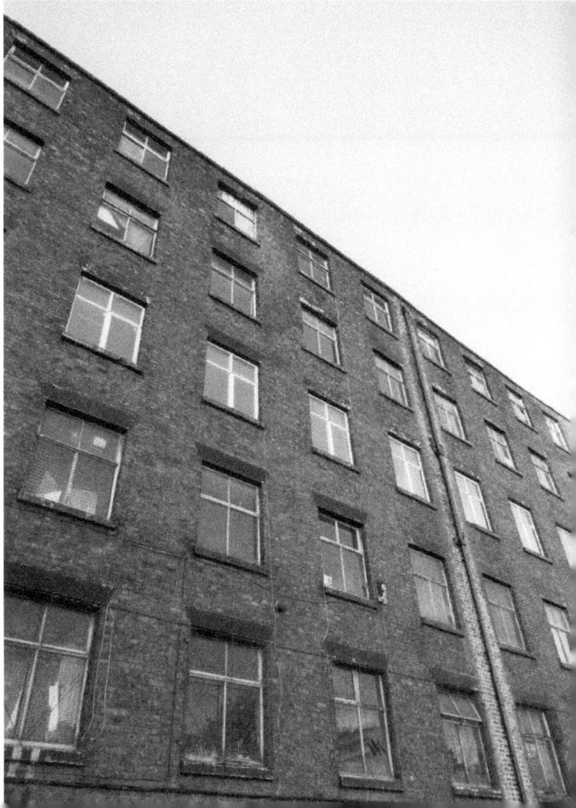

Street. The site just off Oldfield Road was close to several other cotton mills in the area, taking advantage of the adjacent River Irwell.

The following year (13 October 1824), the mill partially collapsed due to the failure of some of the cast-iron beams in the upper part of the structure. Nineteen workers were killed (sixteen women and three boys). Poor casting was alleged to have caused the collapse and Gough suspected negligence. The collapse is said to have caused delays in the widespread utilisation of fireproofing in cotton mills due to uncertainty about their efficacy. A second mill was constructed later to the rear of the main building, along with an engine house and stables.

Today, the mill buildings house the Islington Mill Arts Club, which began to utilise the buildings in 1999–2000. The complex consists of artists' studios, galleries and performance spaces. In 2014, the mill was granted £1 million from Arts Council England to further develop aspects of the as yet unused space at the building.

9. Buile Hill House

Charles Barry built Buile Hill House, located within Buile Hill Park, for the Potter family in 1825–27. It was described by Pevsner as 'restrained and refined'. The style is Greek Revival and is the only house of this design by Barry. It complements Barry's Royal Manchester Institution (later Manchester City Art Gallery). The main block of the building is symmetrical with a recessed west wing. The house was placed on raised ground within the park and the exterior design is quite plain, with the exception of

Buile Hill House, now closed and its future in doubt. (© Matt Ratcliffe)

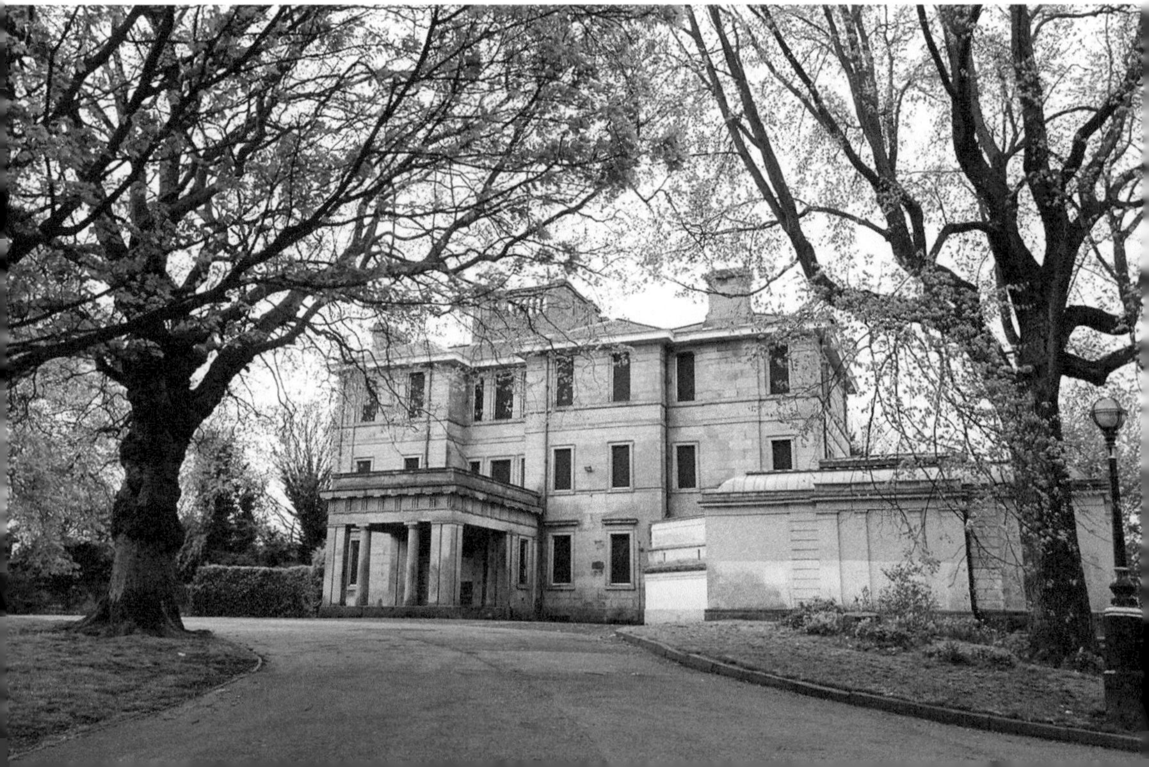

the garden front, which is more decorative. Projecting bay windows on this side have shallow balconies along with tripartite windows. The roof has projecting vertical chimneys and an unusual open balustraded lantern. The building is of ashlar stone and a brick and concrete balustrade and stone steps were added in the 1930s.

Edward Walters added a third storey and a porte cochère (with Greek Doric columns) in 1860. The extra storey is similar in style to Barry's and constructed from the same stone. The park was sold to Salford Council in 1902 for £20,000 and opened as a public park in 1903. The mansion was converted to a Natural History Museum and opened as such in 1906. This was replaced by the Museum of Mining in 1975 and closed in 2000. The future of the house remains in doubt – there have been several proposals for a hotel, apartments and conference centre in recent years, but these have not yet come to fruition.

10. Salford Magistrates' Court

The building was originally designed as a market hall by Richard Lane in 1825–27. It was commissioned by Lord Nicholas Bexley, Chancellor of the Exchequer, who gave his name to the square in which the building stands. It was

Salford Magistrates' Court, now apartments, but retaining the friezes of laurel. (© tigergrowl.wordpress.com)

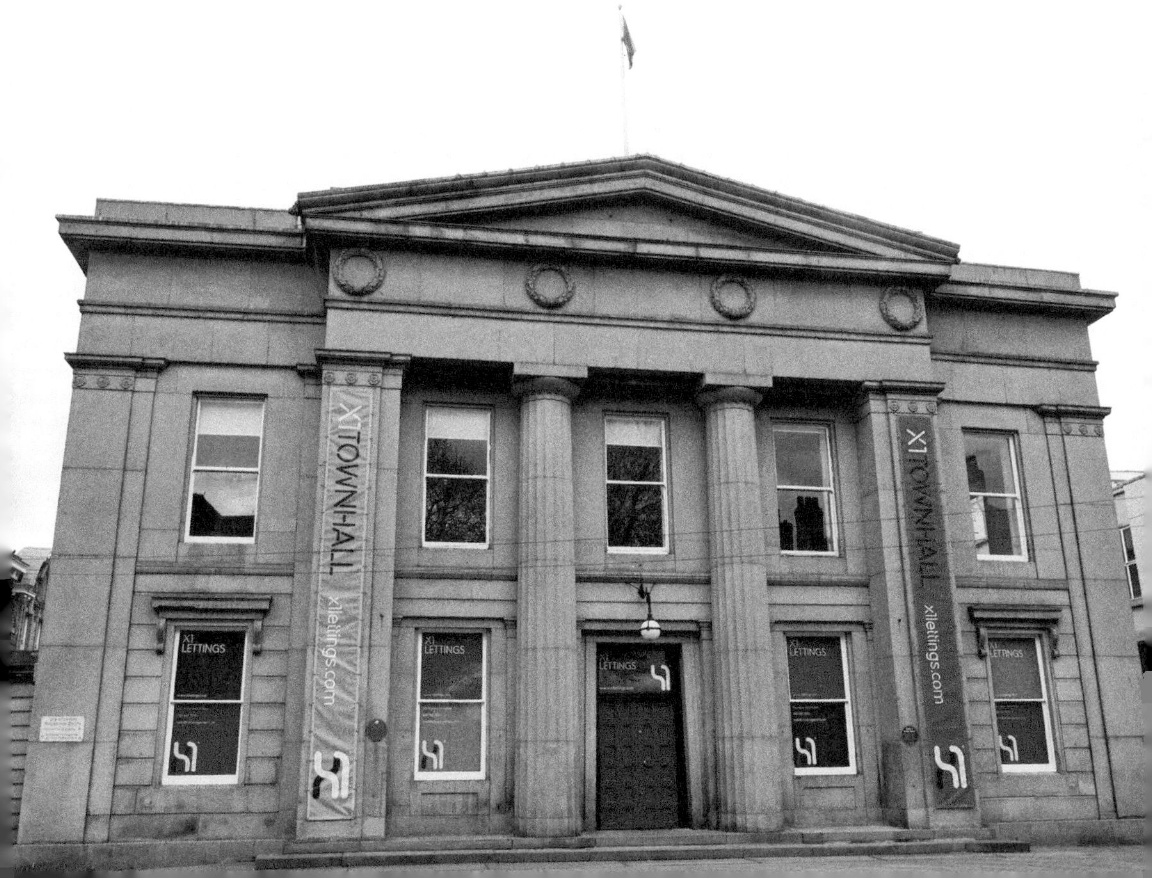

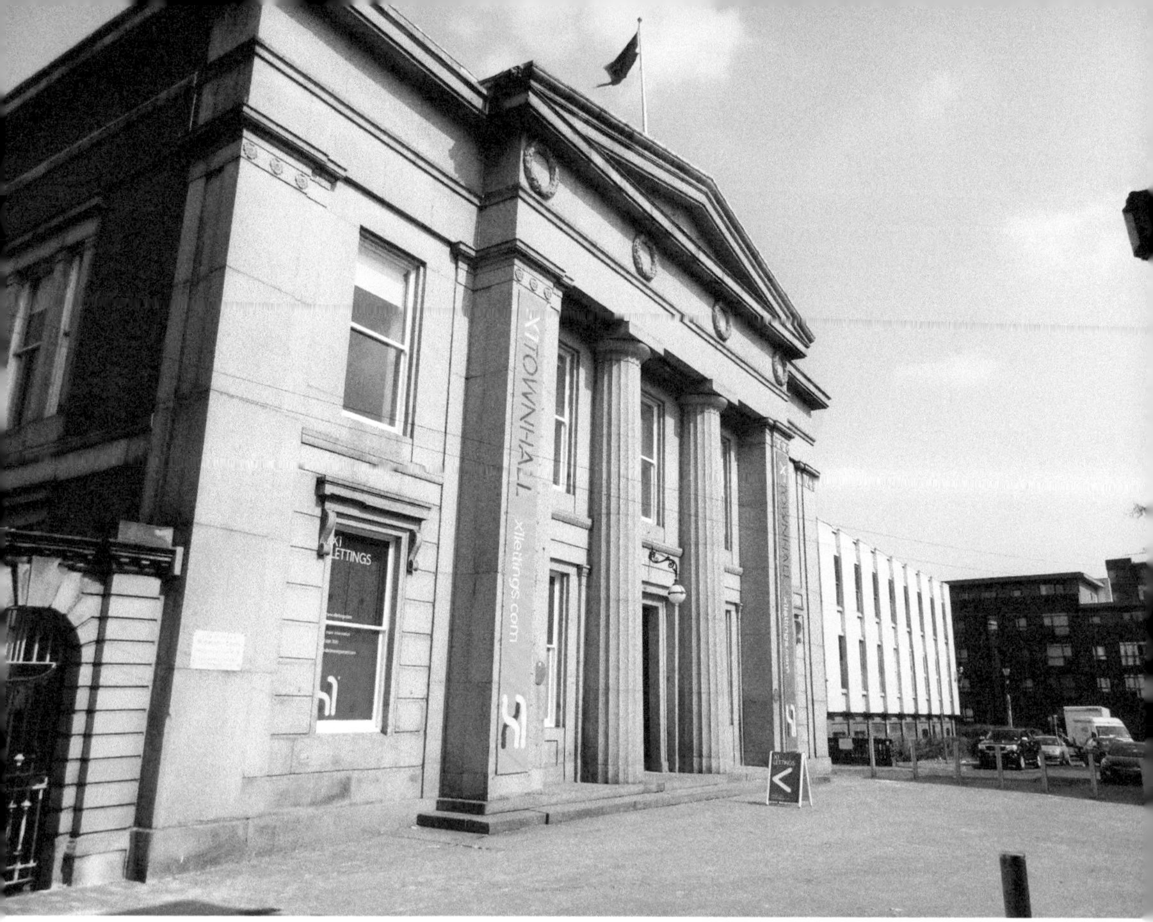

Salford Magistrates' Court, a former market hall. (© Tony Reeves)

Lane's first architectural commission and he would go on to design another Town Hall in Chorlton, Manchester. From 1835, it was used as Salford Town Hall and as a Magistrates' Court in 1840. The building was later added to in order to suit new usage, but the façade and the first bay remains as Lane designed them. The building is of classical, mostly Doric, style and is believed to be based on a Doric portico in Athens, which Lane had observed in a book. The frieze of laurel wreaths on the entablature is an interesting feature.

It was extended in 1865 by the Salford borough surveyor James Evans and was further enlarged by the borough engineer A. Fowler in 1874–75. Some of the ornate plasterwork ceiling still survives. Local man Mark Addy received awards for his bravery in rescuing people from drowning in the nearby River Irwell at the courthouse in 1878. In October 1931, it was the scene of the 'Battle of Bexley Square' during which unemployed workmen clashed with local police.

The court closed in 2011 when Salford and Manchester magistrates merged and all cases were transferred to the new Manchester Courts building. The building was sold to developers and has been recently converted into private apartments.

11. St Thomas's Church, Pendleton

This church and its spire are one of the main focal points of Pendleton. It was originally a Commissioners' Church, having been given a grant by the Church Commissioners for its building. The church was designed by Francis Goodwin and Richard Lane in 1829–31 at a cost of £7,673. It is built of ashlar stone in the Gothic Revival style. Goodwin, a Londoner, also designed St Peter's in Ashton-under-Lyne. It is believed that Lane, a local architect, did most of the work and it fits well with his other nineteenth-century work, notably St Mary's in Oldham. Somewhat auspiciously, the theme of the sermon preached at the consecration of the church by Bishop Sumner was 'how dreadful is this place'.

The nave has five bays, although only one chapel is currently in use for services. This chapel's stained-glass window is decorated with scenes from the life of St Thomas and was designed by John Hardman & Co., one of the world's leading stained-glass manufacturers. The rest of the church is used as meeting space. The churchyard contains a memorial cross to the local men who died in the First World War.

The church (known locally as Pendleton Church) now stands in a very built-up area and is now sadly surrounded by a dense network of busy roads.

St Thomas's Church, Pendleton, built in the Gothic Revival style. (© Ian Roberts)

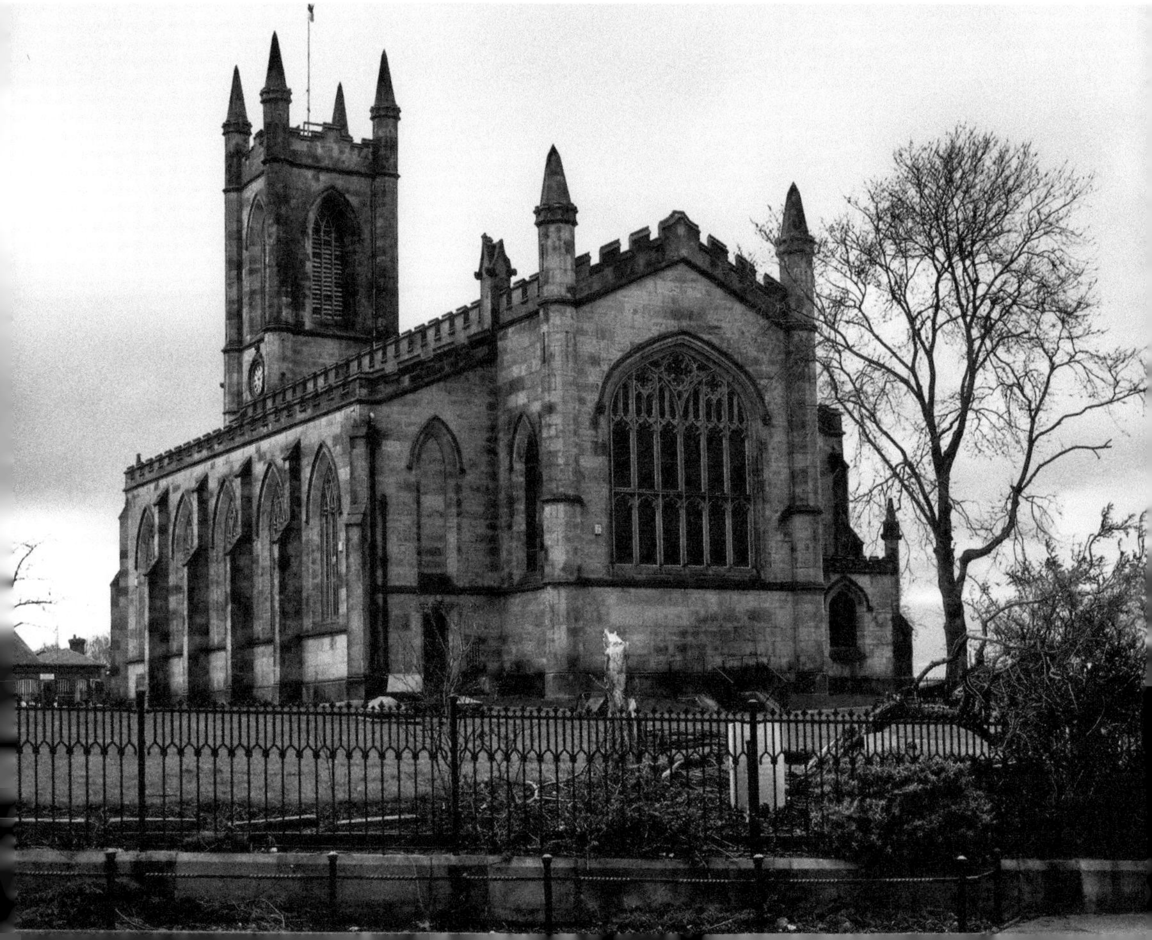

12. Salford Royal Hospital

Salford is often regarded as synonymous with a single building, known throughout the city, but in many cases across the world – the Salford Royal Hospital. It is a building not well known for its architectural merit, with its block-like structure commanding the corner of Chapel Street and Adelphi Street, but more for those who have passed through its doors over the many decades it was open.

The hospital began its history on 10 September 1827 when it opened as the Salford and Pendleton Dispensary. This was an attempt by a number of Salford citizens to found a medical charity to help those whom its first president William Garnett described as 'ordained to tread the dreary steps of penury by the sweat of their brow and to whose heavy burden of poverty are superadded sickness and the consequent inability to reap the slender reward of daily industry'. It was certainly nothing like a hospital we think of today as funding was very limited. Only outpatients were treated and mainly those suffering from industrial injuries where drugs and bandages were dispensed and also included a number of home patients. In its first year alone, 2,014 outpatients were treated and 967 home patients with the funds coming from a variety of sources. This included a Mr Green who was a well-known balloonist who made an ascent from the Cloth Hall, which became the site of the Victoria Bus Station, in 1829 and handed over half of his takings from spectators – a total of £43 15*s* 4*d*. In the same year, William IV gave permission for the title 'Royal' to be added and agreed to contribute to its annual maintenance with a contribution of £25 every year.

On 23 April 1830, the foundation stone was laid for the hospital building we know today, but it was not until 29 March 1845 before the first ten beds were installed and inpatients were admitted. Funding was still very limited, and the hospital expanded only gradually. Old buildings were demolished and in 1865 two new wings were added, and by the 1870s it changed its name to the Salford Royal Hospital but was often known locally as the 'Salford Infirmary'. In 1886, there was yet another extension, this time funded by a bequest from John Pendlebury and a new nurses' home was added in 1904. By 1913 the hospital had 260 beds for inpatients. During the First World War, the hospital treated many casualties including sixty wounded Belgian soldiers. During the Second World War, the hospital took a direct hit in an air raid, killing fourteen nurses. A plaque on the Chapel Street side of the building commemorates the event and points out that fourteen beds in the hospital were endowed in their honour. Salford's most famous nurse was Edith Cavell who was based at the hospital at the beginning of the twentieth century. Her name is inscribed on the war memorial at nearby Sacred Trinity Church.

The hospital eventually came under the administration of Salford Hospital Management Committee on the establishment of the National Health Service (NHS) in 1948, and in 1974 the hospital was recognised as an undergraduate teaching hospital. Salford Hospital Management Committee was succeeded by

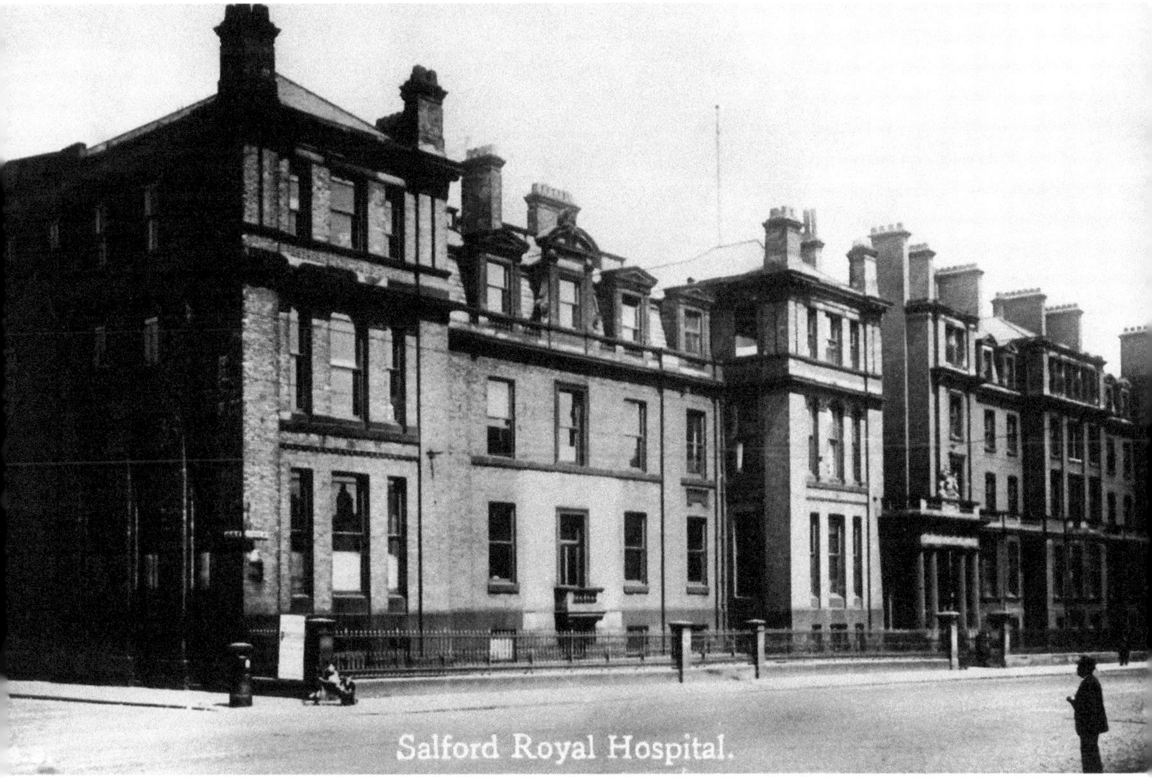

Above: Salford Royal Hospital, opened in April 1830.

Below: Salford Royal Hospital during Victorian times.

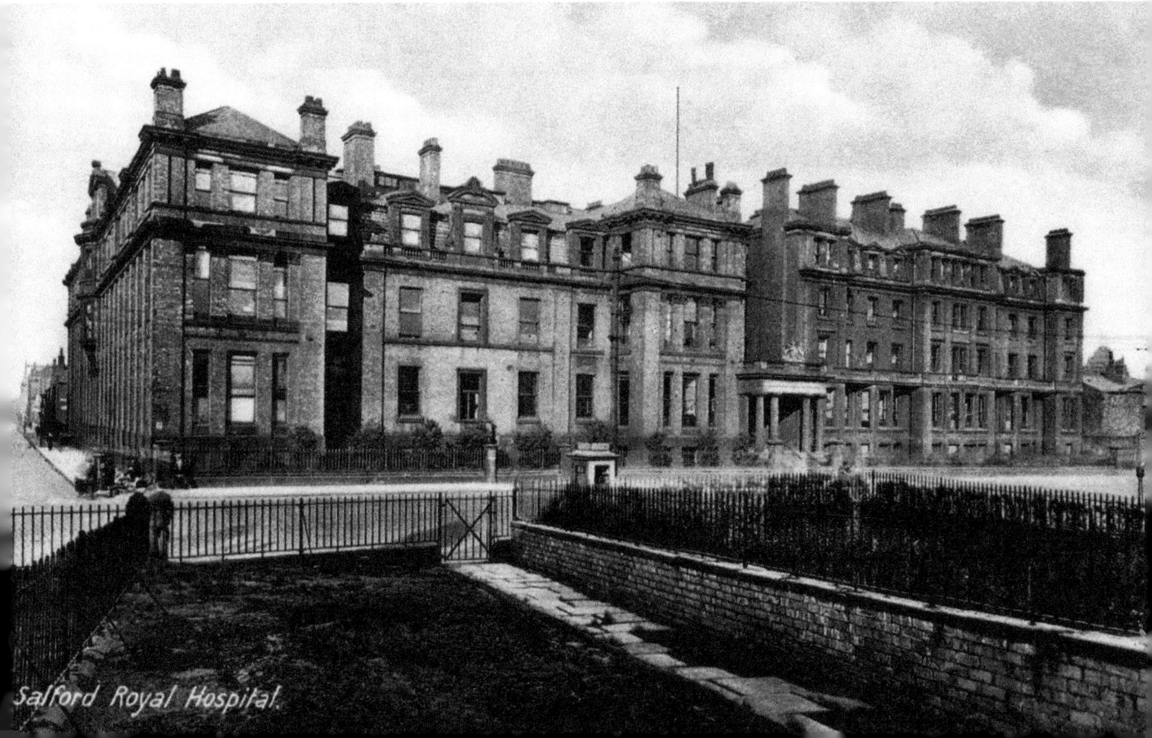

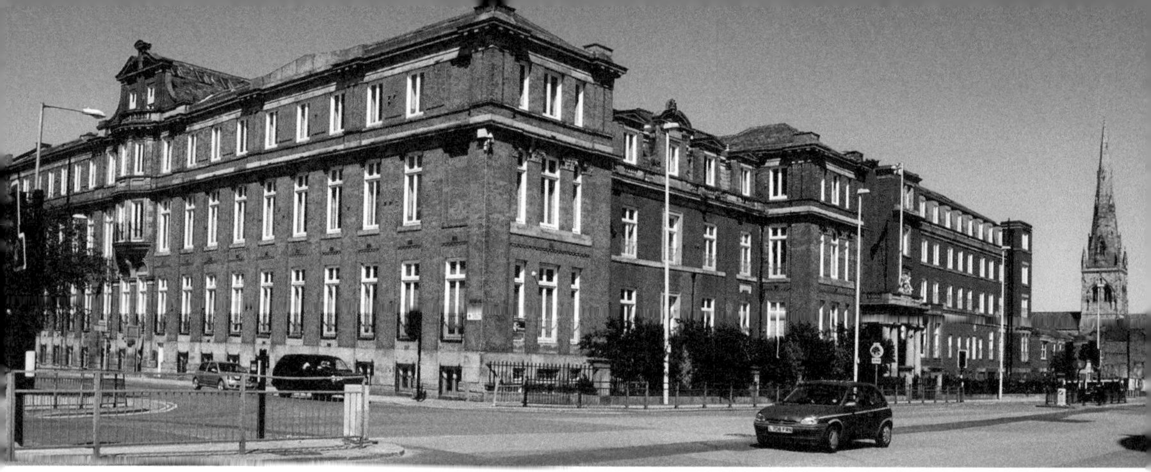

Salford Royal Hospital, converted into apartments after its closure in 1993. (© Rich Daley)

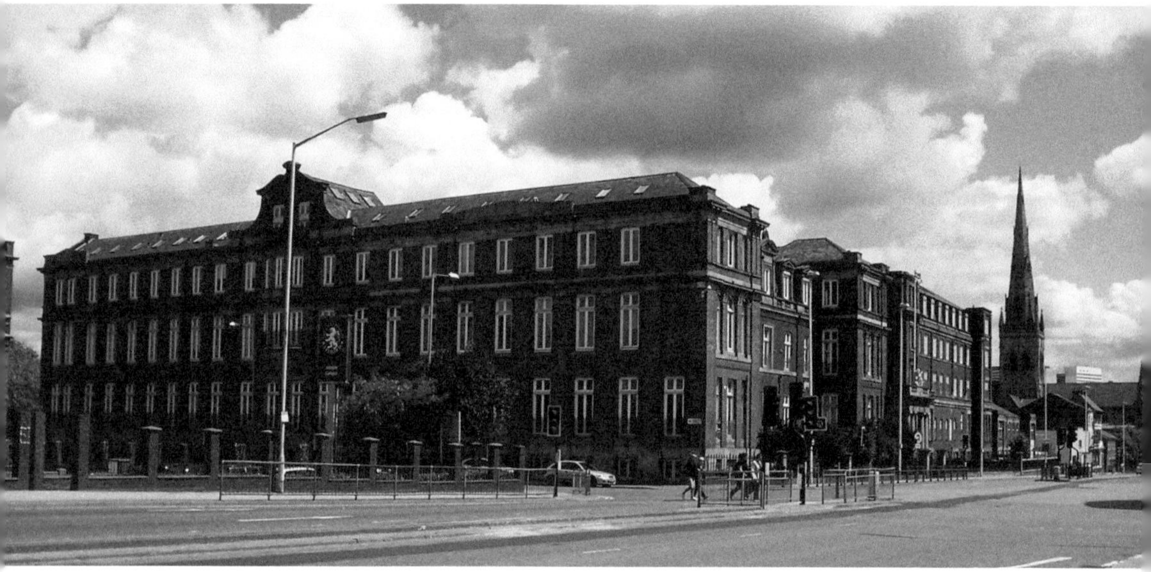

The former hospital is now apartments. While not architecturally impressive, they are an important part of Salford's history.

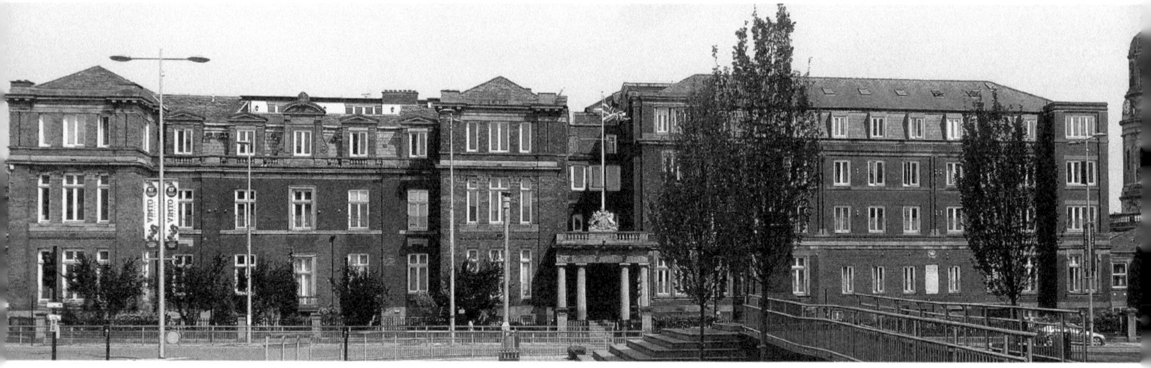

Still an important building today.

Salford Area Health Authority (Teaching) under the North Western Regional Health Authority, and in turn was succeeded by the Salford District Health Authority (Teaching), and then Salford Health Authority. Despite its reputation, the hospital closed in 1993 when Hope Hospital was enlarged and rebranded as the Salford Royal Hospital Trust. Following its closure, the building was eventually converted into apartments.

13. Kersal Bar Tollhouse

The area of Kersal remained a rural area up until 1840 when most of the land began to be sold off by the Clowes family for development. Merchants and manufacturers commenced building larger houses and mansions here and around Higher Broughton. There were many restrictions laid down, with the number of public houses considerably restricted, as well as the higher ground reserved for the wealthier residents. Singleton Road and Moor Lane were at the time the only roads connecting Bury Old Road and Bolton Road and on the corner of Bury Old Road was a toll bar. When Bury New Road was eventually built in 1831, a gate was erected and travellers had to pay a toll to the turnpike to pass through.

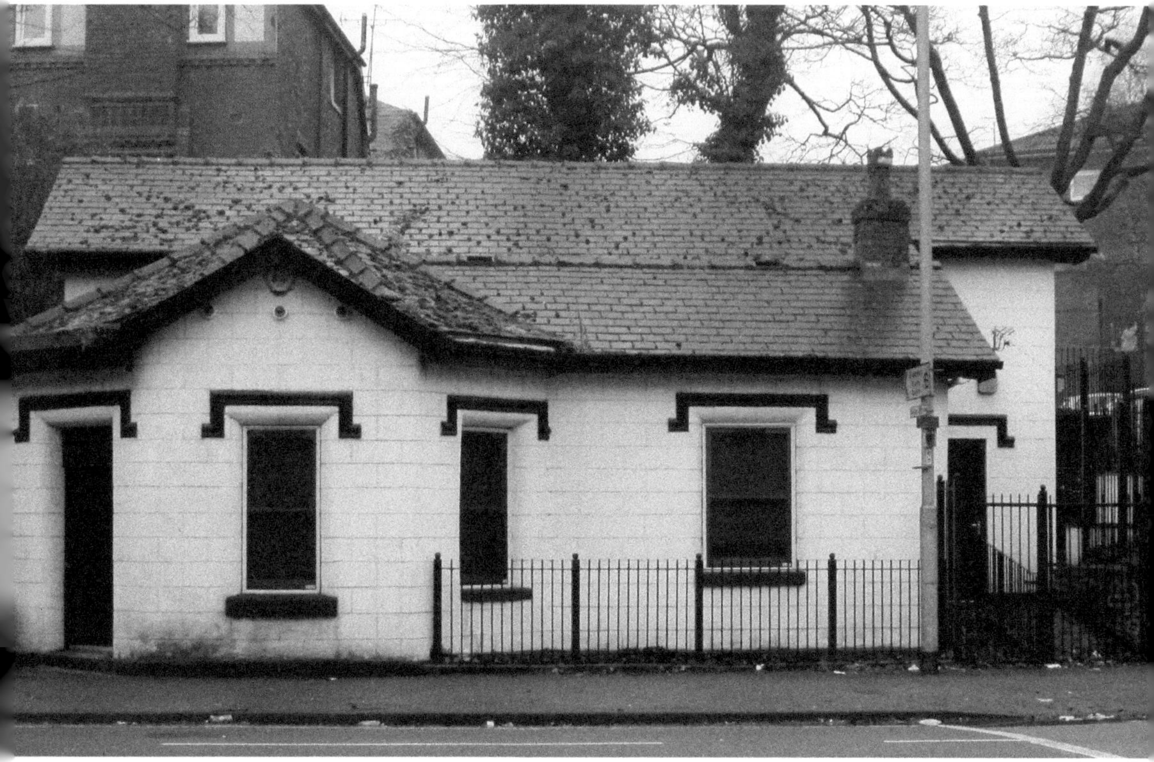

Kersal Bar Tollhouse, which had many uses over a number of decades.

A tollhouse was erected with a bay window projecting out so that the collector of the tolls had an open and clear view of the road. Kersal Bar was also the Higher Broughton terminus of the region's first horse-drawn tramway in 1877, and was also the first out-of-town terminus for the new electric tramcars in 1901.

However, by 1848 tolls were abolished when the local authority took over the road. The building remains here to this day and has changed very little. Designed with stucco over brick, it became a plumbing and cycle-repair business, a general store and eventually a newsagent's shop. It was the only shop in the area where there were restrictive covenants preventing any commercial development. It was restored in 2007 with an extension added and is the only remaining tollhouse in Manchester and Salford area.

14. Salford Cathedral

Salford's Roman Catholic cathedral is occasionally known as the Cathedral Church of St John the Evangelist, and is the seat of the Bishop of Salford. The neo-Gothic church was built between 1844 and 1848 and designed by architect Matthew Ellison Hadfield (1812–85), best known for his work on Roman Catholic cathedrals and churches. Hadfield's design for his new church in Salford was the first cruciform Catholic church to be built in England since the Reformation. His design was very much based on several notable medieval churches, including Howden Minster in the East Riding of Yorkshire and Selby Abbey in North Yorkshire, as well as a number of decorations copied from the Church of St Jacques in Liege, Belgium. At the time of building, the tower and spire were the tallest in Lancashire and are derived from the church of St Mary Magdalene, in Newark on Trent, Nottinghamshire.

It was two local businessmen who donated £1,000 each towards the cost of the church – Daniel Lee and John Leeming. This money went towards the cost of the church and its furnishings and both men are commemorated in the cathedral. To the east end of the building, the east window of 1856, was by William Wailes of Newcastle and depicts the history of Catholic Christianity in England, from the conversion of Ethelbert by St Augustine in 597, to the restoration of the Catholic hierarchy in 1850. The final cost of the building was £18,000 with the foundation stone laid in 1844 by Bishop James Sharples. The church was eventually opened on 9 August 1848 and was elevated to cathedral status in 1852. Serious damage was caused to the cathedral's spire in October 1881 after a severe storm leading to the need to raise funds for repairs as well as works to the building itself.

By early 1890 the last £1,000 of the original debt was paid off for the building of the cathedral, leading to its consecration in the same year by the second Bishop of Salford, Herbert Vaughan, who later became Cardinal Archbishop of Westminster. Many further repairs were carried out to the cathedral over the

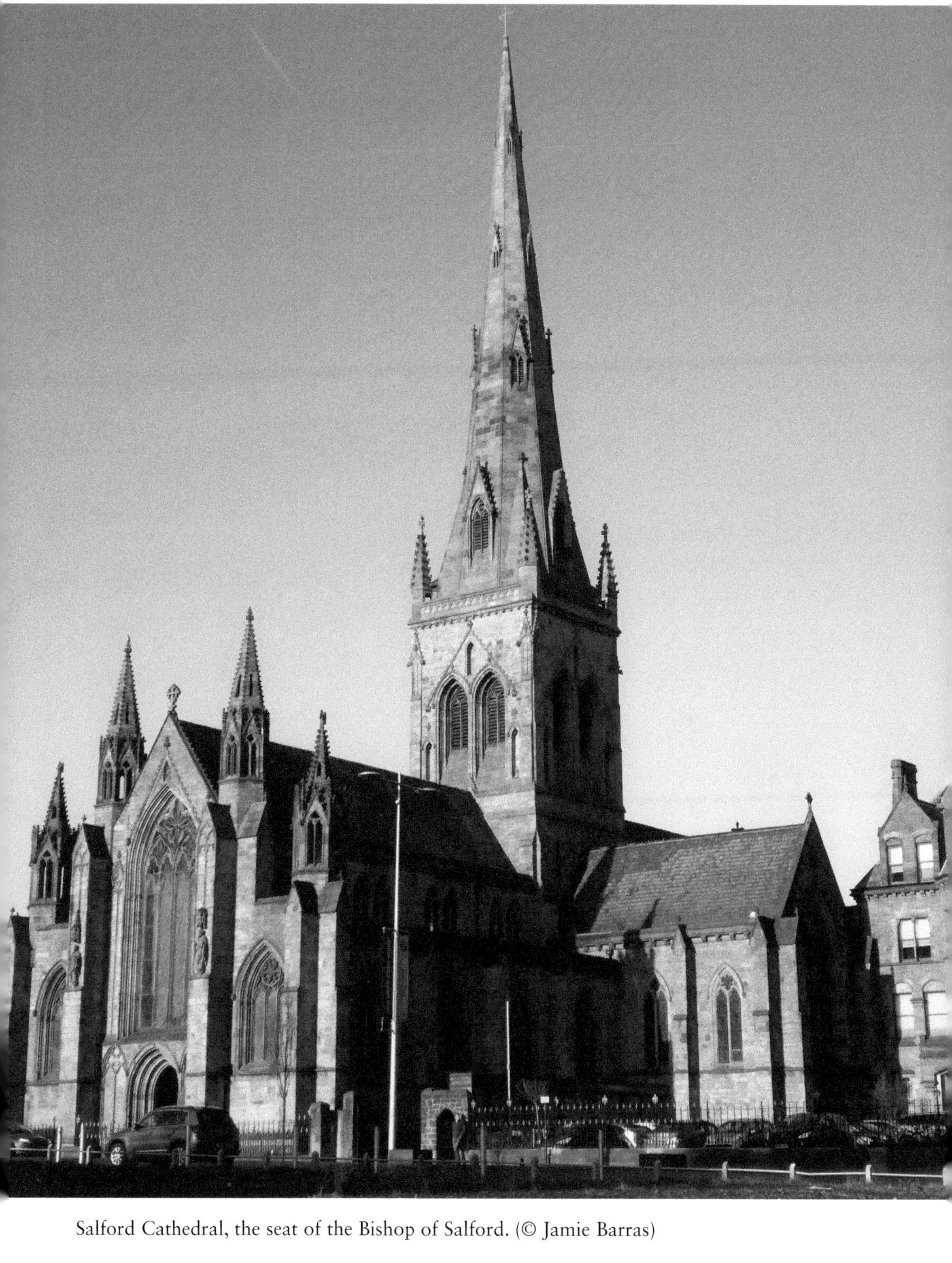

Salford Cathedral, the seat of the Bishop of Salford. (© Jamie Barras)

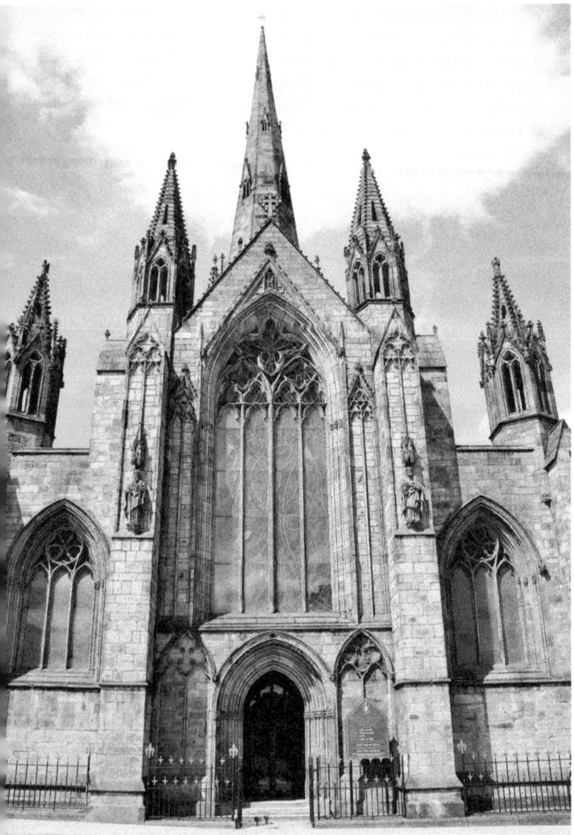

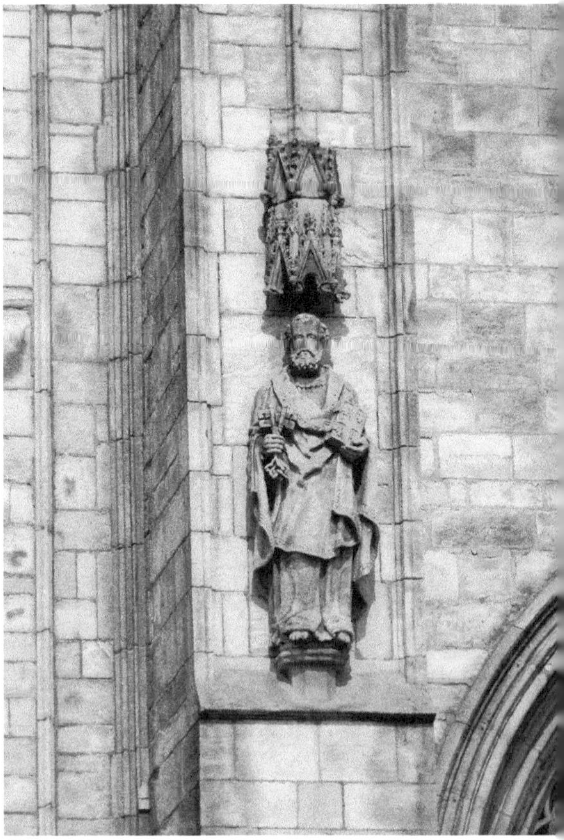

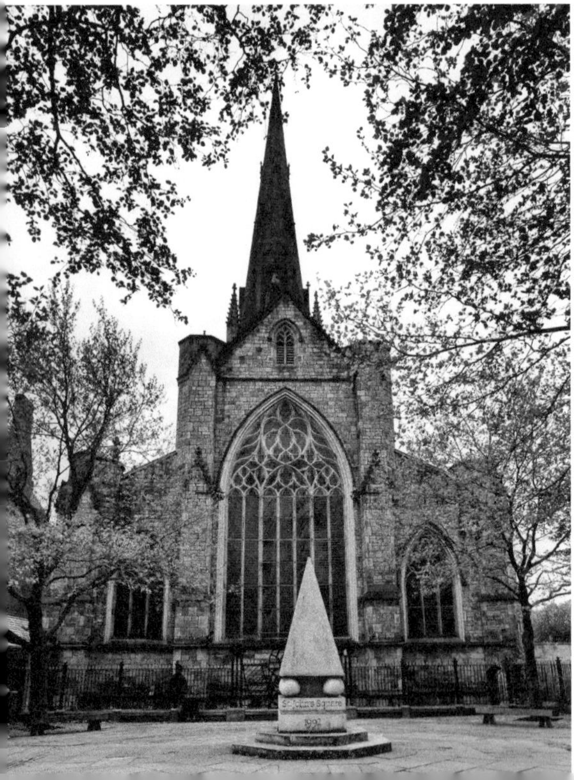

Above left: Salford Cathedral's main entrance, displaying its fine neo-Gothic details. (© Ben Abel)

Above right: Salford Cathedral and one of the many figures that adorn this fine building.

Left: Salford Cathedral with considerable damage that was caused to the spire in October 1881 after a severe storm. (© https://tigergrowl.wordpress.com)

following years including in 1919–20, work under the supervision of Charles M. Hadfield, grandson of the cathedral's original architect. In 1994, a new stained-glass west window was installed commemorating the 150th anniversary of the laying of the cathedral's foundation stone. Its title is 'When I am lifted up I shall draw all to myself', depicting in a rather abstract way, the crucified Christ flanked by the Virgin Mary and the cathedral's patron, St John.

One of the more unusual aspects of the cathedral was the introduction of a new four-manual digital organ in 2002. These are generally uncommon in cathedrals, but it has replaced previous traditional organs installed in 1951 and before that in 1938.

15. Salford Museum and Art Gallery

The Salford Library was founded in 1849, a year before the Public Libraries Act of 1850 and called the Royal Museum and Library. As a result, it was in none other than Peel Park that the first municipal free library in the country opened in January 1850 and the museum opened the November the same year. Four years earlier, Peel Park was opened as one of the first public parks to be opened in the country 'for the enjoyment and recreation of the public ... without charge or restriction'. It was named in honour of Sir Robert Peel, the former prime minister. The library was initially based in Lark Hill House, a mansion built in the 1790s and erected by

Peel Park arch, sadly demolished in 1938.

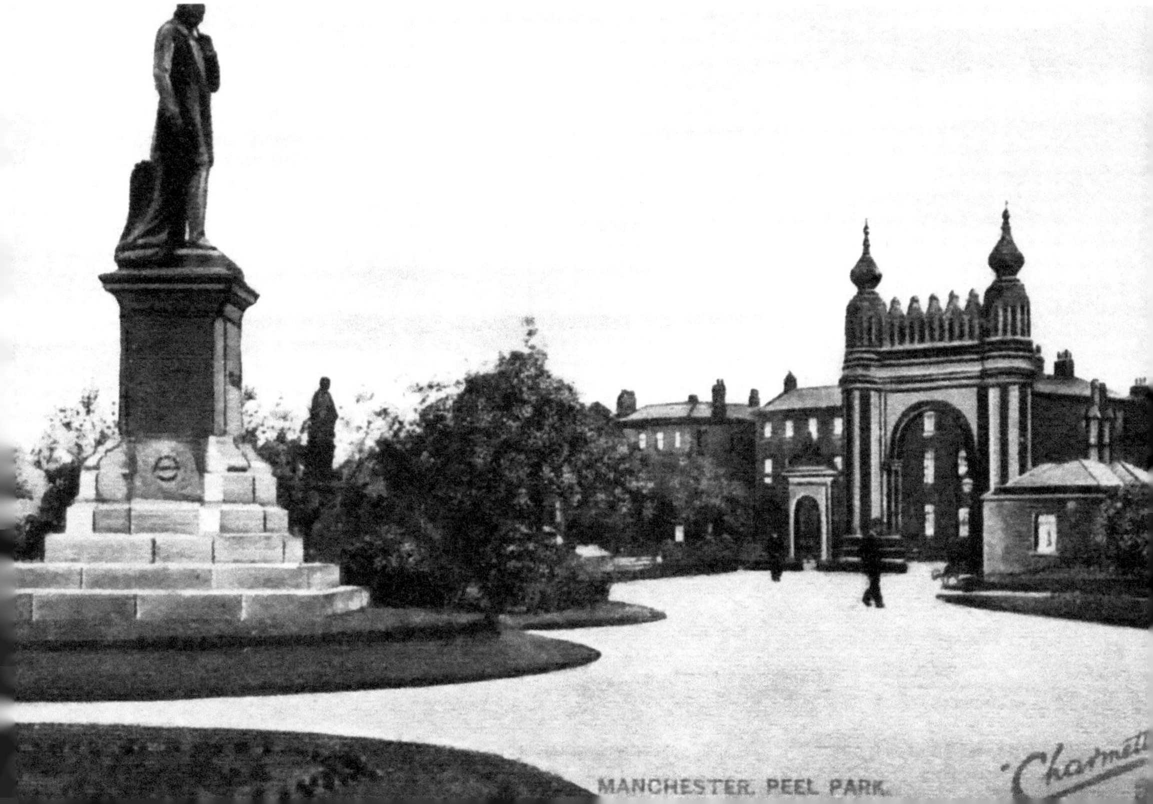

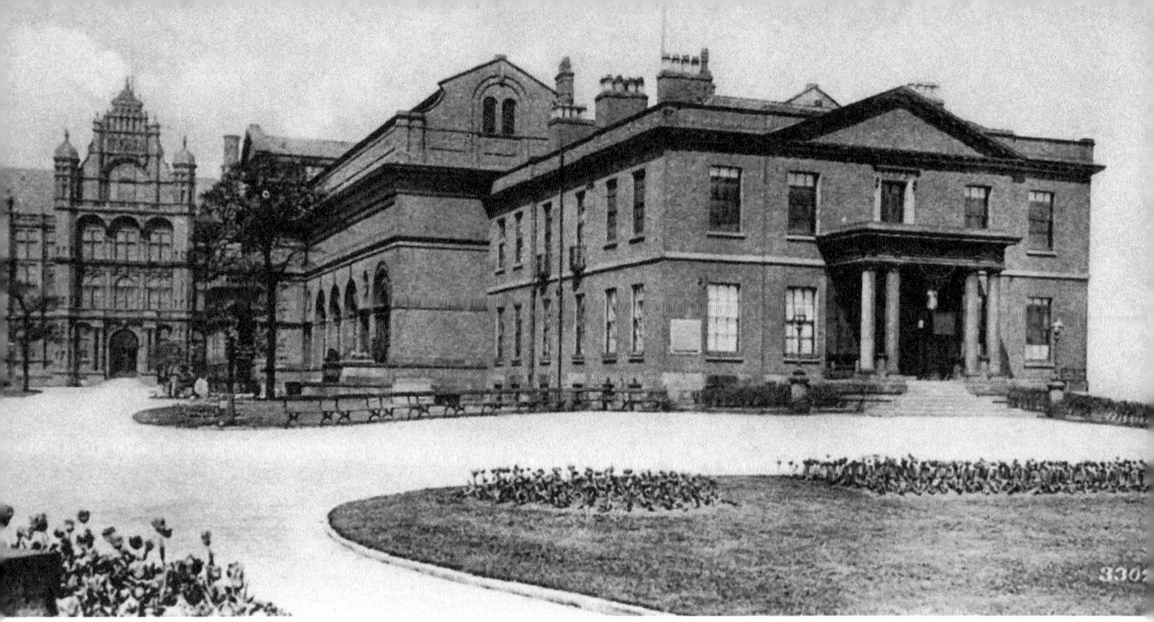

Above: The library and Peel Building, with the former built in Italian Renaissance style.

Below: The building now houses Salford Museum and Art Gallery.

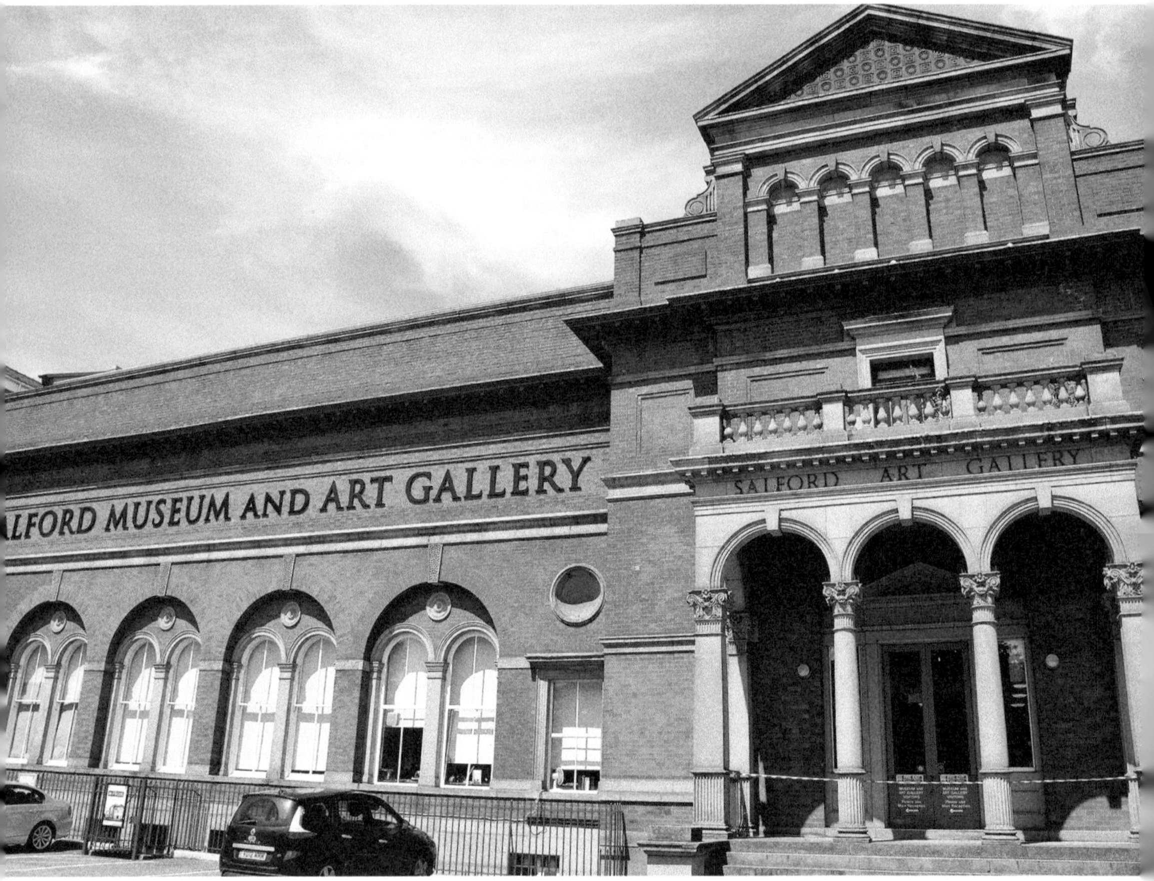

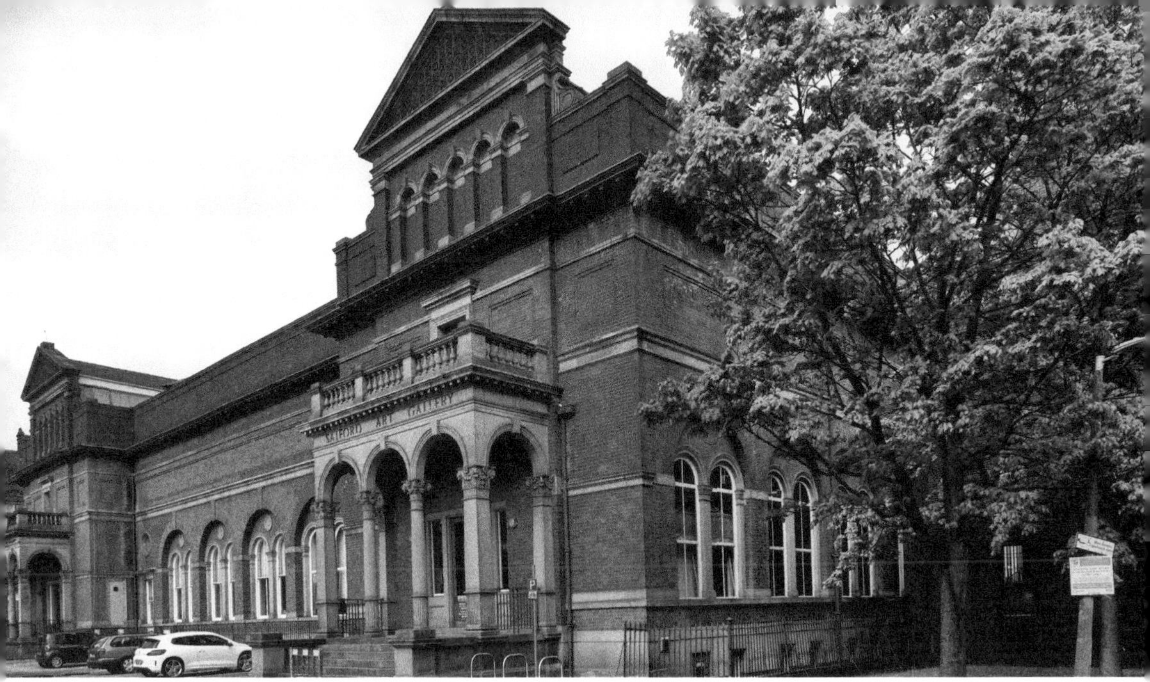

Once the home of a large Lowry collection, the museum has a large collection of Salford's social history. (© https://tigergrowl.wordpress.com)

Colonel James Ackers, which was purchased by public subscription, leading to the grounds becoming used as a public park. The collections were to grow considerably with many gifts from local families and a number of extensions were required to house the many artefacts. In 1852, the first of a number of extensions was commenced by architects Travis and Mangnall, which was to lead to the appearance of the building we see today. A building built in the Italian Renaissance style, it has two handsome arched entrances and has some similarities to the museums in South Kensington in London. Queen Victoria and Prince Albert visited in 1851, with 82,000 children gathering in Peel Park singing 'God Save the Queen'. It was described later by the queen herself as 'the most original and striking spectacle ever presented to do honour to Royalty in any age'. In recognition of this event, the Victoria Arch was erected at the park entrance in 1859, designed by Thomas Groom Barker and in the style of the Brighton Pavilion, designed by John Nash.

The buildings and park were to flourish for many years but sadly the park was to decline in the twentieth century, with Victoria Arch demolished in 1938 along with Lark Hill House. Salford University erected a large tower block, the Peel Tower, which overshadowed the museum and art gallery, eventually demolished in 1994. The Art Gallery hosted a large collection of paintings by L. S. Lowry until they moved to the Lowry Centre on Salford Quays. Now a combined art gallery and museum, it covers much of Salford's social history, although originally the museum did have a much wider remit when it came to collecting artefacts from all over the world. One of its finest displays is the reconstructed street, Lark Hill Place, which contains thousands of museum objects to recreate the feel of a Salford street in the latter part of the Victorian era.

16. St Paul's Church, Kersal Moor

The church was designed by Andrew Trimen (who specialised in religious buildings) in 1851–52 and located on Moor Lane, next to Kersal Moor. It was built on the site of the grandstand of the former Kersal Moor racecourse.

The building sits on the highest point above sea level in the city of Salford. The large west tower has a recessed spire and an interesting octagonal stair turret crowned with a spirelet. This part of the building is over 160 feet in height. Originally, there were three other small spirelets at the corners of the tower, but these blew down over the years and were never replaced. The paired bell openings are reminiscent of Magdalen Tower in Oxford. The interior consists of an arcade of four bays with octagonal pillars. The reredos is flanked by scenes from the life of St Paul in mosaic tiled panels by Walter J. Pearce.

The extensive graveyard surrounding the church contains some 4,000 graves and many of prominent citizens from Salford and Manchester. These include members of the Holt brewing family, Edwin Waugh, the Lancashire dialect poet and Alexander Cussons who invented Cussons Imperial Leather soap in his Kersal Vale/Moor Lane factory. The 1923 graveyard extension on Moor Lane contains some interesting art deco memorials from the 1930s.

St Paul's Church, Kersal Moor. (© David Dixon)

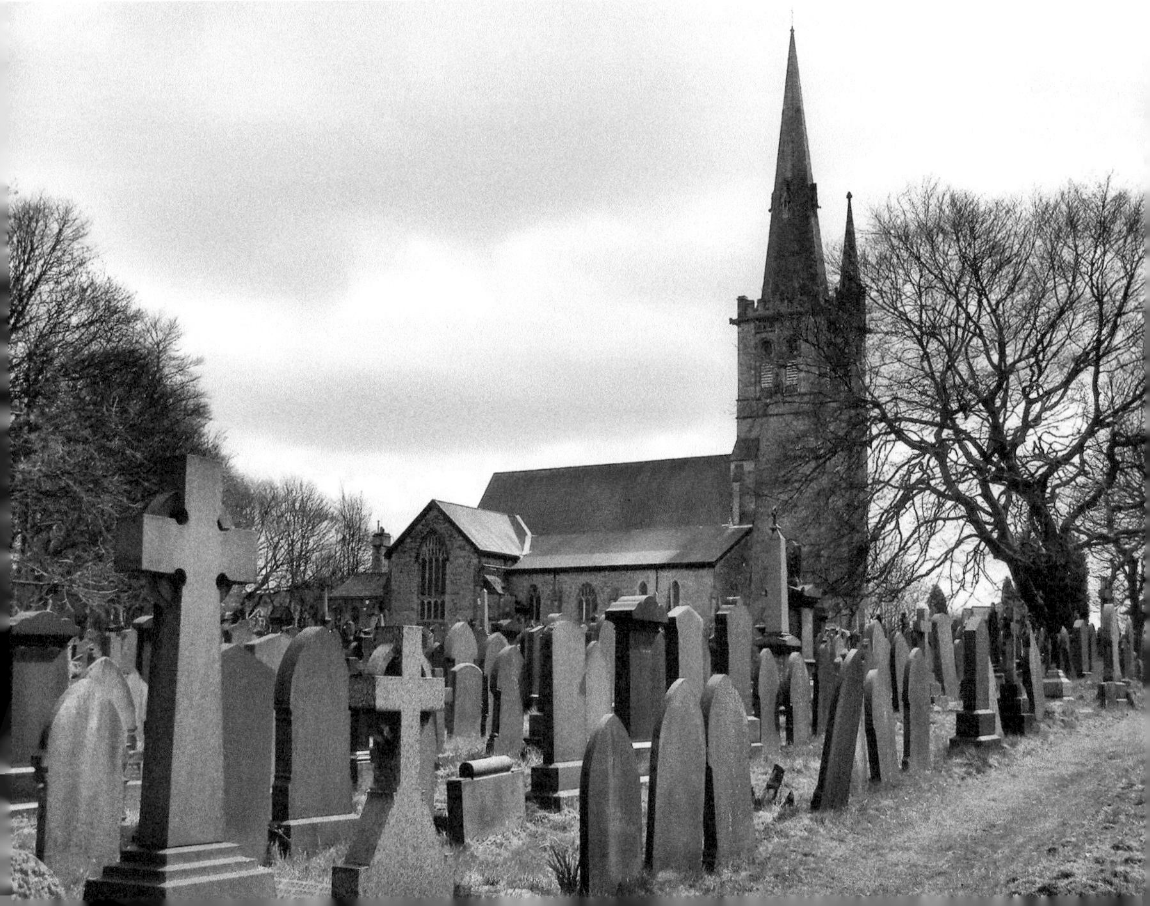

An arson attack in 1987 badly damaged the church and resulted in the loss of the entire clerestory, much of the stained glass was destroyed and the bell fell, breaking the stone font. Only the north transept window survived. The subsequent rebuilding meant that the church is now confined to the east end of the building with the rest of the space designated as meeting rooms and community spaces.

17. Greengate Baths

Of immense historical and architectural importance and somewhat hidden away in an almost forgotten back street, yet only a short stroll from Manchester's busy Deansgate, is the boarded-up and virtually derelict Greengate Baths. The building is the oldest surviving public baths in Britain, and one of only five public baths to be listed Grade II*. Incredibly, it only operated as baths for barely twenty-five years, and spent the following hundred years or so as a warehouse. It is, though, the sole surviving example of the earliest generation of public baths in the mid-nineteenth century. The surroundings of the building today are very different, with an adjacent dual carriageway, industrial units and new developments forming part of the Greengate Embankment regeneration area. This area was once one of the most deprived and densely populated parts of the city in the 1850s. And yet unlike their counterparts in London, Birmingham, Liverpool or Preston, neither of the local authorities in Manchester or Salford were prepared to adopt the 1846 Baths and Washhouses Act. Instead, in 1854 local philanthropists and businessmen stepped into the void by forming the Manchester and Salford Baths and Laundries Company, with 7,000 shares of £5 each.

Greengate Baths was its first venture, for which the company hired an untested but promising local architect, Thomas Worthington (1826–1909), whose front elevation and chimney design clearly shows the influence of his recent tour of Italy. Unusually, the first- and second-class pools were of equal dimensions, at 53 feet long (to suit the site rather than any stipulated minimum), but as was the norm, no provision was made for women, other than in a separate slipper bath section at the side. The baths were incredibly popular. In its first five months, it was used by 16,000 people, and as it had cost barely a third of Cornwallis Street in Liverpool or Kent Street in Birmingham, the company was more than pleased. One of its leading shareholders, an engineer, declared that Greengate would be an 'example across the kingdom, and was much superior to any of the baths he had visited in London'. However, he was mistaken. With a number of problems arising with ventilation in particular an issue – remedied by Worthington in his two other baths for the company – Salford Corporation, who took the baths over in 1877, built new baths on nearby Blackfriars Road instead. (These opened in 1880 and in 2001 were converted into offices.) From 1880 until around 1990, Greengate served as a warehouse, and then stood empty and exposed to the elements and vandalism. Its chimney had already been demolished in the 1980s

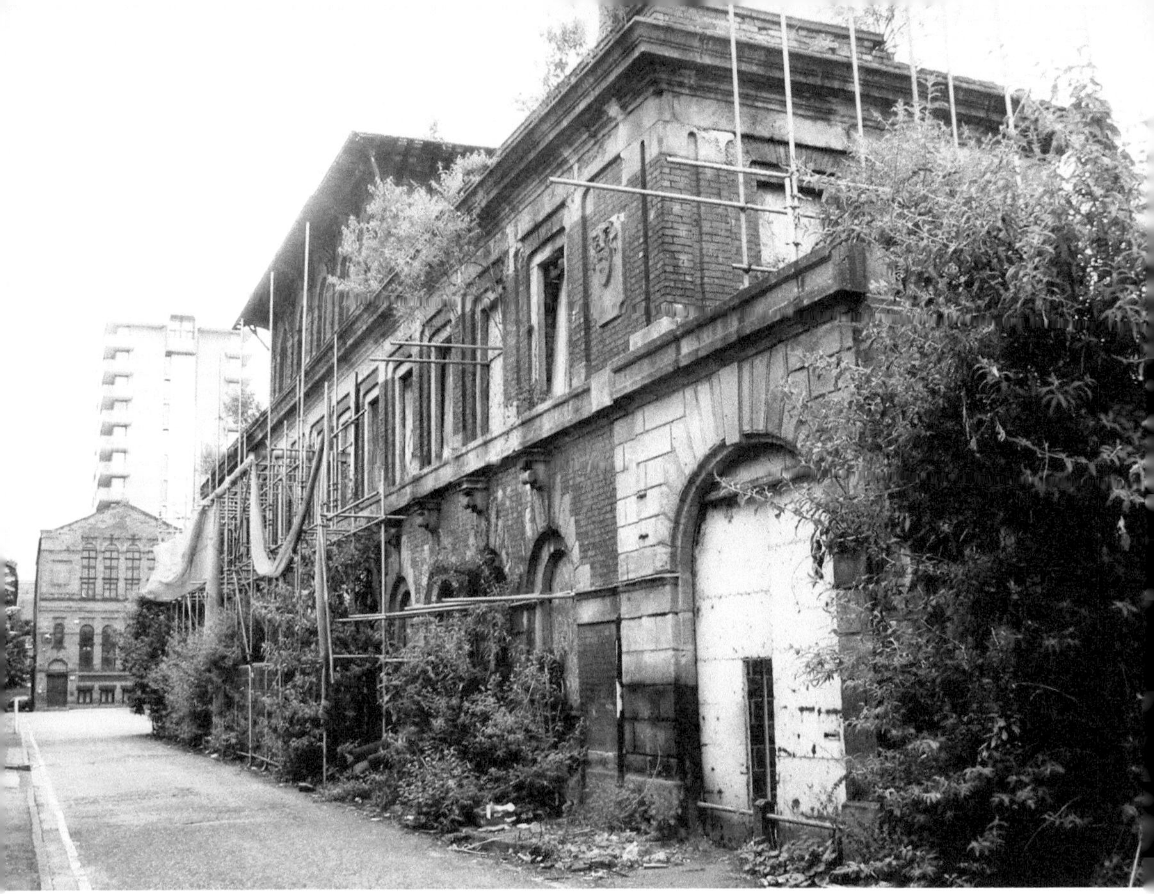

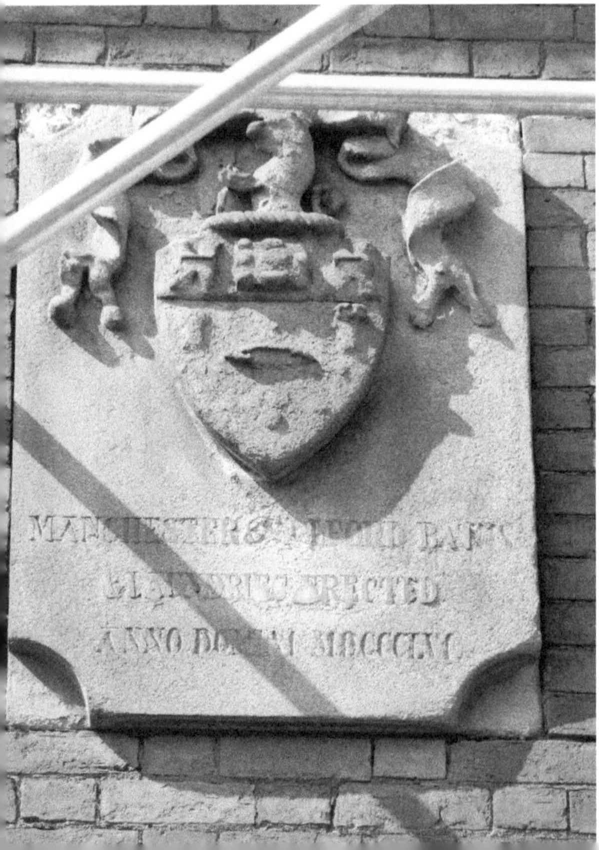

Above: Greengate Baths, the oldest surviving baths in the country, now derelict.

Left: Greengate Baths – a distant memory. (© Tony Reeves)

and in 1998, it was placed on English Heritage's Buildings at Risk Register. Three years later it was bought by Ask Developments. They spent £400,000 on securing the fabric against further deterioration, but after considering various options to convert the shell into offices or residential units, a collapse in the property market in 2008 left its future uncertain. The building's deterioration has been dramatic and it has since been listed in the top ten of the most at risk Victorian buildings in the country.

18. Greek Orthodox Church of the Annunciation, Bury New Road

This interesting building was designed by Clegg and Knowles, who had a reputation as builders of warehouses and commercial premises in Manchester. The church was built in 1860–61 and reflects the social and economic power of the Greek community in Salford at this time. It is the oldest Greek Orthodox church in England. It was funded by donations from Greek immigrants who had begun to arrive into Britain from 1800. The design was deliberately kept simple so as to respect the wishes of the Greek community to integrate into British society.

The building is dominated by Corinthian columns on the portico and Corinthian pilasters on the side and makes a strong classical statement. The iconostasis (a screen or partition where the icons are placed) was painted by noted Greek painter Theodore Vryzakis. Some of the interior was replaced in the mid-

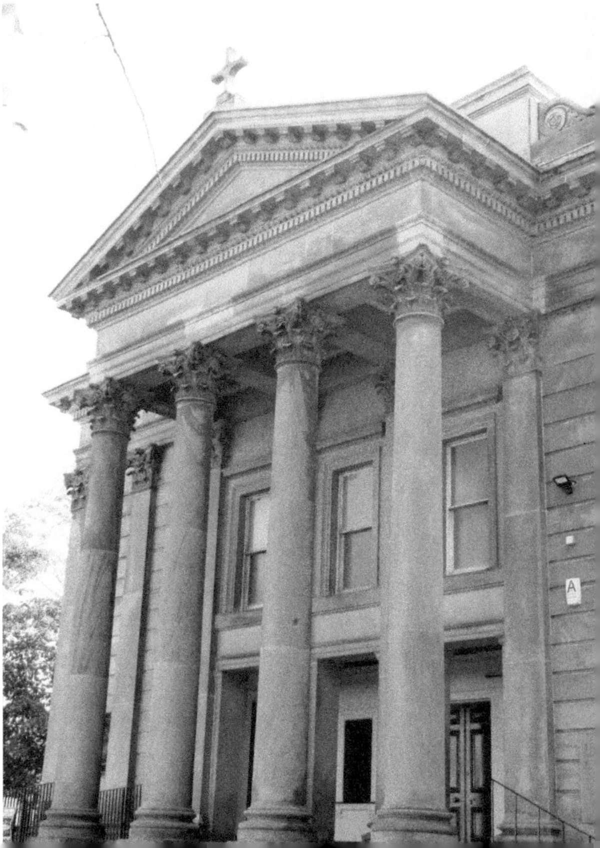

The Greek Orthodox Church of the Annunciation on Bury Road – the oldest of this kind in the country. (© Carole O'Reilly)

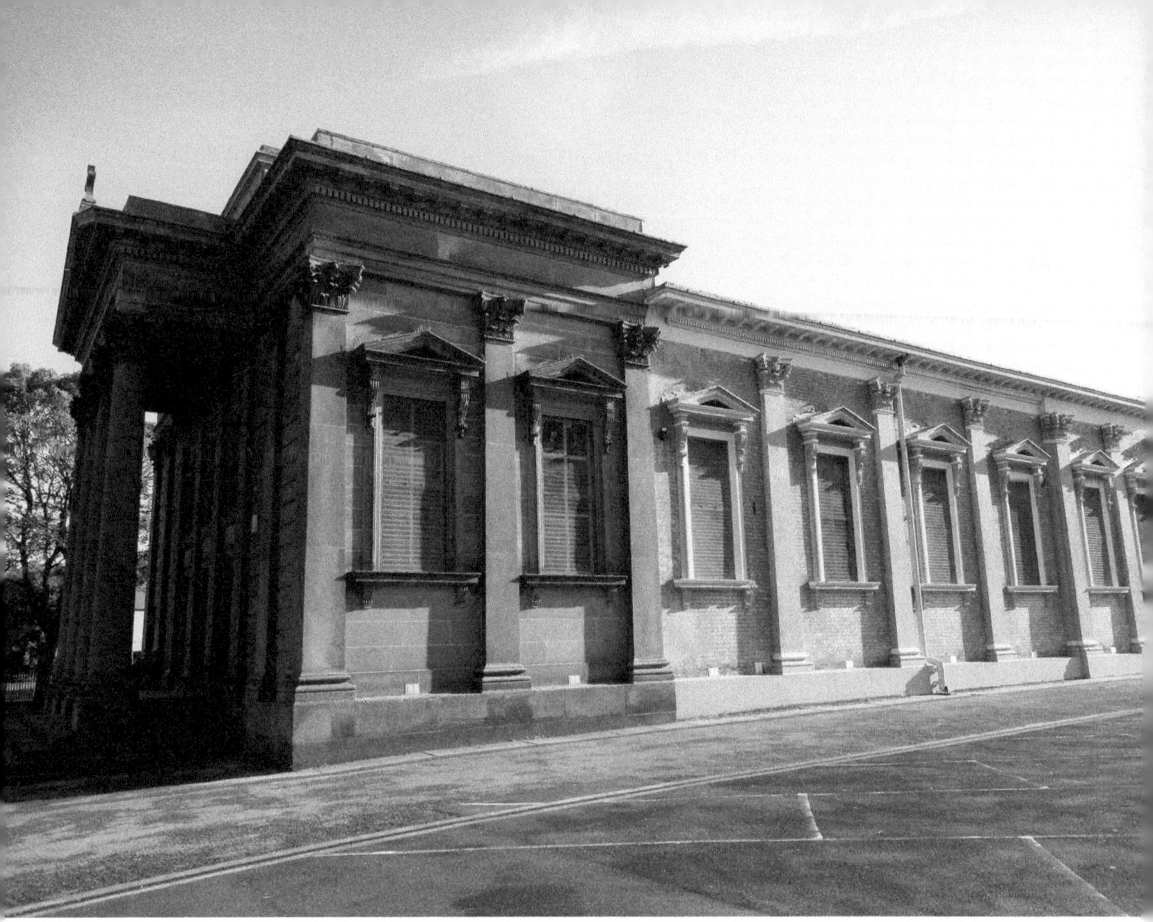

The Greek Orthodox Church of the Annunciation. (© Carole O'Reilly)

twentieth century, following a fire. The original domed ceiling with its mural was destroyed by dry rot and replaced by a pitched roof in 1962. The building was renovated with support from Historic England and the Heritage Lottery Fund in 2009.

The church continues to provide a place of worship for the local Greek community.

19. Ainscow Hotel (formerly Watson & Woodhead Brewery)

Many of the workers in the cotton and other related industries were consumers of a popular liquid industry – the brewing of beer. Many innkeepers brewed their own beer but, by 1790, there were at least four quite large independent breweries in Salford. Twenty years later, nine of the fifteen breweries in Manchester and Salford were in the latter town and was to grow further over the next twenty years. Breweries included Lupton and Adamthwaite. John M. Threlfall, who acquired the Greengate Brewery, took over the Cook Street premises and Joule & Son were early brewers at New Bailey Street. Many of these brewery buildings have since disappeared but one of note remains. The building, now the Ainscow Hotel,

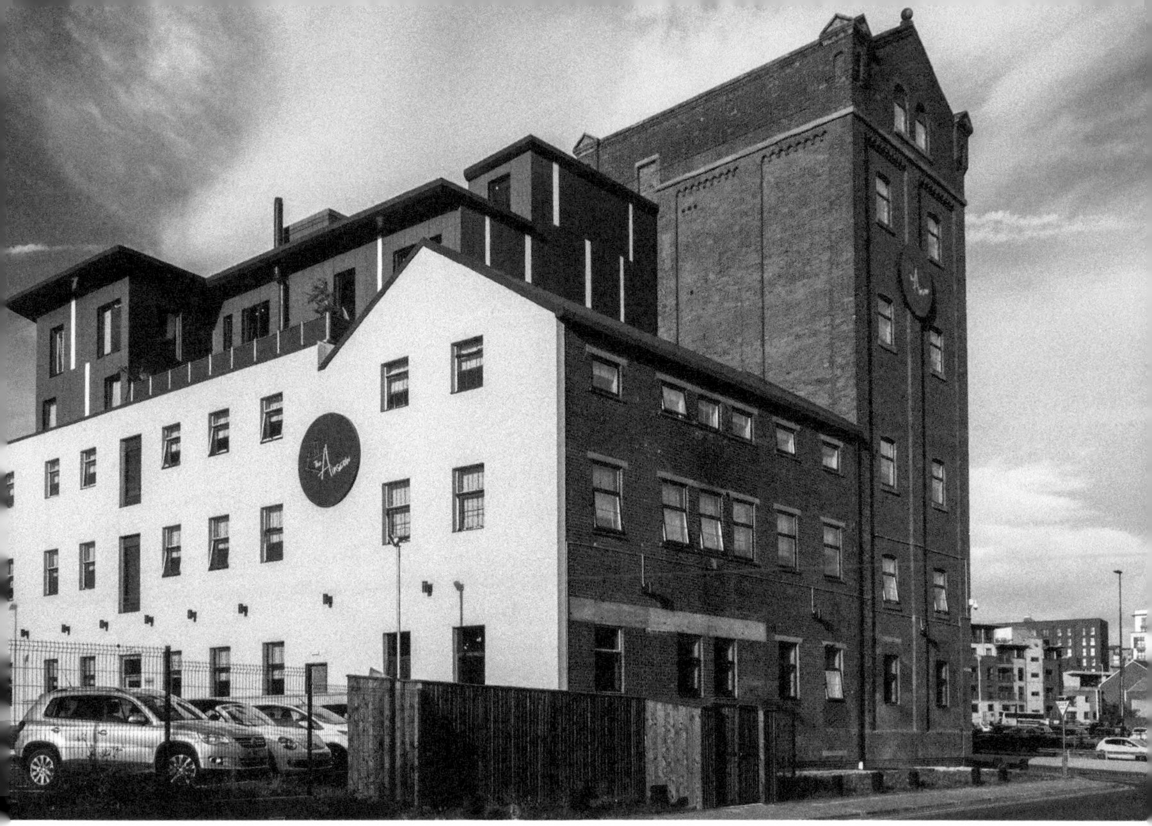

Above: The Ainscow Hotel, once a former brewery. (© Peter McDermott)

Right: The Ainscow Hotel. (© Martyn Hilbert)

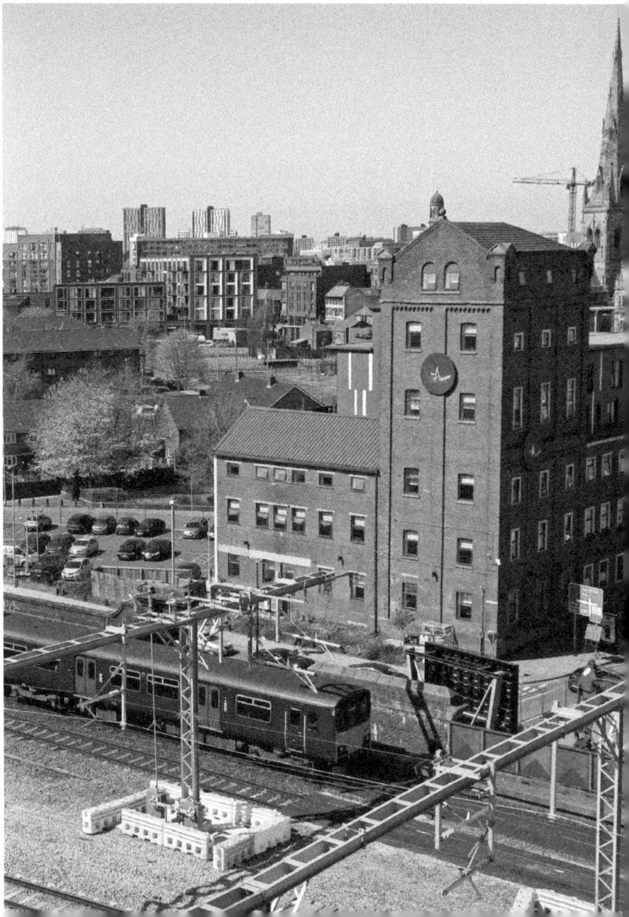

opened as a brewery for Watson and Woodhead in 1876. During its lifetime, it has been used for many purposes, including a jam factory (1927–55) and an auto-parts shop. Mackie & Sons Fruit Preservers occupied it and this was followed by Brown Brothers Auto Parts until 1986.

The building's location was key. On the corner of Trinity Way (former Irwell Street) and Chapel Street, it was close to the border with Manchester and this explains its popularity as a central convenient commercial premises.

The building was recently refurbished in 2014 and now operates as the popular Ainscow Hotel.

20. Baerlin's Warehouse, No. 10 Blackfriars Street

The nearby city of Manchester has plenty of warehouses, but this one is unusual for being in Salford and of very different design to those in Manchester. The warehouse was built in 1877–79 by Oldham and Wilson. The building is not in the Italian style of most warehouses but of Flemish Renaissance and Tudor design. It is constructed in sandstone ashlar and rises five storeys in height with an attic. The building is strongly vertical, which is emphasised by the octagonal piers that rise above the parapet. Oriel windows on the first and second floors mark the main offices. The fourth-floor centre bay has a large Dutch gable with fine carving by E. Williams.

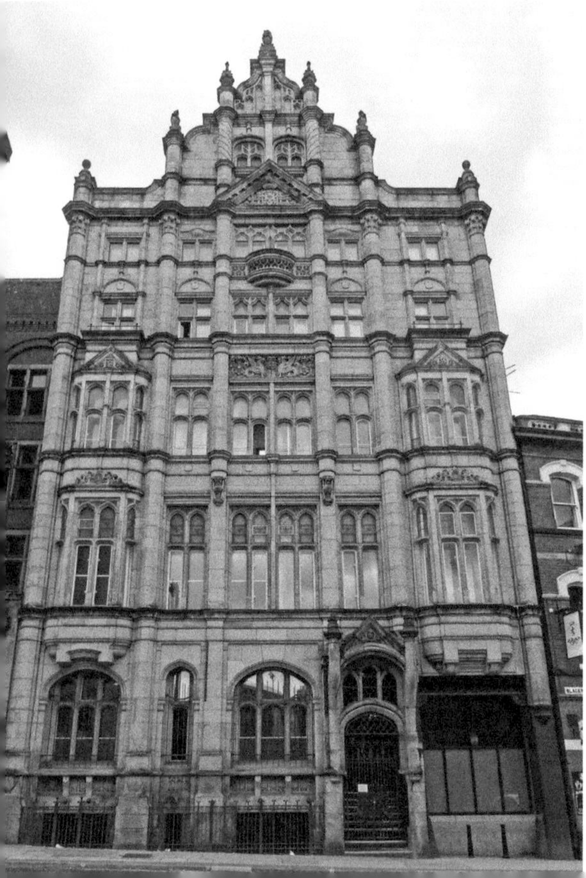

Baerlin's Warehouse, an imposing building at No. 10 Blackfriars Street. (© Tim Green)

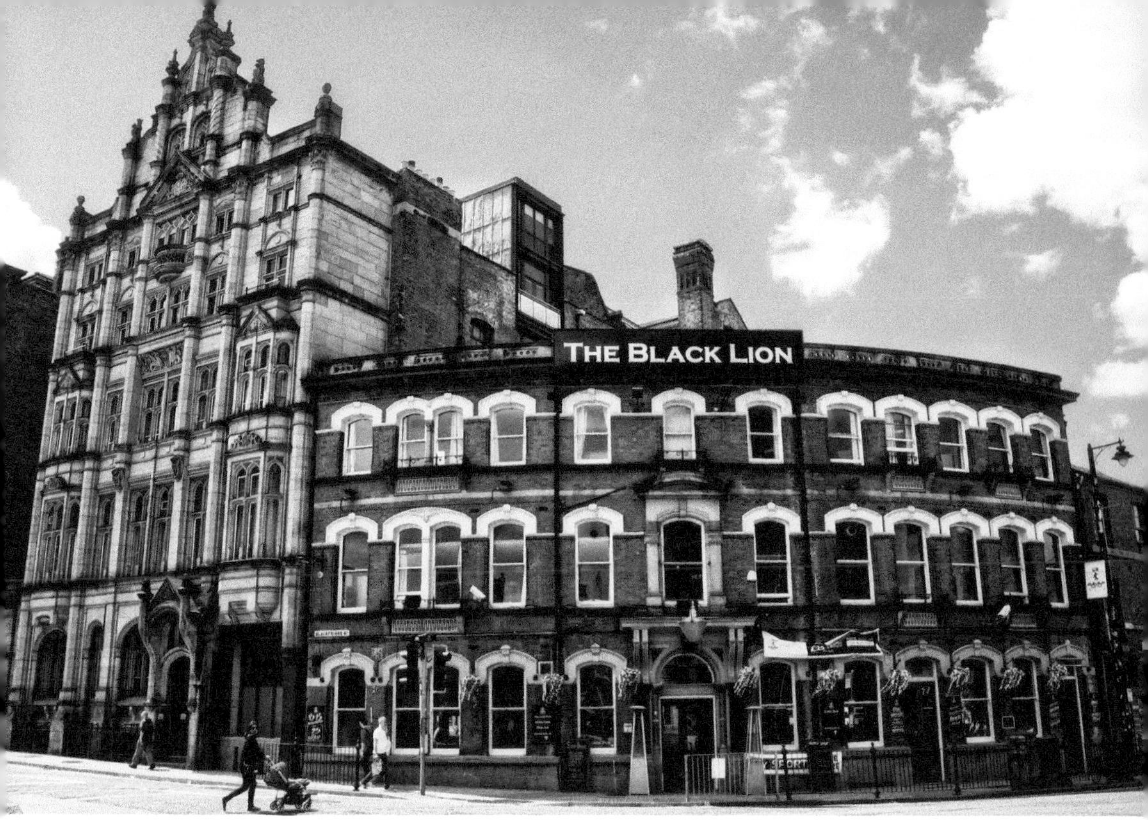

Baerlin's Warehouse, now apartments adjacent to the Black Lion public house, an imposing part of the Salford streetscape. (© Mike Rampton)

Baerlin & Co. occupied this warehouse, which was outside the traditional merchant district. Following a fire in 1883, the rebuilt premises still stand as a fine example of Victorian period architecture in stone. The firm were 'merchants, engineers, drysalters, cotton and flax waste dealers, exporters of all classes of cotton yarns, machinery, rollers and chemicals for printers, dyers, etc. also of cotton waste, importers and dealers in flax waste and other materials for paper makers etc'. Maximilian Baerlin lived at The Limes and Sigmund at Hope House, both on Eccles Old Road.

This beautiful building was eventually converted into apartments, known as Textile Apartments.

21. Arlington House (former Gas Board Offices), Bloom Street

The former Corporation Gas Works Office building at the northern end of Bloom Street is now Grade II listed and one of the finest buildings in Salford. An elaborate building, it has on occasions been described as 'a hidden architectural gem'. It was built in 1880 and is attributed to reputable Salford architect Thomas Worthington. He is best known as the architect responsible for Manchester's Albert Memorial, which was unveiled in Albert Square in 1867 – only a year before Alfred Waterhouse was appointed to design the new Town Hall on the northern side of the square. Worthington was born in Salford and was articled at the age of fourteen to local architect Henry Bowman. After completing his articles, he worked with Sir William Tite, who was most famous as being the architect of the Royal Exchange in London. Worthington's work was described of the time as having a 'pronounced Italian influence ... evident in much of his architecture,' and that he was 'a versatile pluralist, equally at ease with the Renaissance palazzo mode as with Venetian Gothic'. A significant influence on his life's work was also his religion. He was a committed Unitarian, and had a particular interest in social reform, encouraged in him early on by J. P. Kay (later Kay-Shuttleworth) and Mrs Gaskell and her husband, William, a Unitarian minister in Manchester. Concerns over housing conditions and amenities for the poor were a significant issue for him. Writing in his book of 1857, *Dwellings of the Poor*, Worthington wholly condemned back-to-back housing, and advised against the 'mere cleansing, painting, and whitewashing' of such properties, advocating instead 'improved drainage and structural alterations'.

Worthington's other works in the area are impressive and include the City Police and Sessions Court in Minshull Street, Manchester (1867–73), the Nicholls Hospital Building, Manchester (1881) and the Jubilee Fountain in Albert Square (1896–97). He was responsible for a number of Unitarian chapels on the outskirts of Manchester and was also president of the Manchester Society of Architects in 1875. His impact and reputation were considerable, including being invited to

Below left: Arlington House, designed by Salford architect Thomas Worthington.

Below right: One of the most impressive buildings in Salford, designed by Worthington in High Gothic style.

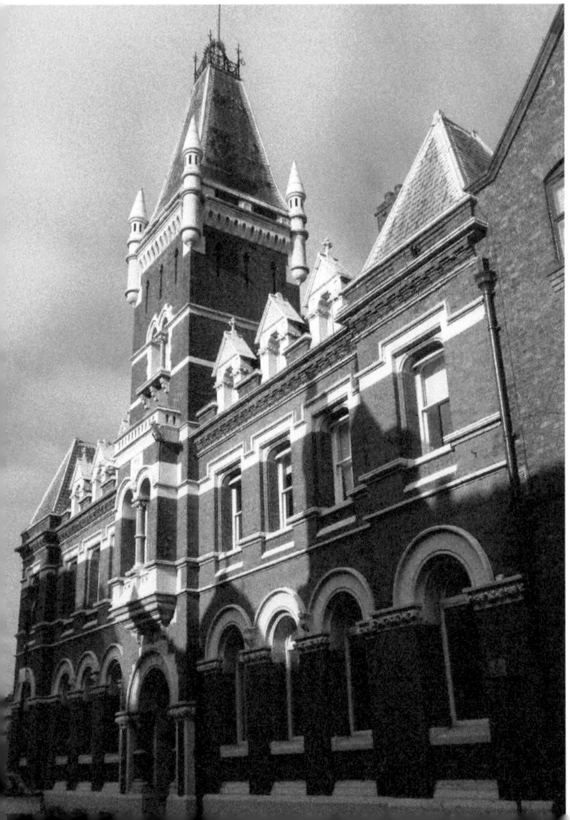

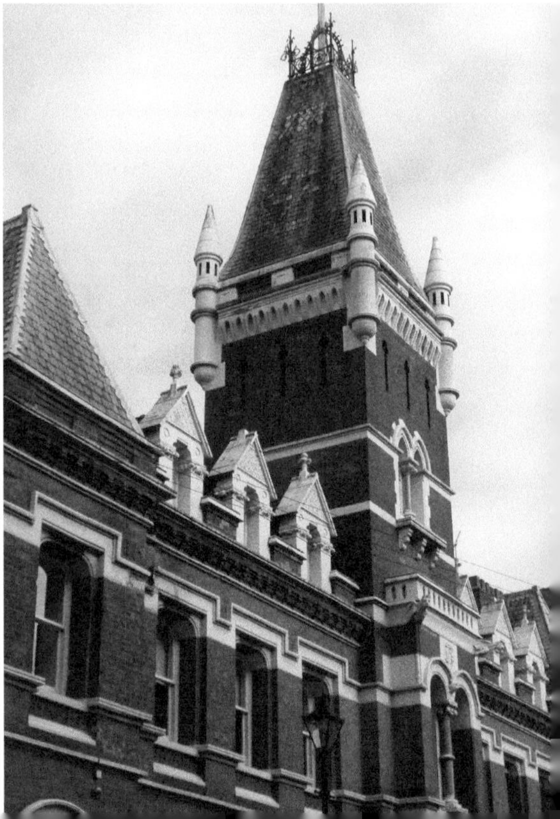

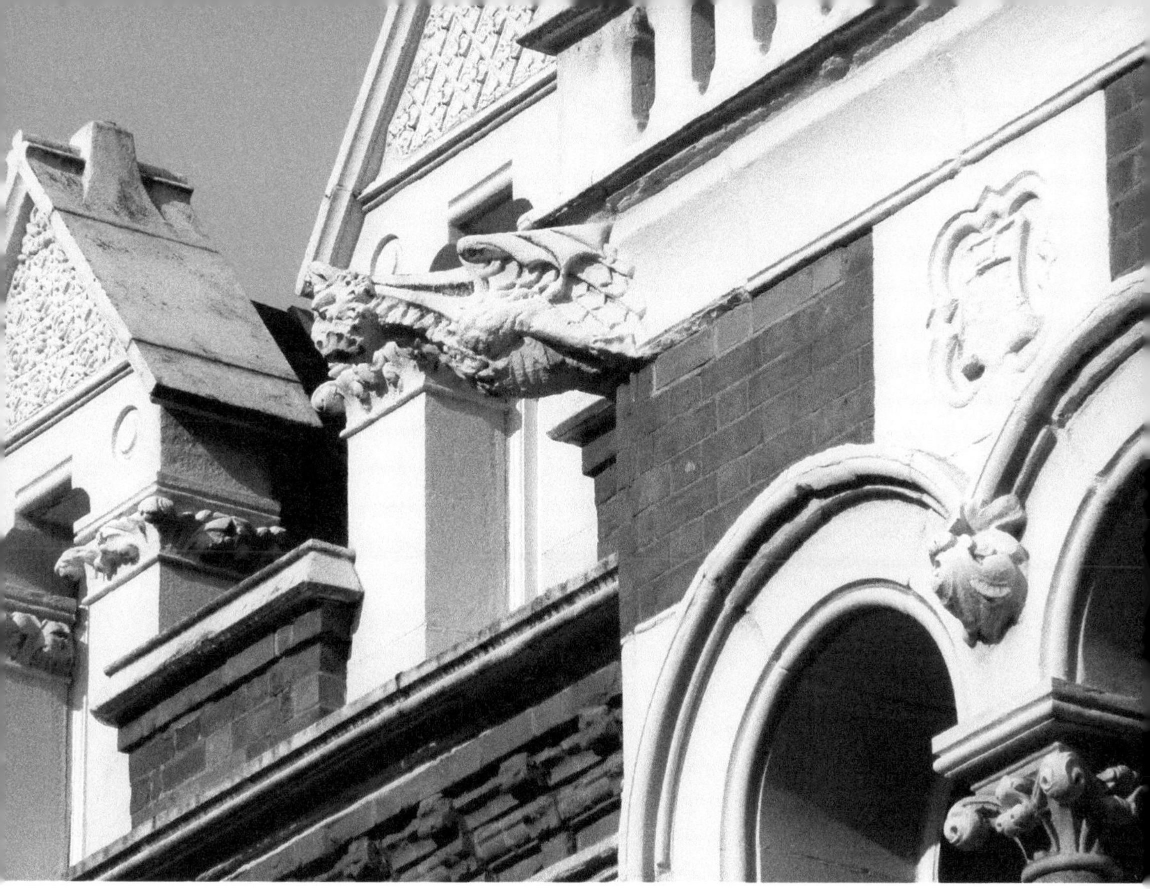

The building is adorned with Gothic features, adding to its character.

design the new Manchester Town Hall (Waterhouse's design selected instead) as well as submitting a design for the Great Exhibition in Hyde Park in 1851 (Joseph Paxton's design selected). He died in 1909 with his eldest son Percy (1864–1939) and youngest son Hubert (1886–1963) both becoming distinguished architects.

Worthington's building on Bloom Street, along with Minshull Street and the Nicholls Building, are all designed in the High Gothic style with impressive yet similar towers. Today, Arlington House belongs to Kenworthy's Legal Chambers.

22. Manchester Tennis and Racquet Club

This fine building on Blackfriars Road has been the home of the Manchester Tennis and Racquet Club since 1880. The club itself began life at a location in Miller Street in May 1876 after being formed in 1874. However, at that time only two 'racket' courts were available and did not include a tennis court. It was simply known as the Manchester Racquet Club. Sadly, the following year the London and North Western Railway obtained a compulsory purchase order on the new club so that they could build the approach road to Exchange station. However, the club members, undeterred, decided to build again and formed a limited company, the Manchester Racquet and Tennis and seek a new building.

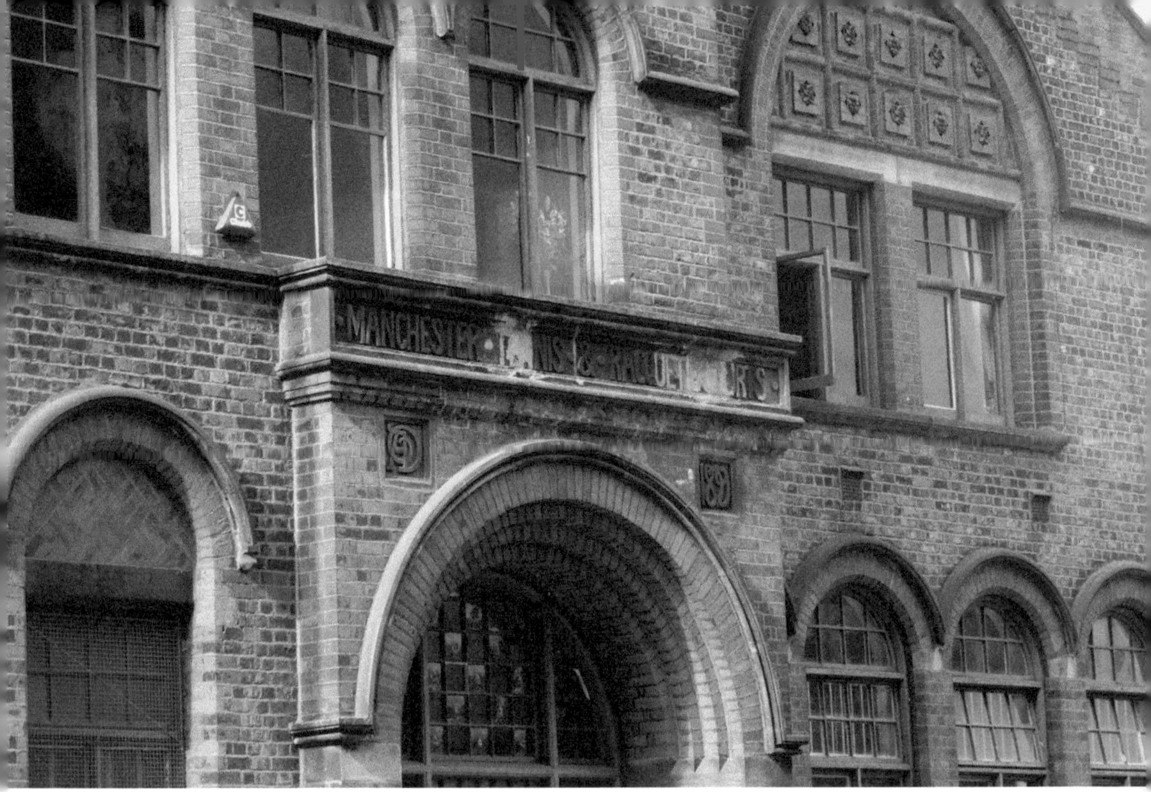

Above: Manchester Tennis and Racquet Club, dating from 1880.

Below: An unusual building and a hidden gem in Salford.

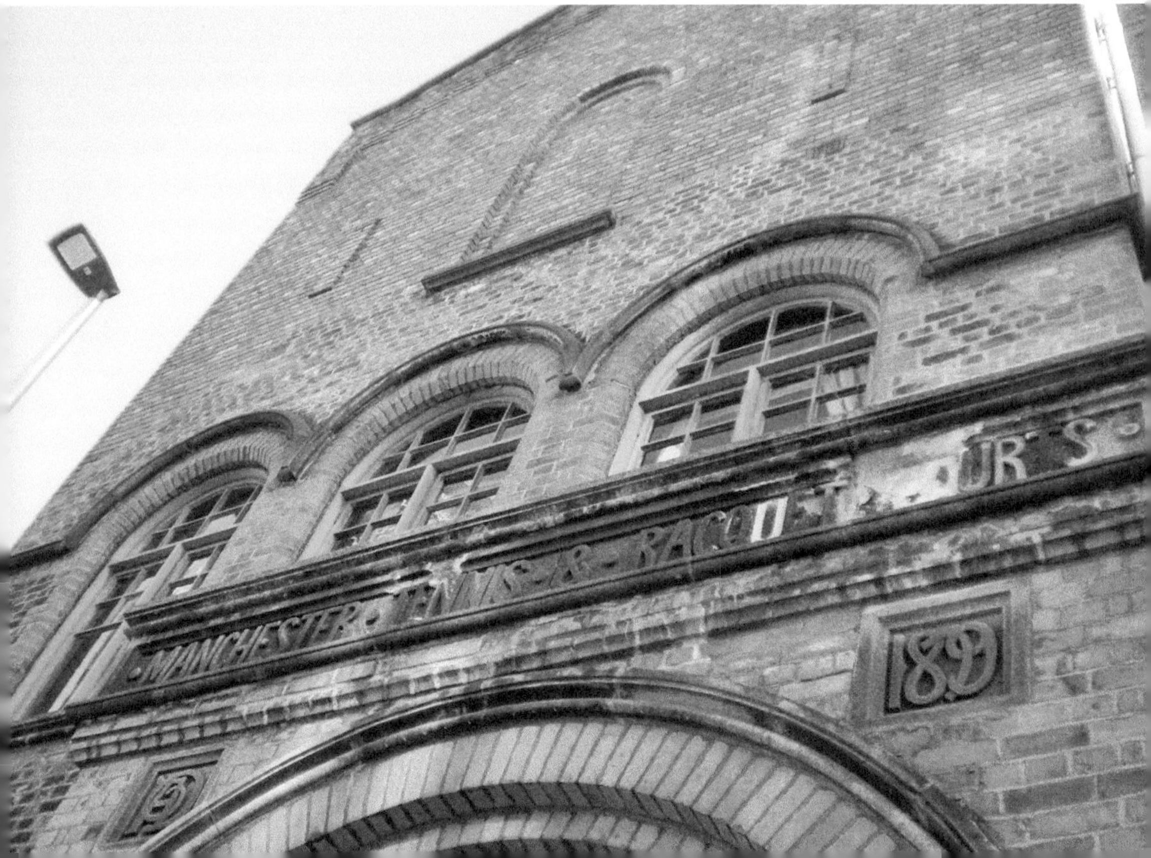

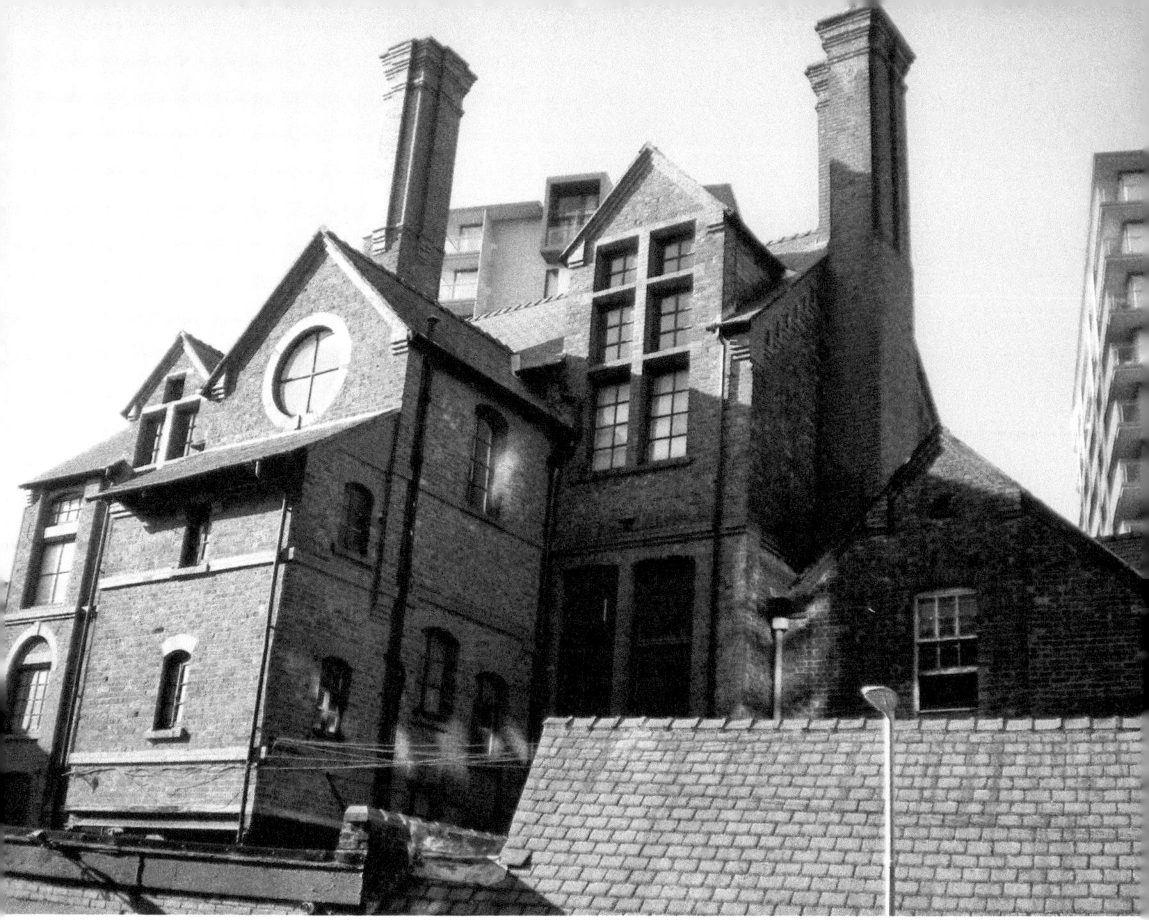

The home of the Manchester Tennis and Racquet Club since 1880.

Their eventual new building was designed by architect George T. Redmayne and when the club moved to Blackfriars Road in 1880, they only had one 'racket' court, but did have the addition of a real tennis court. In 1925, a squash court was added as an upper floor. Today, it is Grade II listed and was described by Pevsner as having an interior that is 'a delight, with a grand entrance and staircase hall, club rooms, dining room, changing rooms, etc. as well as extensive wine cellars. The double-height tennis court has a gallery on one side'.

Rackets is described as the 'purest of all the indoor court games'. Salford has the only operating rackets court in the north of England. The game is the forerunner of squash, and is played in a much bigger court with a smaller and faster ball. The Salford-based club is also one of only twenty-seven real tennis courts in the UK and forty-six in the world. It is considered the precursor of the modern game of lawn tennis.

23. The Black Friar

The once popular Black Friar pub occupies a corner of the busy junction of Blackfriars Road and Trinity Way and has been closed for several years. This Grade II listed building was designed by Manchester architect William Ball and is constructed of red brick and red sandstone and features a slate roof in a Vernacular Revival style. On the side of the building is a stone plaque that commemorates it was rebuilt in 1886 but suggests that it is a modification of or a replacement for an earlier building; in this case, possibly the Old School Inn, which is shown on the Ordnance Survey of 1848.

The building itself has a number of decorative features that do seem to imply an earlier date than 1886 including a carved stone tympanum depicting a friar holding a banner with the words 'The Black Friar' and a second tympanum that features a hound and a deer on either side of a shield. The shield features corn sheaves and bees, although these are very difficult to make out now. The Blackfriars is listed in the 1872 Directory of Manchester and Salford in the category of hotels and the licensee at that time was Ann Porter.

In 1975 the now named Blackfriars Hotel was described as an 'attractive smoke-blackened building' with 'You may go further and fare worse' engraved on the front wall. It was often said that the 'Boddington's bitter was so good in the Blackfriars Hotel that keg ale and lager was not even available'.

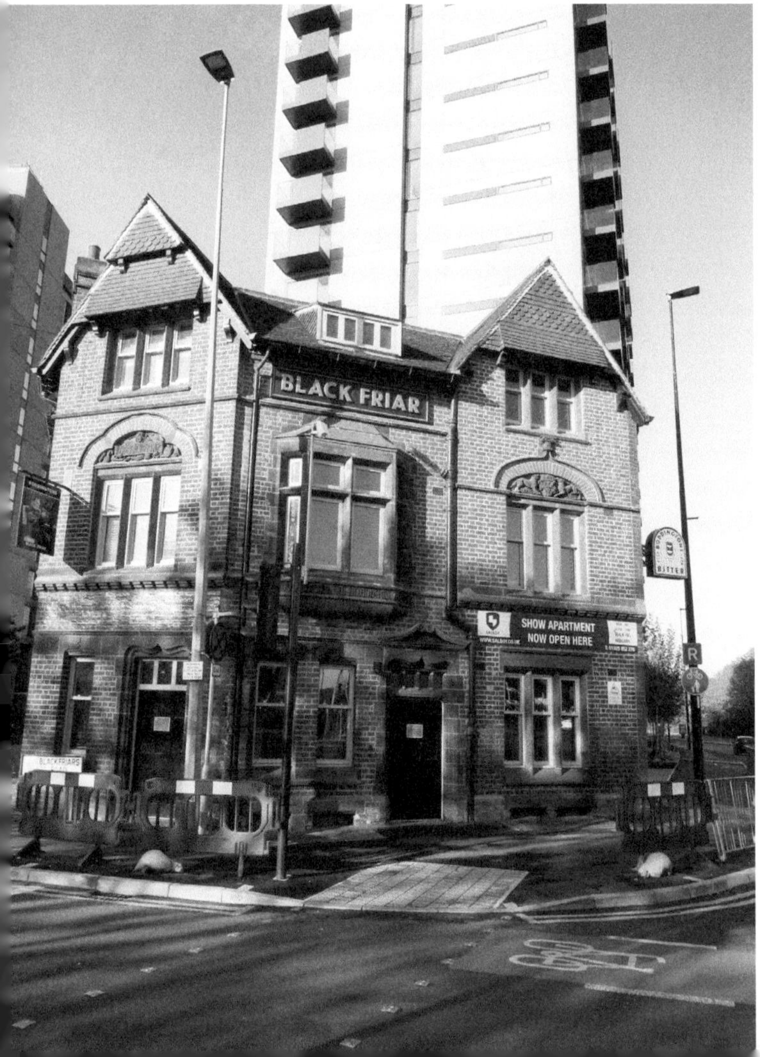

The Black Friar, now surrounded by significant new development. (© Carole O'Reilly)

By 1989, Trinity Way had been constructed and the pub had reverted back to the Black Friar, and a popular Boddington's house, yet it remained a thriving community local despite the changes going on around it. Today, the pub remains a Grade II listed building but sadly remains closed although it is being incorporated into Salford bookie Fred Done's latest residential development on Trinity Way and to be used as offices.

24. Brunswick Wesleyan Schools, Broad Street, Pendleton

The former school dates from 1887 and was possibly designed by Walter Sharp, to whom the adjacent Wesleyan Chapel was attributed (by Hartwell, Hyde & Pevsner, 2010). This is disputed by the Salford History website, which lists

Brunswick Wesleyan Schools, built in the Gothic style, but with some dispute over who the architect was. (© Carole O'Reilly)

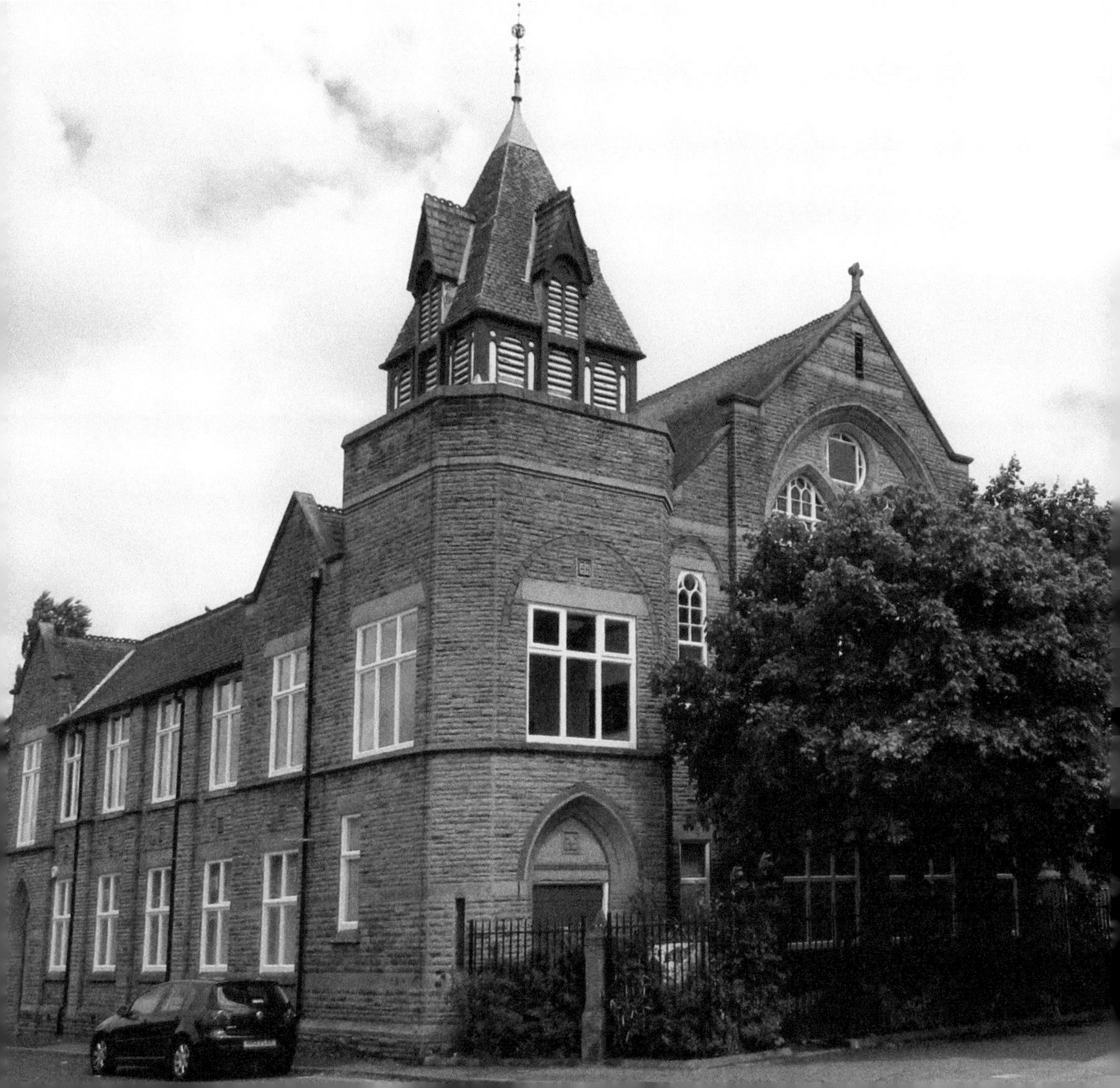

Richard Knill Freeman from Bolton as the architect of the demolished Brunswick Wesleyan chapel and of the schools. Freeman was born in Derby but based himself in Bolton. He designed St Andrews Anglican Church in Moscow in 1884.

The school building is of Gothic design with a steep roof of Welsh slate and pointed gables. The windows are mullioned and transomed, giving the building an ecclesiastical feeling. There are two storeys, with the principal being on the first floor. The building is capped with a tower, which is crowned by a wooden lantern. The doors are set back into the building, underneath moulded archways. The building is now used as offices.

25. Pendleton Co-op, Broughton Road

This was the principal building of Pendleton Co-operative Industrial Society, built in 1887. The main part of the building was designed by F. Smith with the extension by W. H. Walsingham added in 1903. The building is mostly of brick with stone and terracotta dressings and a Welsh slate roof. The Dutch gables and the large octagonal turret are both distinctive. The five principal bays were built in two phases

The Pendleton Co-operative building, dating from 1887, with terracotta dressings to the façade. (© Steven Robertson)

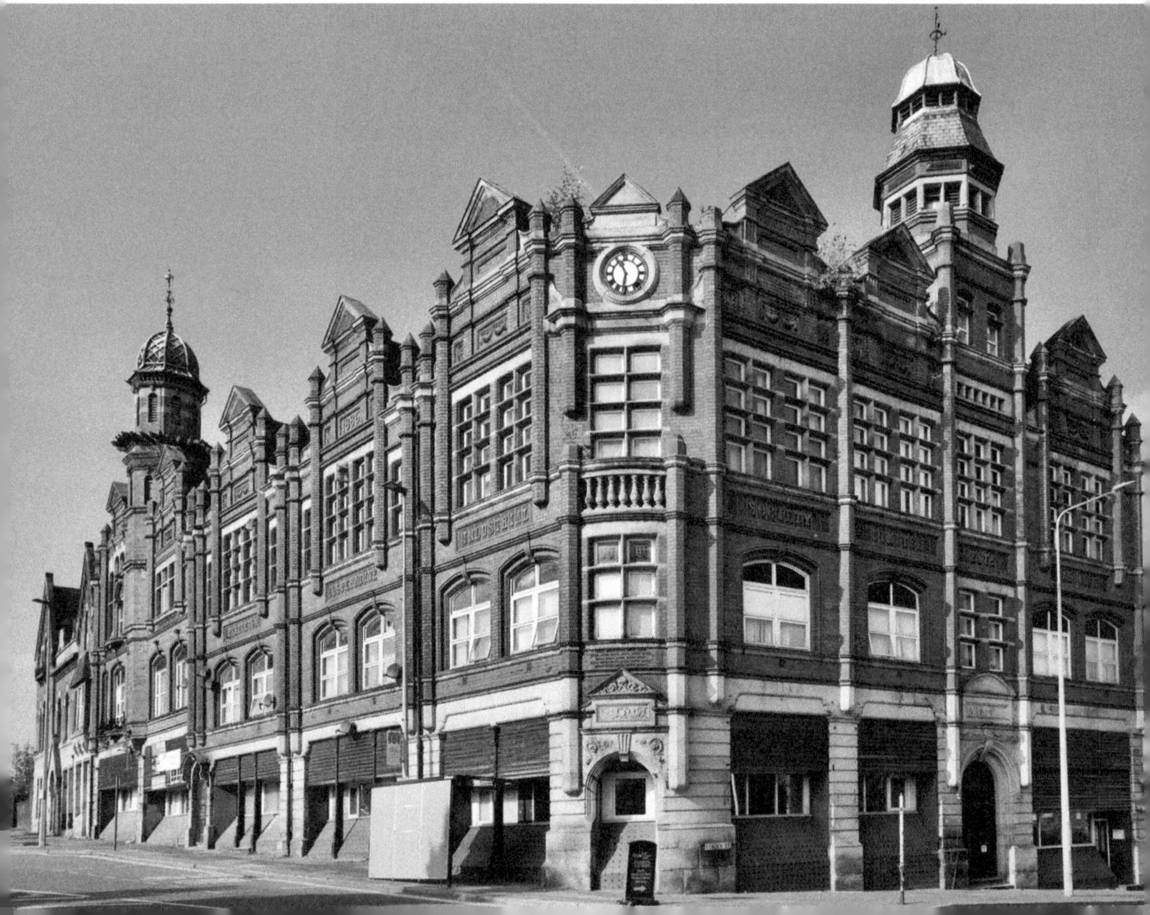

but are very similar in style. The original part of the building held offices, shops, store rooms, an assembly room and a board room. The extension contained show rooms, committee rooms and more offices and shops. The need for extra space was a testament to the success of the Co-operative movement. The street corner location slopes rather steeply and this is accommodated well by the design.

The building was augmented by others nearby, including the bakery and dairy buildings on Agnew Street and the Co-operative butchers on the corner of Littleton Road and Gerald Road. The butcher's shop was constructed in 1909 by W. H. Walsingham and is typically colourful with yellow and green terracotta on red brick. An octagonal domed tower rises from the angled corners and the building makes a pleasing use of its location.

The main Pendleton Co-operative Building is currently used as apartments, while the butcher's shop is now a restaurant.

26. Monton Memorial Schools, Monton

The school dates from 1888 and was designed by Salford architect Thomas Worthington and his partner J. G. Elgood. John Garrard Elgood was a native

Monton Memorial Schools, another building by Salford architect Thomas Worthington. (© Carole O'Reilly)

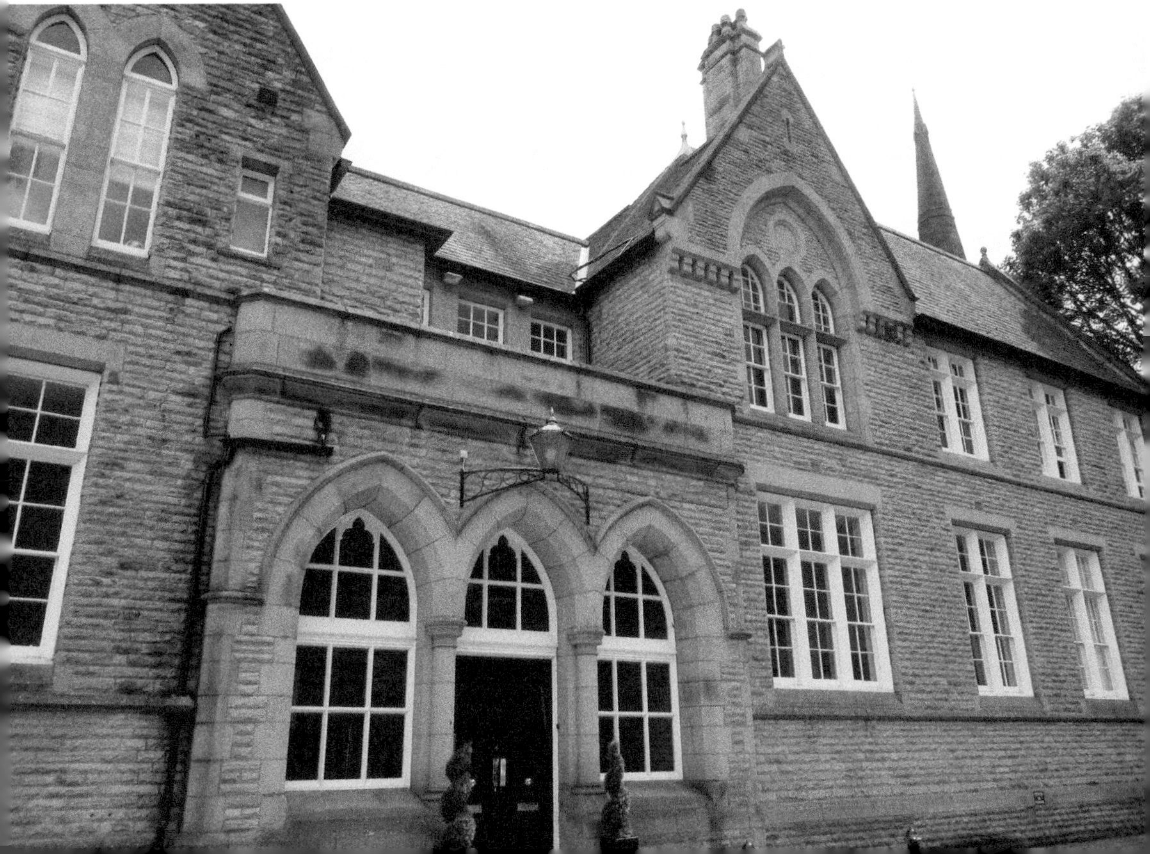

of Leicester. Early in his career he was a pupil of Bowman and Crowther of Manchester, to whom he was articled in 1847 for a period of seven years. During this time, he was largely employed on their well-known work *The Churches of the Middle Ages*. In 1855 he became assistant to Worthington and, after twenty-five years as his assistant, he became his partner in 1880. The partnership between Thomas Worthington, J. G. Elgood and P. S. Worthington under the style of Worthington & Elgood was dissolved in January 1893. The circumstances are recorded in Elgood's obituary notice in *The Builder* on 8 April 1893:

> In the autumn of last year (1892) Mr Elgood contracted a severe chill; which was followed by a serious illness necessitating an operation, and his illness having lately assumed a critical form, he died on the 8th ult. He was unmarried and though of a singularly modest and quiet disposition, his professional knowledge and attainments were very considerable. He was a man of calm, sound judgement, had a rare appreciation of the details of Gothic architecture and was an accurate and most conscientious draftsman. He was well-known among his professional brethren of the Manchester Society of Architects and had taken a very warm interest in the amalgamation into one body of the senior and junior societies in Manchester. Elected an Associate of the Institute in 1874, he became a Fellow in 1890.

The memorial school, designed by them, was in the Gothic Revival style and is made of distinctive rock-faced stone (stone that has been dressed by the use of a hammer). The building is two storeys throughout and has steep roofs. The tall chimney stacks are ridged. All of the windows retain their original glazing bars. The building is located within the Monton Green Conservation Area, which includes the Green itself and the Unitarian Church.

Part of the schoolhouse is now luxury apartments with some offices.

27. Men's Model Lodging House, Bloom Street

Next to the former Gas Board Offices is a large apartment block that promoted a 'New York lifestyle in Salford' when they first became available. Located on Bloom Street, the current apartments are a far cry from the origins of this building, which opened in 1893 as a men's lodging house. During the Victorian era there were particular concerns about the health of the working classes, but in particular transient and single people forced to live in privately owned lodgings that were far from healthy. As a result, across the country, a number of 'model lodging houses' were built to provide accommodation for primarily single men and, on occasions, single women. Glasgow had many examples, but they were described as 'dark and ill-ventilated' as well as 'hotbeds of vice', though provided a bed for each lodger and people were able to use the facilities including a large dining room and kitchen.

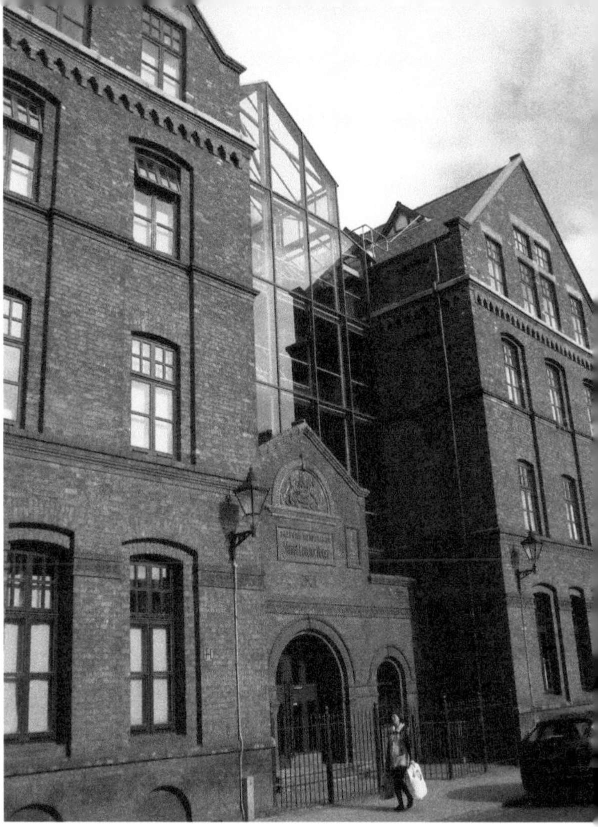

Right: Opened in 1893 as a men's lodging house, built primarily for single men. This was the first of its kind in England.

Below: The model lodging house, now transformed into apartments.

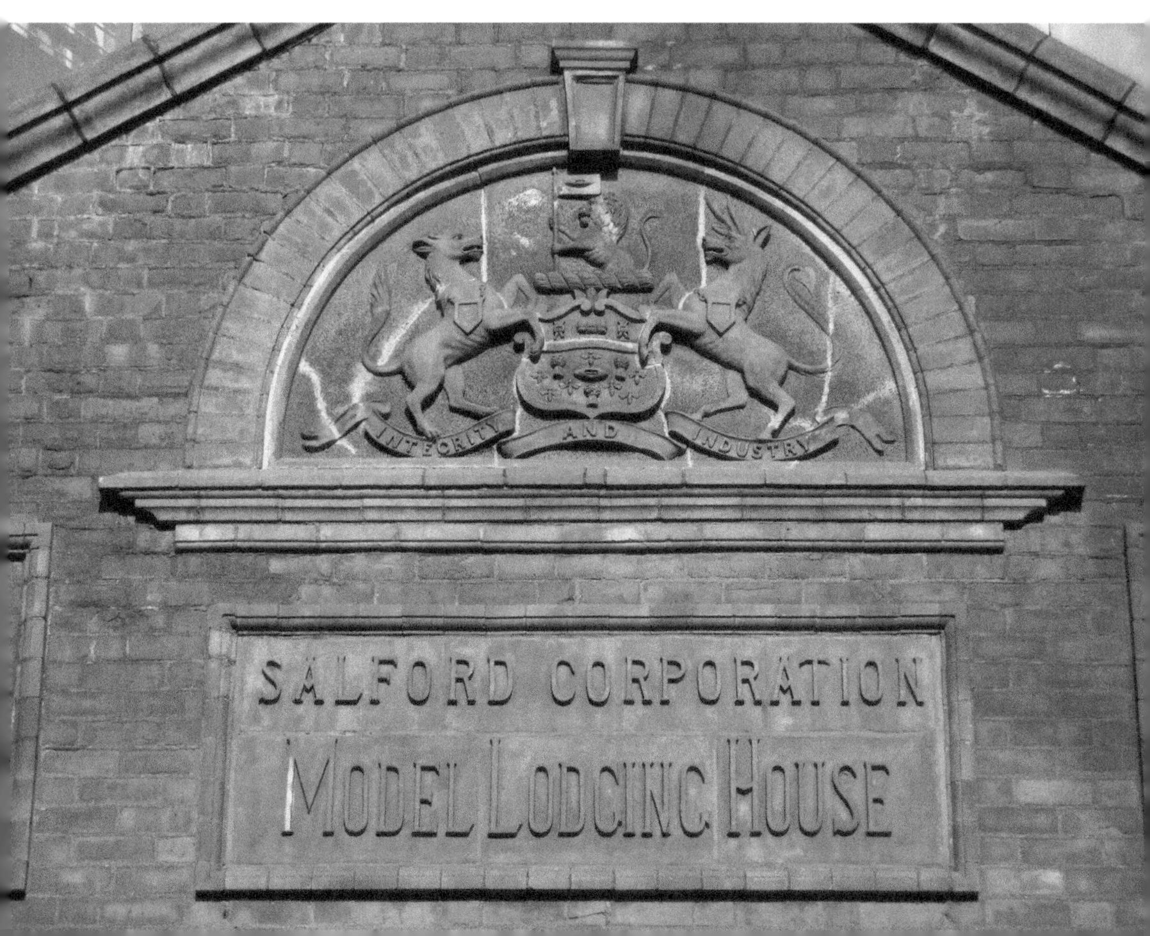

The Model Lodging House in Salford, when it opened, was the first of its kind in England and offered accommodation for 285 men, with some having eventually lived there for over twenty years. The *Illustrated London News* of 9 January 1850 described a typical life in one of these model lodging houses as

> Any respectable single man of the working classes, on payment of three shillings to the Superintendent, and a small sum as a deposit for articles of crockery, &c., becomes a tenant for one week, and receives two keys, a larger and smaller. The larger of these opens the sleeping compartment on the upper stories, the number of which corresponds with that stamped on the bow of the key (it will unlock no other). On closing the door, he finds himself in a space eight feet in length, by four feet six inches in width, lighted by half a window (which he can open or shut), and furnished with a substantial iron bedstead, clean bedding, a clothes-box (unlocked by the smaller of his keys), clothes-pegs, and looking-glass. There is also the means of admitting fresh air under his clothes-box, which he can regulate at pleasure.

The transformation of this building has been remarkable with the construction of a glass atrium added to the space between the two bays of the building and many of the original beams exposed in the upper rooms, which have created a striking contrast between contemporary fittings and the original architecture of the building.

28. Irlam Railway station

The existing railway station at Irlam dates from 1893. However, twenty years previously, the original station, named Irlam, was opened by the Cheshire Lines Committee on 2 September 1873 as part of their route between Manchester Central and Liverpool Central. In 1879, the station was renamed Irlam and Cadishead. The construction of the Manchester Ship Canal was to affect the line when it opened on 1 January 1894. The railway line had to be raised in order to provide enough clearance for shipping, so a new line was built but, although parallel, at a higher level. This new line was initially used by goods trains from January 1893, but by March the same year passenger trains were also transferred to the deviation, the original station being closed and replaced by the station we see today. Renamed again in 1954 to Irlam for Cadishead, it eventually reverted to Irlam in May 1974.

Difficult times though lay ahead for Irlam Station House and it fell derelict in the 1990s, but after twenty-five years, the station building was restored and reopened in March 2015 with a railway themed café, with toilets, a cycle hub and

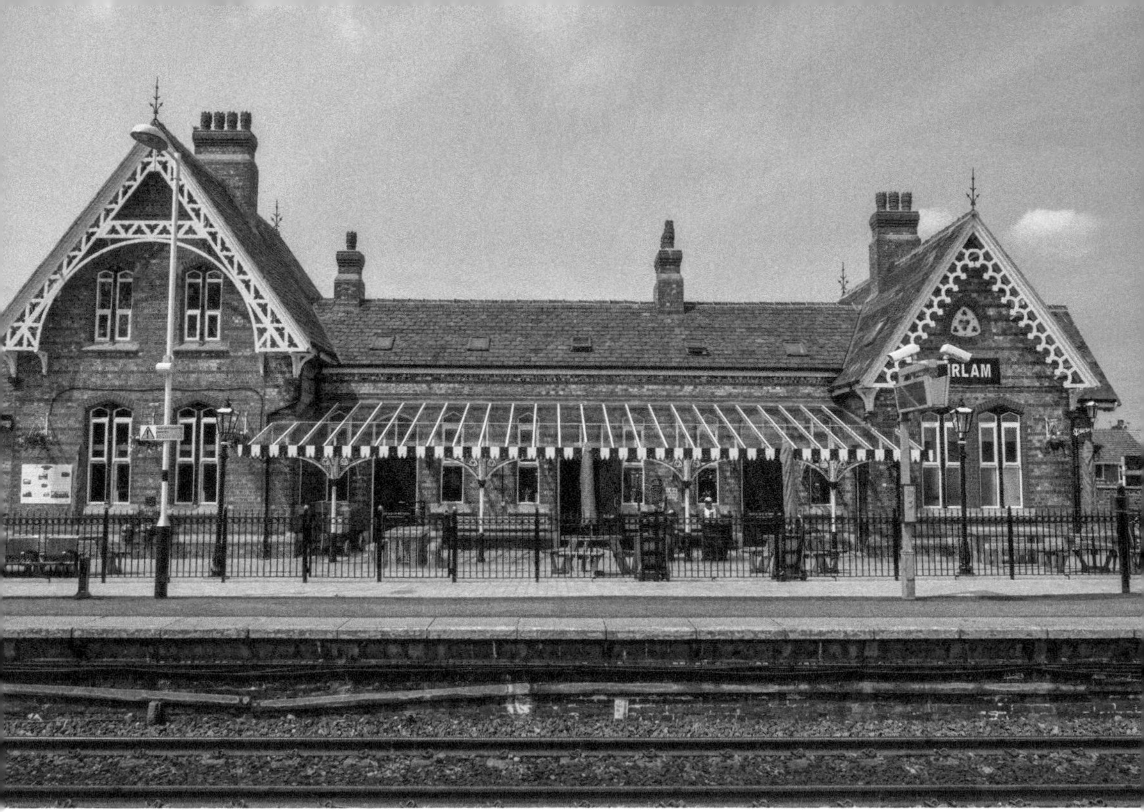

Above: Irlam railway station, restored in 2015 and once again a very busy station. (© Steven Robertson)

Below: Welcome to Irlam, popular with locals and visitors alike. (© Tim Whelan)

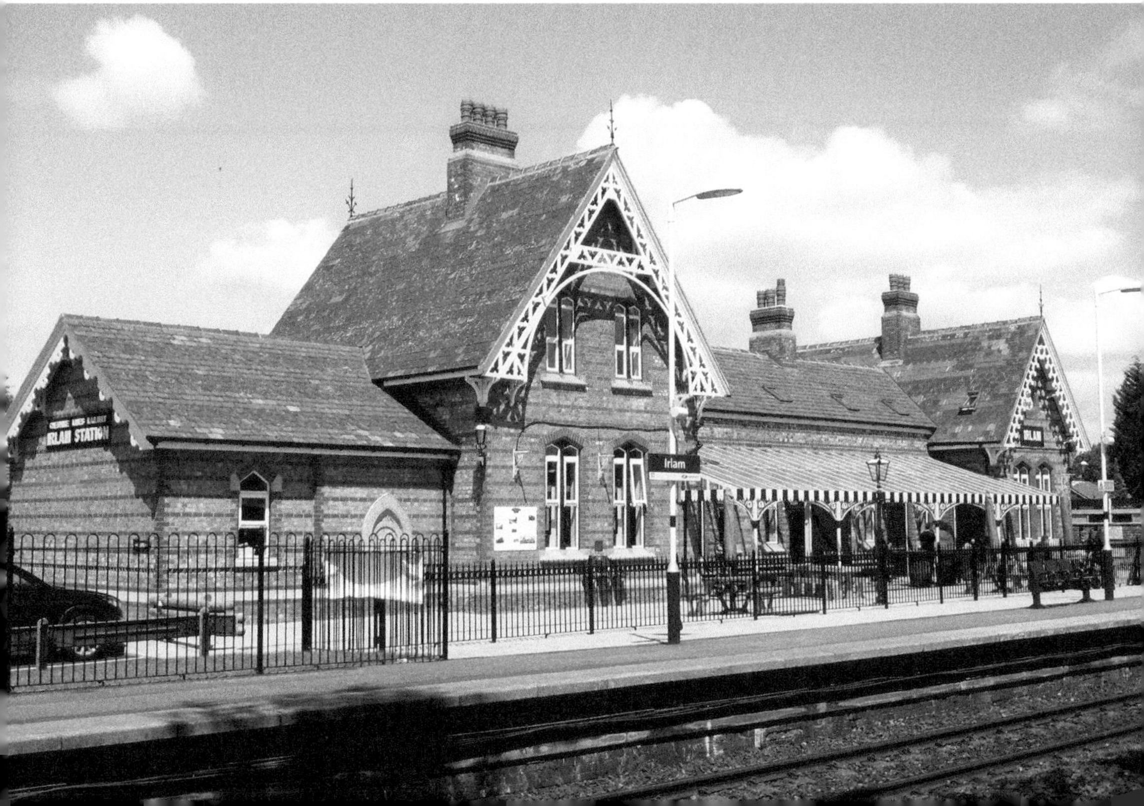

car park. The restoration of the building was partly due to local philanthropy with Irlam-born TalkTalk founder Neil McArthur contributing £1.1 million of the £1.5 million required. Reporting in the *Guardian* in July 2018, 'McArthur bristled. The Irlam he was born into, a good 30 years before he founded the telecoms company that became TalkTalk, was an industrial boom town. Everyone had a job, if not at the steelworks like his dad, then in the factories making soap, margarine, rope or baskets. "It was manically busy," says the 62-year-old, "with thousands of people coming in by train to work." There are many other stations like Irlam that would benefit from similar transformations into multi-purpose community hubs'. Irlam is now one of the busiest stations in the Greater Manchester area, with over 350,000 users annually.

29. No. 62 Chapel Street (former Police Station)

Once a former police station on land between Chapel Street and the Salford Approach to the former Exchange station, this building occupies a prominent position and was built in 1888 by Arthur Jacob, the Salford borough engineer.

The former police station at No. 62 Chapel Street, built by the Salford borough engineer Arthur Jacob. (© Ben Abel)

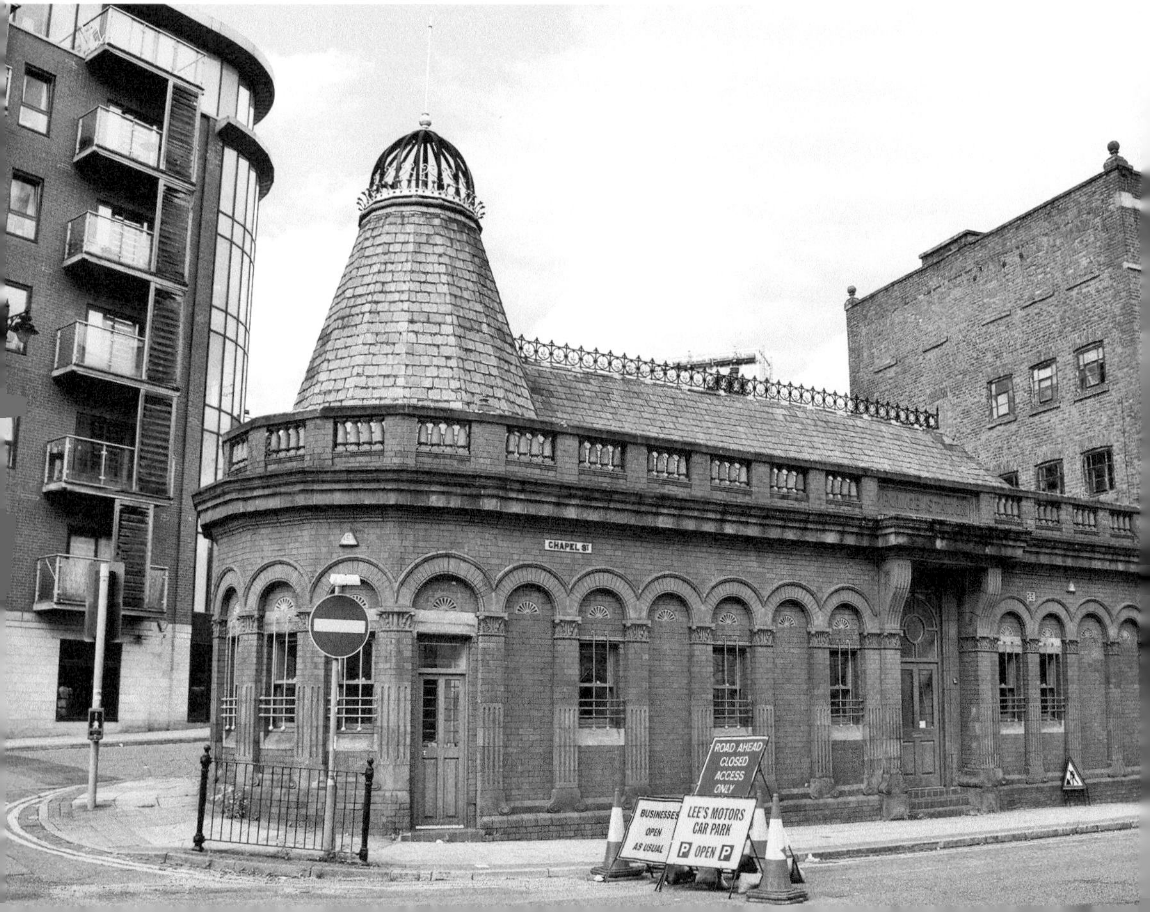

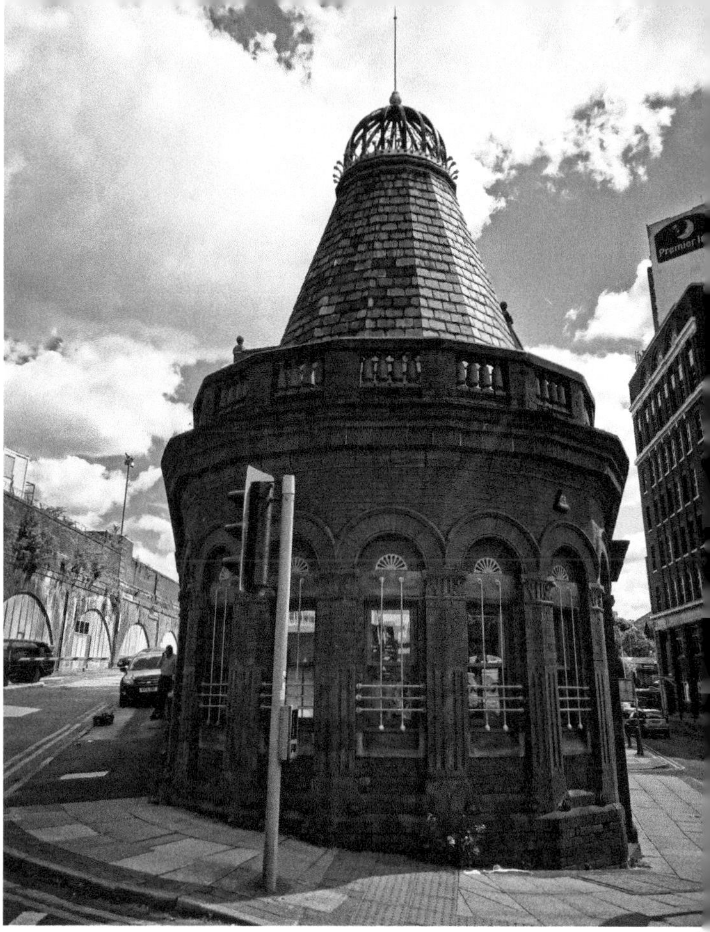

The elevation of the former police station, now occupied by local businesses. (© Mike Rampton)

It has since had a number of uses including a tram ticket office and then as part of a printworks. It has since been converted into offices and occupied by a number of users including local architects.

The Salford Police Force has changed considerably since the day this building was occupied by our local law enforcement. In 1844, the Salford Police Force consisted of a chief constable, four inspectors, and thirty-seven policemen; by 1898 this total had risen to 330. By 1868, the Borough Fire Brigade were also the responsibility of the police, which was staffed by fifteen 'fire policemen' who had two manual fire engines for use in Salford – one for Broughton and another for Pendleton. The Salford Police Force was eventually amalgamated with Manchester's in 1968 and the fire brigade joined the Greater Manchester Fire Service in 1974.

30. Salford Education Office

The principal buildings of Salford are primarily found along Chapel Street as the city lacks a centre. On the northern side of the street some of the finest buildings in Salford can be found, and possibly the most outstanding of them all is the former Education Office, built in 1895 and designed by Manchester architects John Henry Woodhouse and George Harry Willoughby. It was not until the Education Act of 1870 that the schooling of children really changed. In Salford and elsewhere, schooling had been primarily the responsibility of the churches and the schools of each denomination were generally in the styles chosen for church buildings. As the new state schools were non-denominational, the new buildings' styles were considered to be more appropriate in a secular style rather than an ecclesiastical character. Many of these new buildings were therefore designed in the Queen Anne style; however, in the case of the Salford Education Office, architects Woodhouse and Willoughby opted for a French Renaissance style, with a building that consisted of three storeys above a basement. Its façade is faced in yellow terracotta and consists of an oriel window and central wrought-iron balcony. Now Grade II listed, the Salford Education Directorate operated out of the building until 2001 and remained empty with plans in 2018 for the building to be converted into retirement flats by the diocese of Salford. The building still remains empty today.

The former education office on Chapel Street where many of Salford's finest buildings are found. (© Tony Reeves)

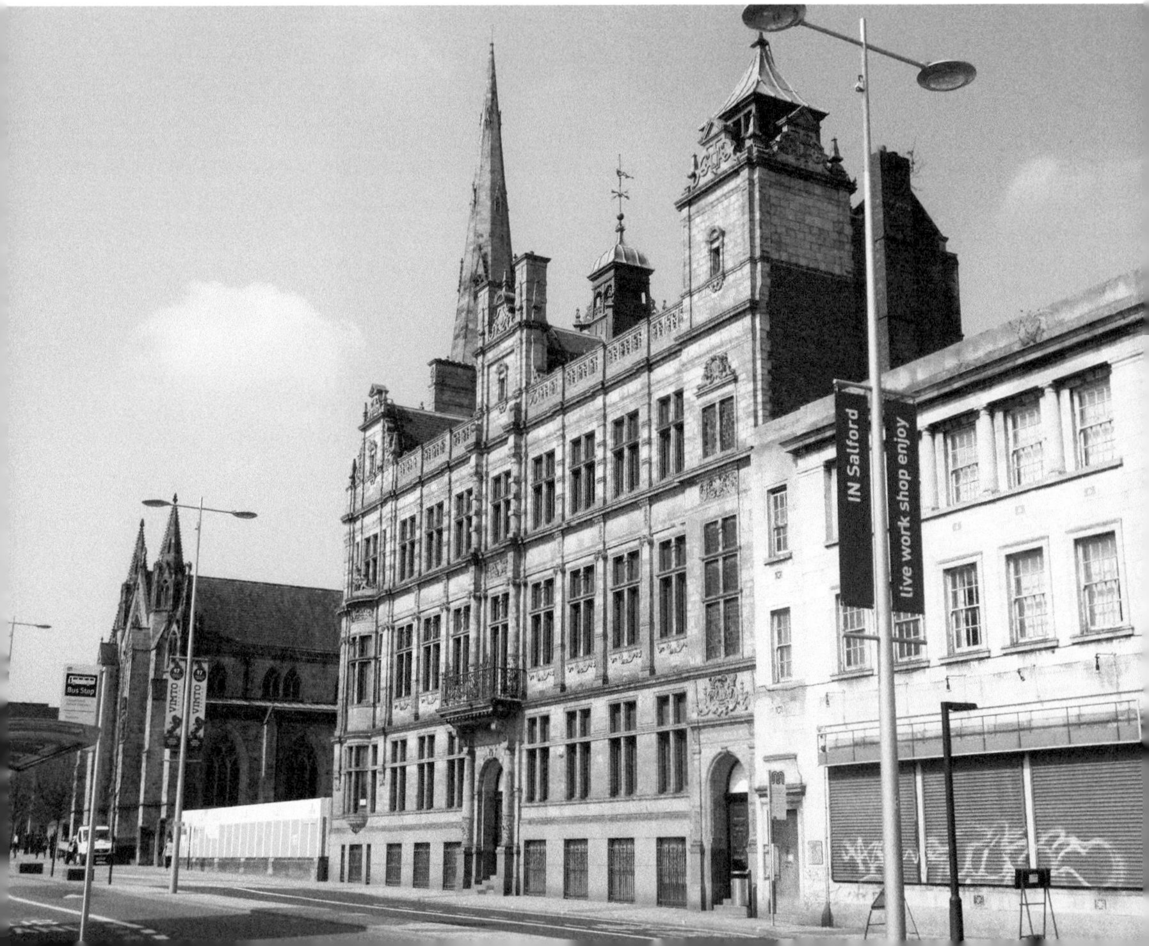

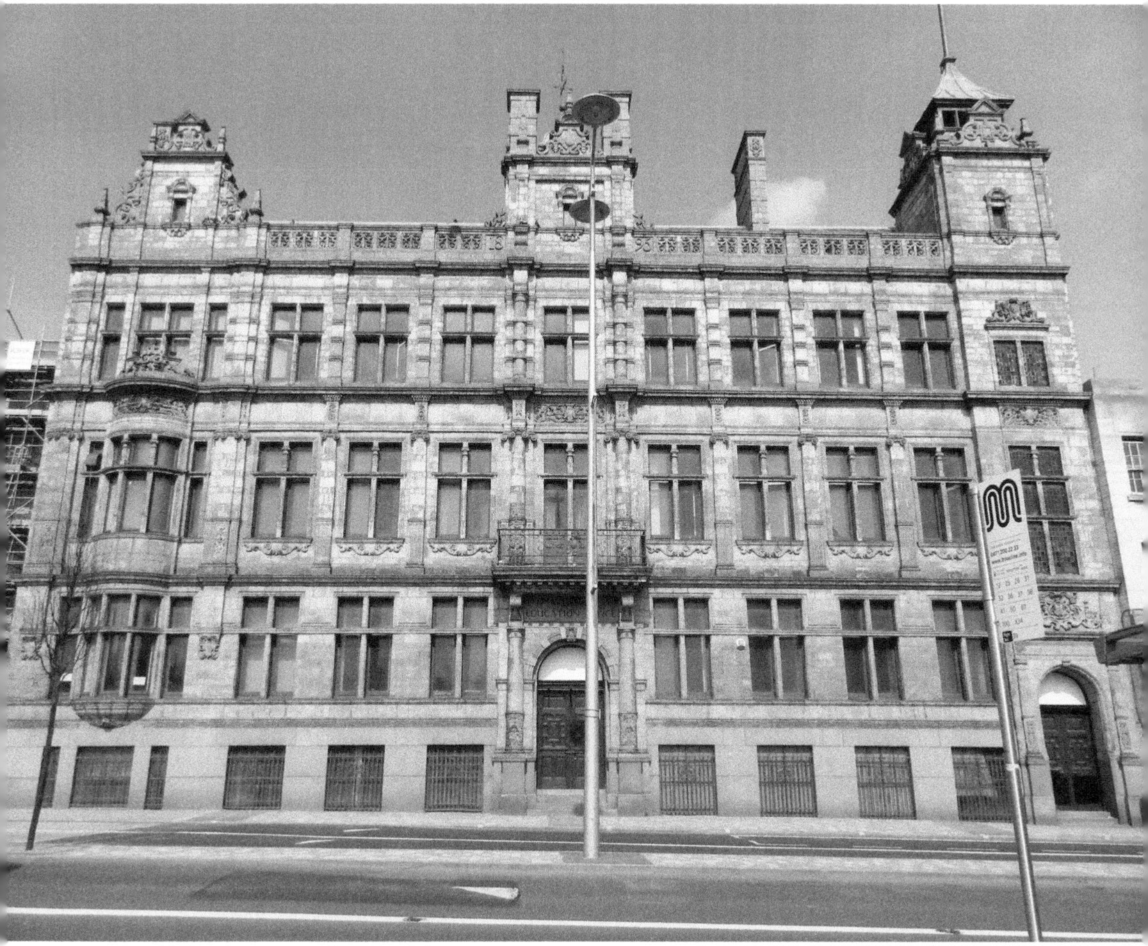

Above: The French Renaissance style of the former education office. (© Tony Reeves)

Right: A reminder of past glories. (© Tony Reeves)

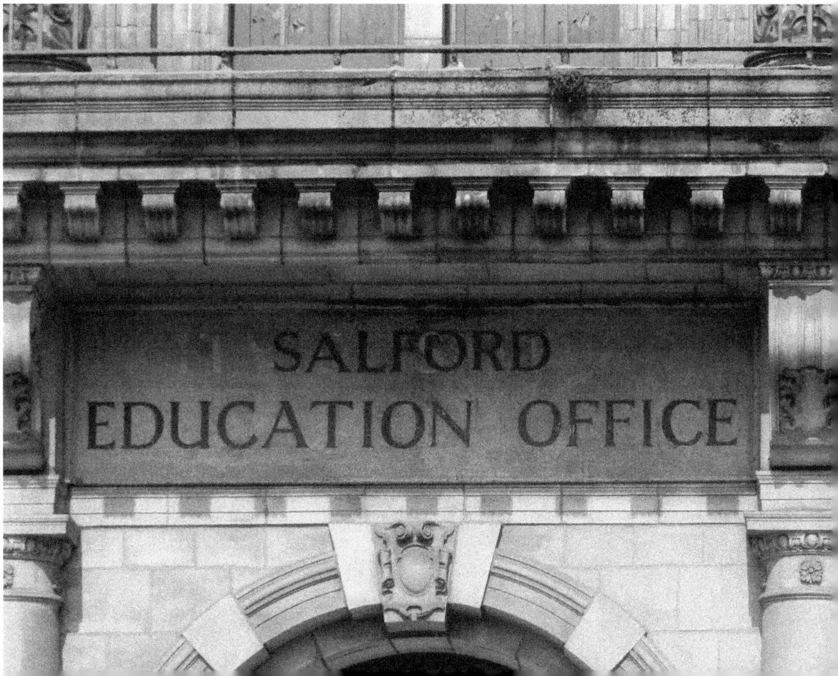

31. Peel Building, Salford University

Founded in 1858, the Salford Working Men's College and the Pendleton Mechanics' Institute (founded eight years earlier) combined in 1896 to become the Salford Technical Institute, which was to be located on the campus at Salford Crescent. The establishment of this new college was funded by local manufacturers and mill owners, with the institutes having close links with local industries in Salford. By 1908, there were further changes as Salford Technical Institute divided into two colleges – the Royal College of Advanced Technology and Peel Park Technical College. The Duke and Duchess of York (later George V and Queen Mary) attended the opening of the Royal College.

The courses on offer were very much influenced by the number and type of industries that were based in Salford at the time, so mechanical engineering, chemical works, textiles and construction were popular. Eventually, the Royal College became the University of Salford in 1967, the Duke of Edinburgh having the honour of being the new university's chancellor. Peel Park Technical College became Salford Technical Institute in 1961, Salford College of Technology in 1970 and eventually University College Salford by 1992. It was only another four years before the full merger of the University of Salford with University College was to occur.

At the centre of the campus today is the Peel Building, which was designed by architect Henry Lord and built in 1896 and remains the oldest building on site. Henry Lord was responsible for many of Salford's most iconic buildings including Salford Royal Hospital, Salford Museum and Art Gallery and the Salford Lads' Club. He was born in Chester on 21 May 1843 and was articled to Charles Reboul

The Technical School, Peel Park, now Salford University.

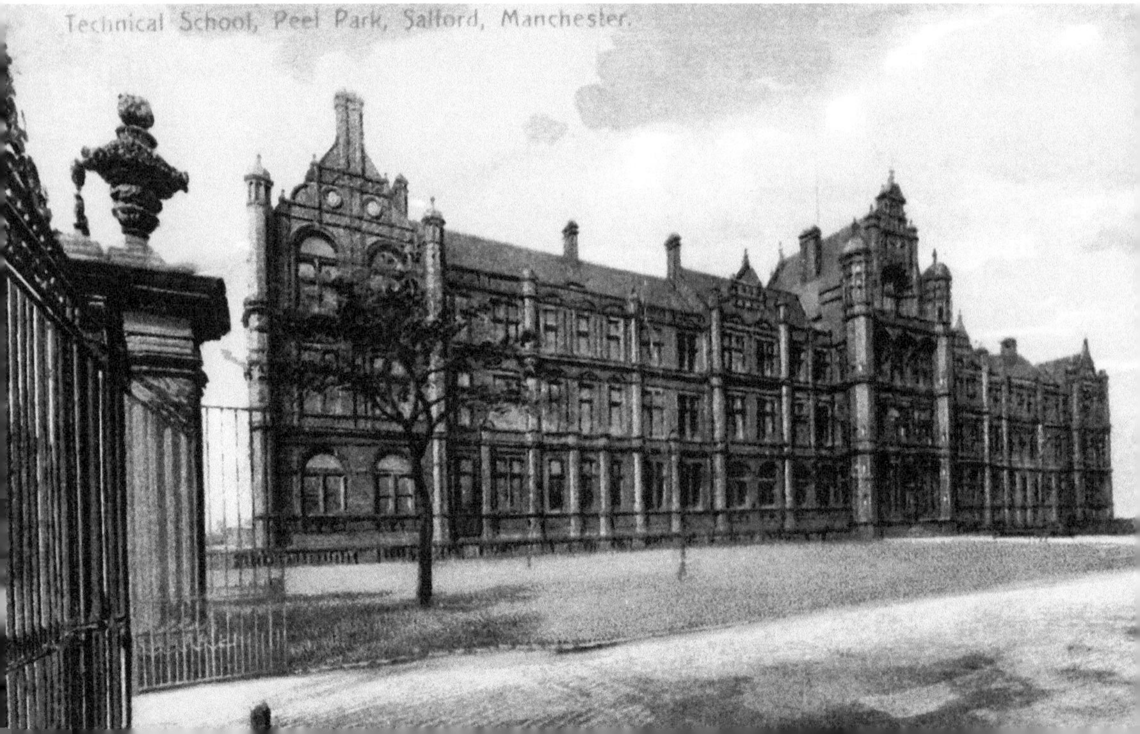

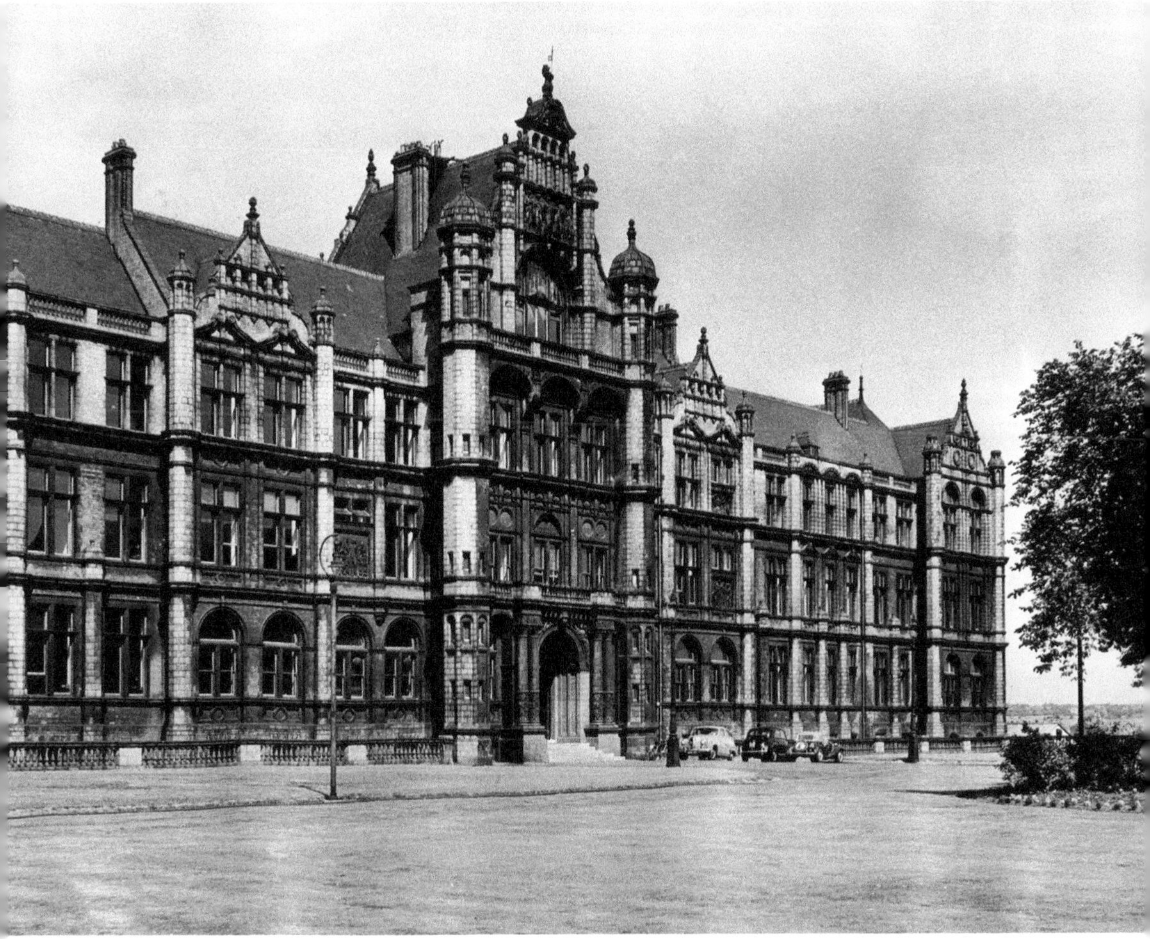

Above: Peel Building. (© University of Salford)

Right: Peel Building, Salford University. (© Ben Abel)

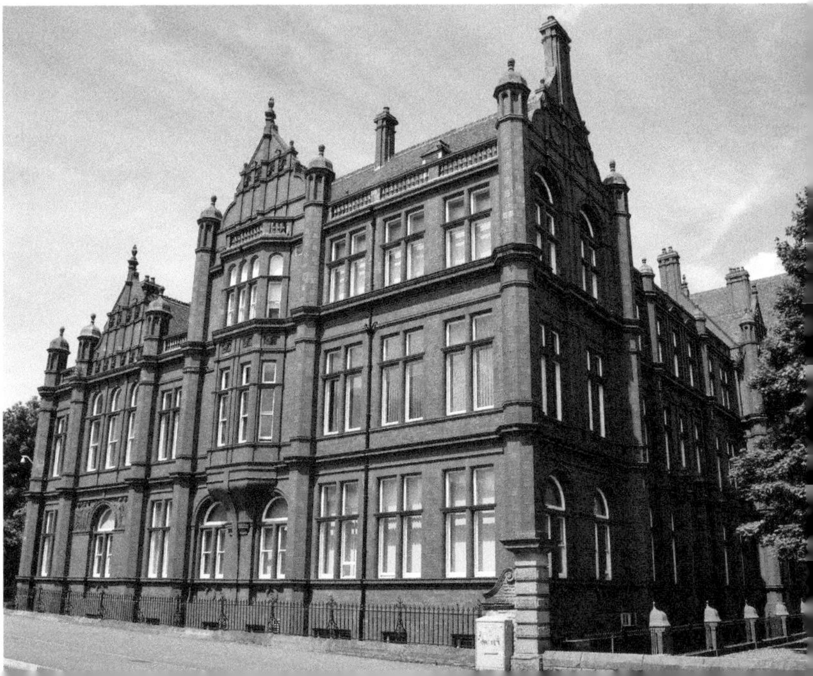

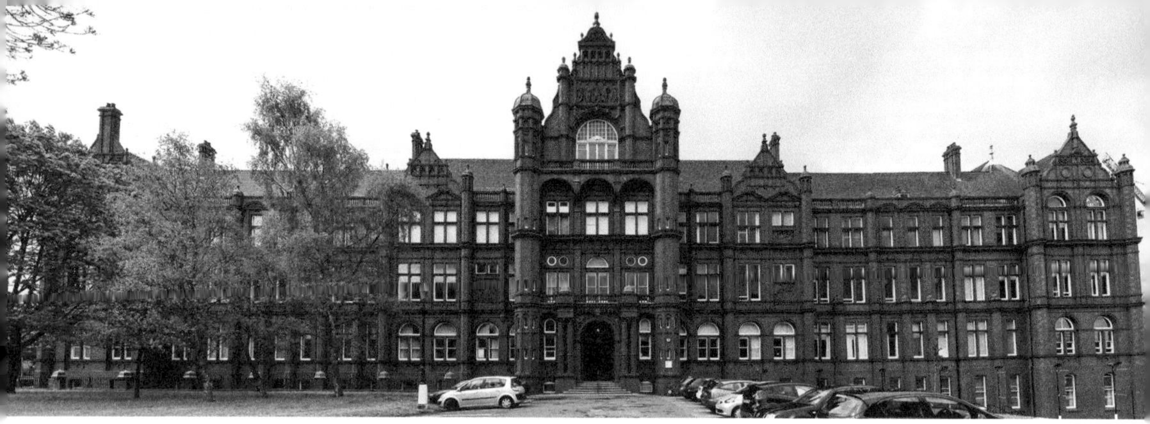

Above: Peel Building and its extensive frontage. (© https://tigergrowl.wordpress.com)

Below: Sculpted terracotta on the frontage. (© https://tigergrowl.wordpress.com)

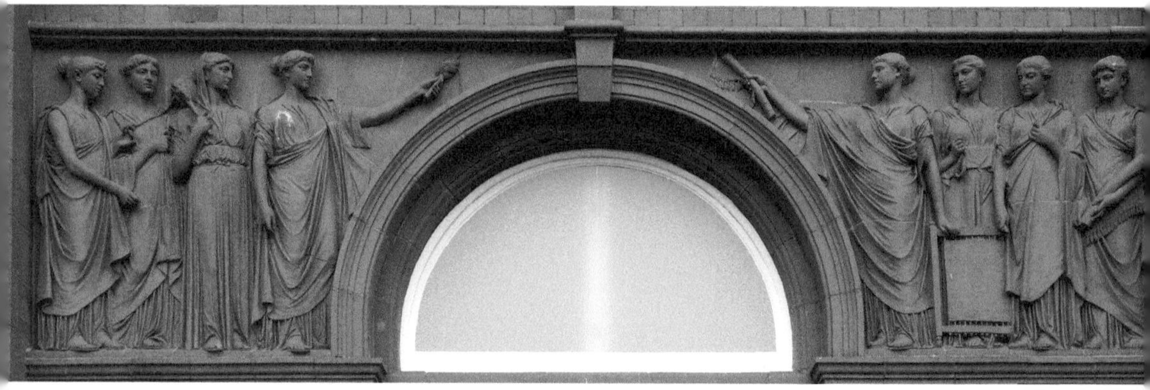

Sacre at Manchester Railway Works, Gorton, initially as an engineer for one year and eventually articled to Ernest Bates of Manchester from 1860 to 1864, where he remained as a clerk until 1867. He ultimately joined the architect's department of the London & North Western Railway where he remained until 1871 to begin his own practice based in Manchester and was admitted to the Royal Institute of British Architects in 1888. The Peel Building is one of his finest achievements.

Eventually renamed the Peel Building, the detailed façade was beautifully constructed using red Accrington bricks and sculpted terracotta with Earp, Son & Hobbs responsible for the intricate detailing of this fine façade.

In 2019, the university has a successful global presence and a turnover of £189 million. Its seven schools, 20,000 students and 2,500 staff continue to serve the needs of industry, commerce and education.

32. Working Class Movement Library (former Queen's Jubilee Nurses' Home), Acton Square

This building was a former nurses' home for Salford Royal Hospital and was built in 1897–1901 by Henry Lord. It was officially opened by Lady Mottram on 26 January 1901. The building was originally known as Jubilee House as it celebrated Queen Victoria's Diamond Jubilee and was funded with a collection to celebrate the event. Its official name was 'The Salford Royal Nursing Home' and it belonged to the Manchester and Salford Sick Poor and Private Nursing Institution. It is a striking composition of three storeys with tall chimneys, mock-Elizabethan timbered gables and terracotta motifs. The cellar has a rack where nurses could hang their cloaks to dry in wet weather.

District nursing was initially introduced in Manchester and Salford in 1866, when the Manchester Nurse Training Institution was established. District nurses were employed in the Adelphi and St Stephens districts of Salford, two of the most deprived and unhealthy parts of the town. The nurses initially lived within the district in which they worked but by 1891 most were housed within a nurses' home under the supervision of a matron, herself a qualified district nurse. The number of districts slowly expanded. By 1882 over 1,300 cases were nursed and during 1905 the thirteen nurses in the new Salford home were responsible for 85,398 visits to 3,443 patients. This level of activity was not maintained due to the First World War and the economic depression that

The former Queen's Jubilee Nurses' Home, now the Working Class Movement Library. (© https://tigergrowl.wordpress.com)

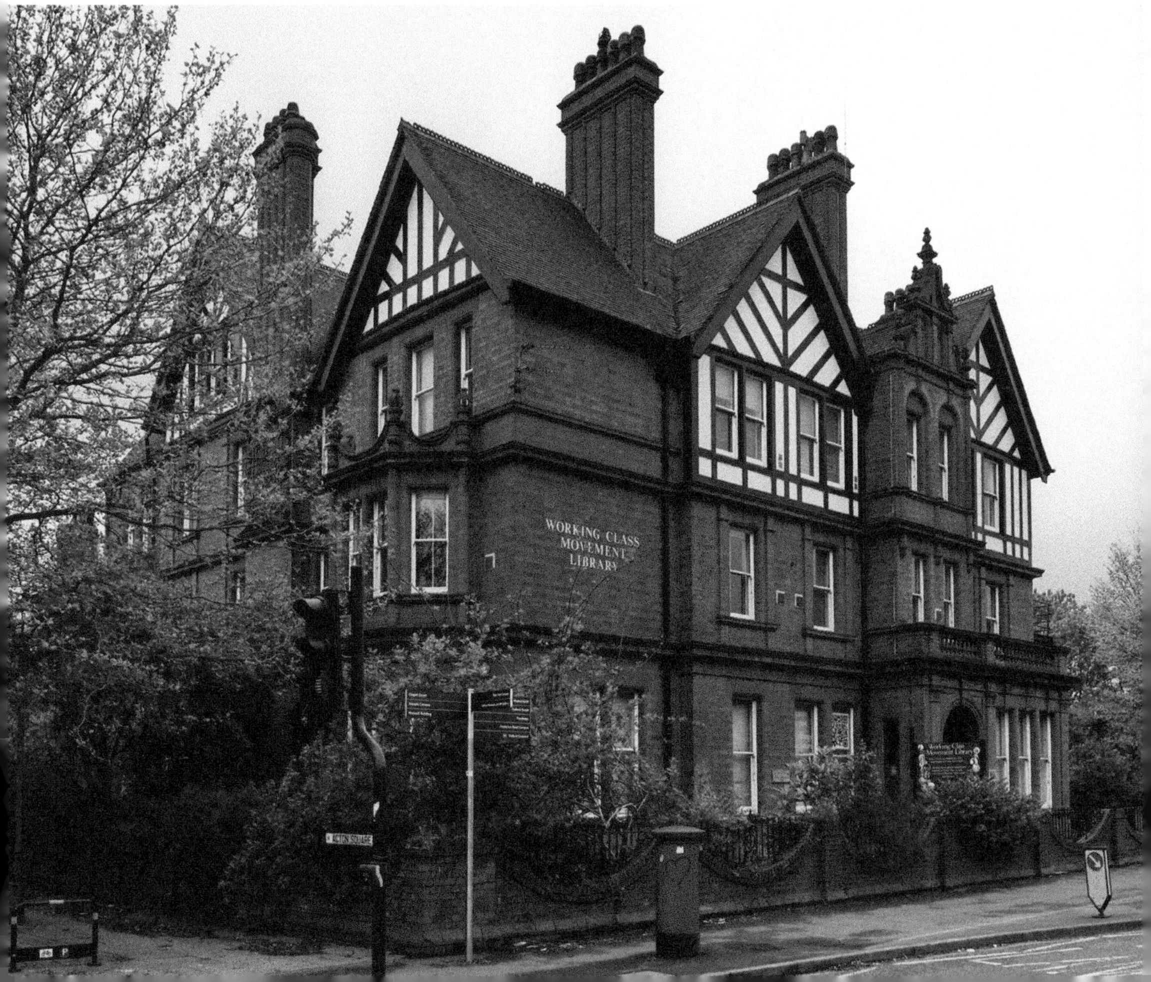

followed, but the number of nurses slowly increased to about twenty by 1939. In 1948, the newly formed National Health Service (NHS) was introduced and district nursing came under the control of Salford Corporation. In 1974 district nursing services were absorbed into the NHS and eventually the building became obsolete as society had changed and qualified nurses no longer wanted to live in nurses' homes.

In 1987, Salford Council gave the house to two bibliophiles, Eddie and Ruth Frow, for their collection of working-class and labour movement materials. The rooms, which had been the nurses' bedrooms, now form the nucleus of the library. It is now the holder of the GMB trade union archives among others and contains material documenting the history of the political, industrial, social and cultural institutions of the working classes. The council leases the building to the library and provides an annual grant.

33. Chester's Brewery, Cook Street

This building, designed by W. A. Deighton, mostly dates from 1898 and was known as the Cook Street Brewery before Chester's moved into it from nearby Greengate. It makes the best use of an awkward site, close to a railway bridge and is designed

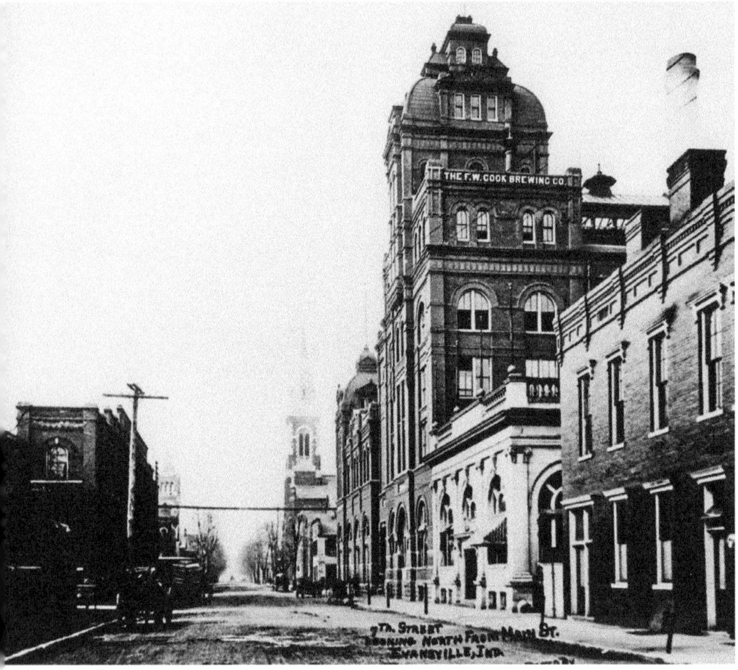

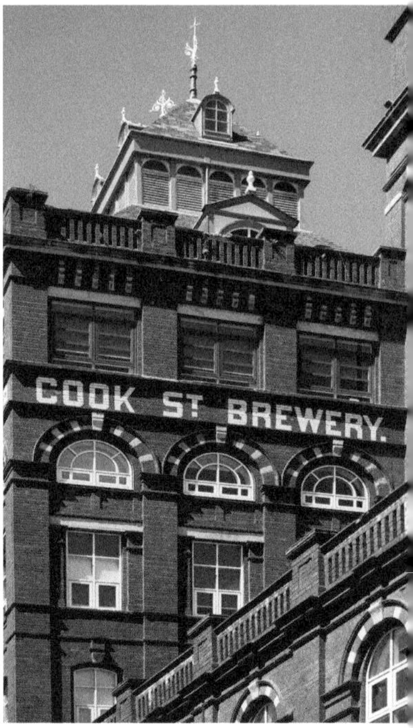

Above left: The brewery of F. W. Cook Brewing Company and its striking tower.

Above right: The remnants of one of Salford's most popular breweries – now offices and a church. (© Rich Daley)

as a T shape. The building is mostly of red brick with roofs of Welsh slate. The striking campanile and five-storey tower are very much a local landmark, along with the copper brewing house. Chester's merged with Threlfall's in 1961. Threlfall's breweries was not only in Salford but also in Liverpool, and was active between 1861 and 1967. It also included the West Cheshire Brewery, Birkenhead Brewery and Mackies off-licence chain and was the eighth largest brewery in the country at the time. The company eventually became part of Whitbreads in 1967, but was known by its historical name of Chester's in response to the CAMRA (Campaign for Real Ale) movement to use local names. Brewing ended in 1988 and the building became surplus to requirements. Today the building is currently known as the Deva Centre Office Park, which houses offices and an evangelical church.

34. Victoria Theatre, Great Clowes Street, Lower Broughton

The theatre was designed by William 'Bertie' Crew in 1899 and had a capacity of 2,000 (this was increased to 3,000 in 1910). Crew was a leading theatre designer of the late nineteenth century and was responsible for the Piccadilly Theatre in London and Manchester's Palace Theatre.

The exterior is quite plain, being of red brick with terracotta details. The real splendour of this building lies with the interiors, which contain many of Crew's hallmarks. The designs of the public boxes are especially elaborate with Corinthian columns, cherubs, moulded figures and ornate, gilded plasterwork. There are two balconies, the first with an unusual balustraded parapet. The roof is of hipped Welsh slate. The wooden sub-stage machinery was designed to facilitate the traps used in live variety theatre.

The building opened in December 1900 and was originally designed as a variety theatre. Within a few years, it was also showing films and it became a full-time cinema in 1913. By 1917, the building was being used as a theatre again, indicating the continuing difficulties in predicting the leisure tastes of the twentieth-century audience. The Victoria was redesigned in 1919 when it became a cinema again with the addition of a café and a newly painted ceiling with scenes from Victorian life and musical instruments.

The cinema finally closed in 1958 from when the building was used as a clothing shop. It returned to its theatrical roots in the mid-1960s when it was bought by a local Salford businessman, Samuel Goldberg, who had a personal attachment to theatre. Goldberg owned Southport Repertory Company, which used the Victoria Theatre as their winter headquarters. An attempt to persuade Salford City Council to buy the building failed and the theatre closed in 1971 when Goldberg died. It was reopened as a bingo hall in 1973. This was quite short-lived until the 1980s when it staged bingo again until 2012 when the building closed for the final time.

In September 2018, the building was sold by auction to a private buyer. A community group is working towards an asset of community value but its future is uncertain, despite its Grade II listed status.

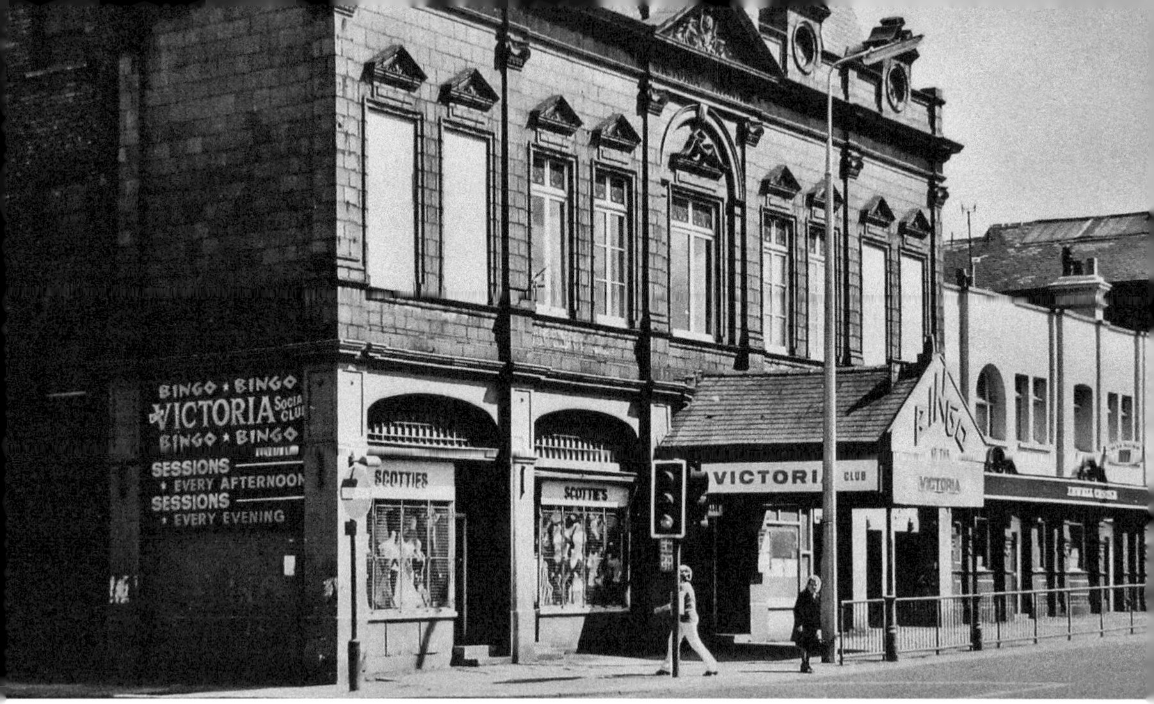

Above: The original Victoria Theatre in the early 1970s, used as a bingo hall.

Below: Much altered, the building has seen better days.

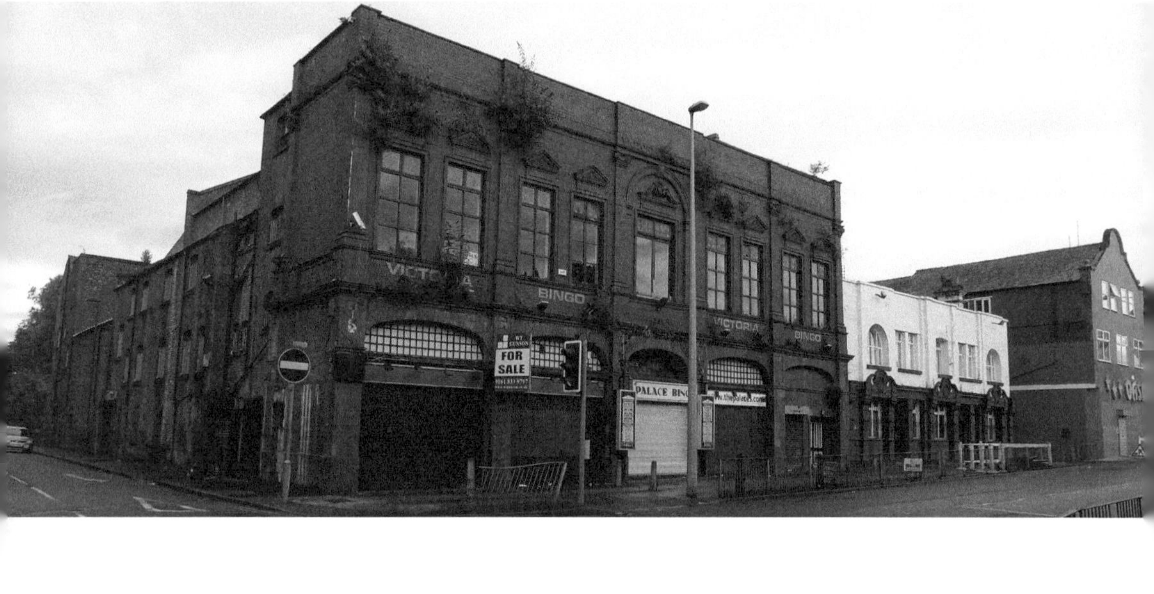

35. Crown Theatre, Eccles

The theatre was built on land bought by Richard Flanagan, a local theatre manager in December 1897. It opened as the Lyceum theatre in 1899 having been designed in baroque style by two local architects, Campbell and Horsley. The theatre seated 2,500 people and contained many modern innovations such as electric lighting and seventeen fireproof dressing rooms. The stained-glass windows used in the building depicted poets and playwrights and were intended to educate those who knew little about culture. Attendance at the early Shakespeare productions was poor at first but improved considerably when more variety and novelty shows were offered. The theatre played host to many eccentric acts such as Dr Walford Brodie, a hypnotist who claimed to be able to cure polio by using magnets.

Flanagan sold the theatre in 1907 to W. H. Broadhead (a former mayor of Blackpool) who renamed it the Crown Theatre. During the First World War, the theatre screened footage of the men of the Manchester Regiment 'going over the top' film, which was both faked and heavily censored.

The 1920s and 1930s was a 'golden age' for the Crown, as it was for many theatres in Britain. In 1923, a young George Formby appeared at the bottom of the bill. By 1932, the theatre was sold again to H. D. Moorhouse and became a cinema only. In 1963, it changed again, this time to a bingo hall.

Another Salford building at risk: the Crown Theatre. Plans to turn it into apartments have yet to come to fruition. (© Philip Wright)

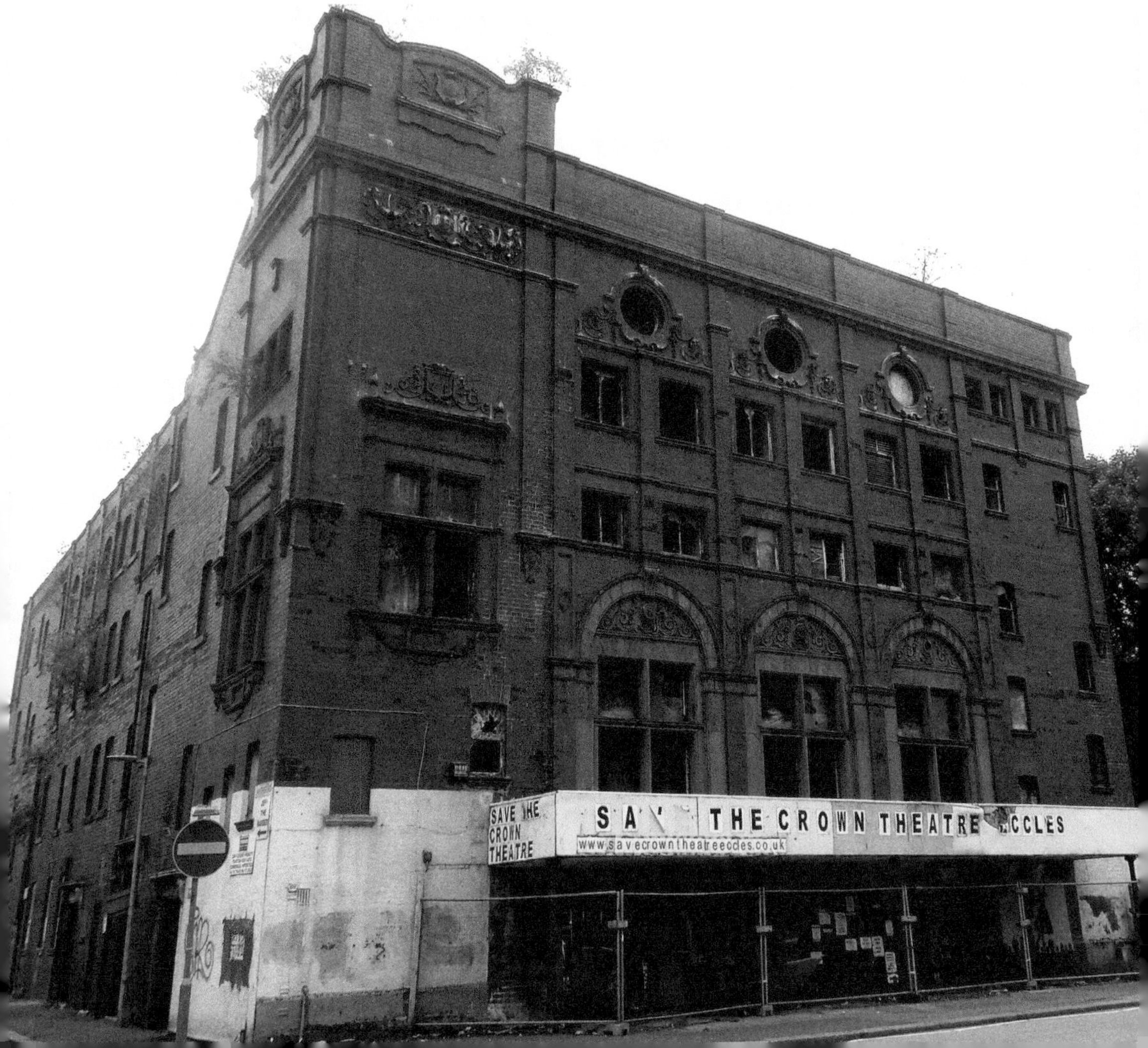

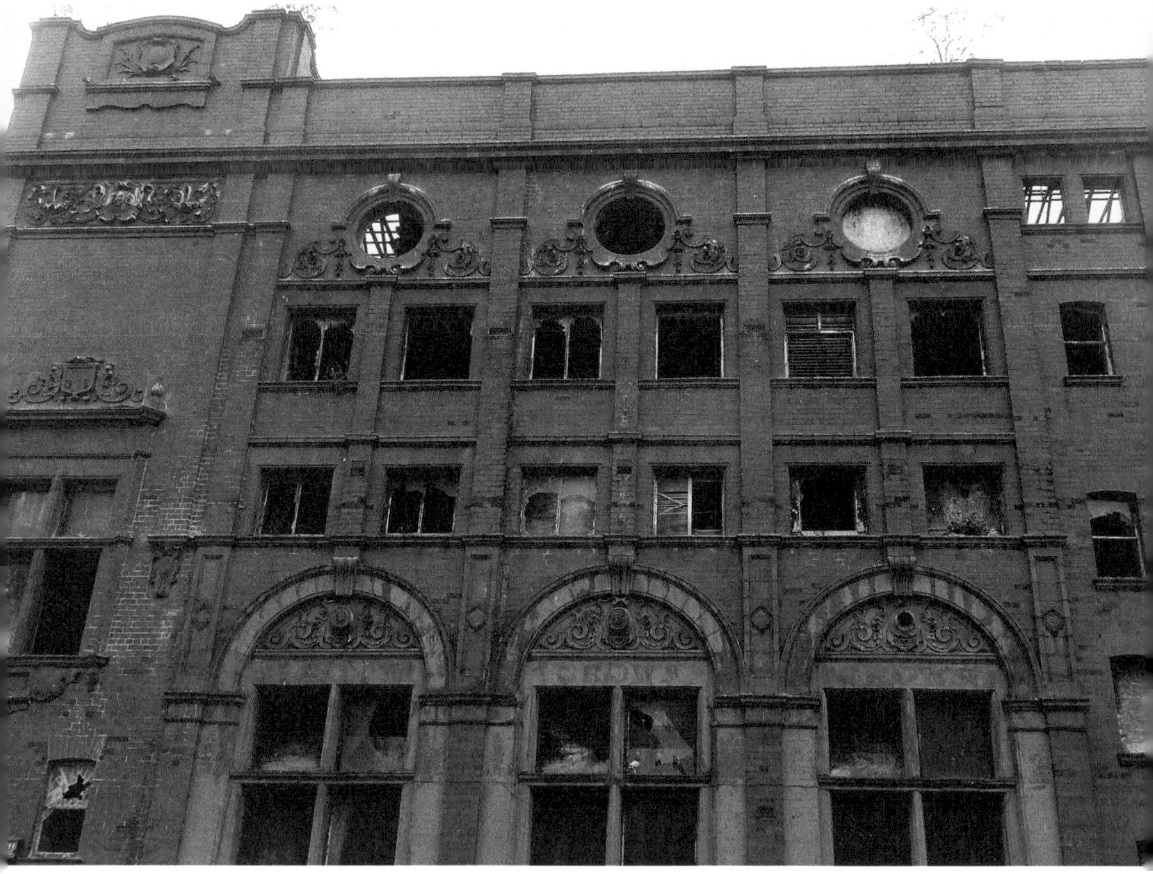

The word 'Crown' can still be seen below the centre arch of the building, a reminder of its heyday. (© Philip Wright)

The Crown closed permanently in the 1980s and was badly damaged by a fire in 2013. The building is at risk of demolition and is the focus of a campaign to save it. In late 2018, a proposal was submitted to save the façade of the building and to convert it into apartments.

36. Agecroft Cemetery Chapel

Agecroft Cemetery was initially known as Salford Northern Cemetery and was opened by Salford County Borough Council on 2 July 1903. It was opened because the existing cemetery at Weaste was virtually at full capacity. The new cemetery that was created here was 45 acres in size and was located in the Irwell Valley and adjacent to Agecroft Road. The cemetery was incorporated into the city of Salford in 1974. Since the cemetery was opened, there have been more than 53,700 interments here with the original Nonconformist chapel converted to a crematorium in January 1957.

Within the cemetery grounds is a large disused mortuary chapel with a clock tower, now derelict and hidden by many trees. Along with many buildings in the cemetery, the Anglican chapel is just one of a group of coordinated buildings designed by the Manchester architects Walter Sharp and Frederick Foster. The range of buildings here also includes the lodge, cemetery office, former Nonconformist chapel (now the crematorium), the imposing entrance gateway and perimeter walls. In addition, there was once a Roman Catholic chapel to the south of the cemetery, which has since been demolished. The mortuary chapel is of particular interest as it was opened in 1903 by Manchester's Bishop James Moorhouse. It was designed as the centrepiece of the cemetery and it is an outstanding building of significant height, dignity and robust construction. The importance of the chapel is reflected in its Grade II listed status and its unique design – a mixture of Gothic, Arts and Crafts and art nouveau influences. Unfortunately, it is still a building very much at risk.

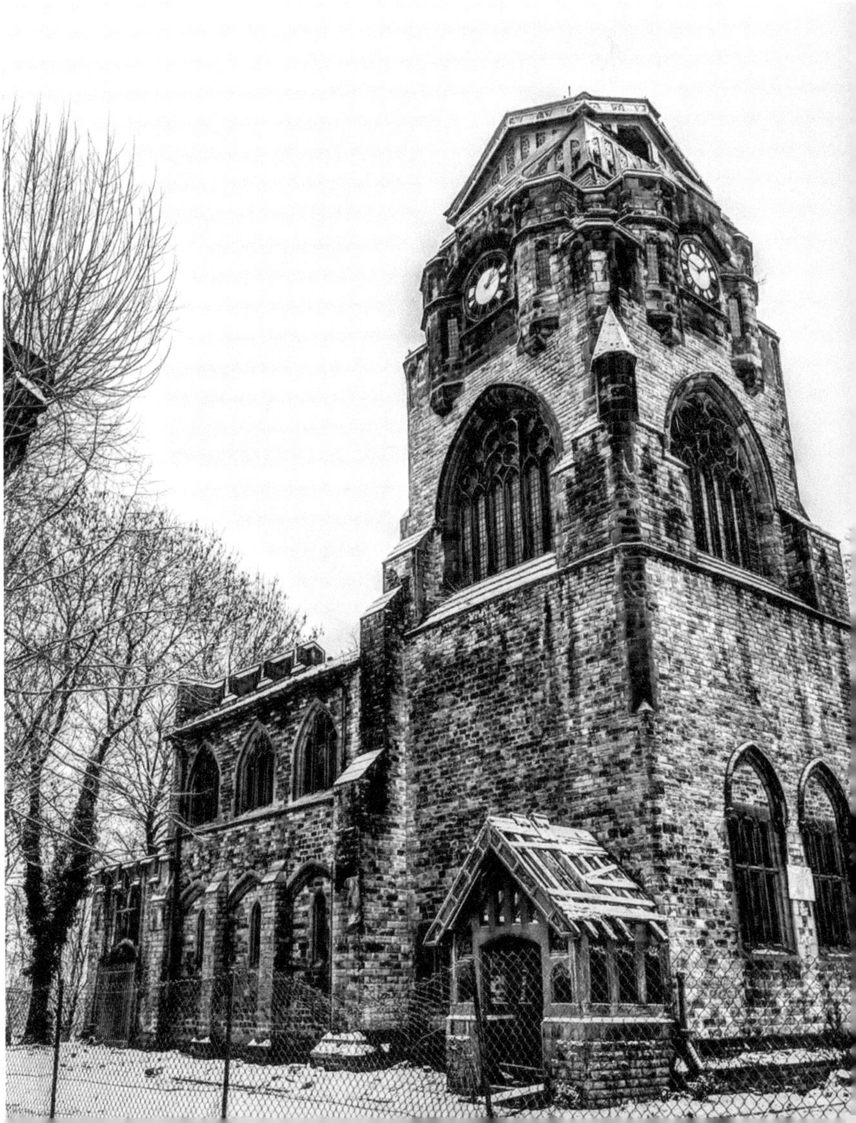

Agecroft Cemetery Chapel. (Courtesy of kyleofsalford)

37. Salford Lads' Club

The iconic Edwardian building known locally as Salford Lads' Club was originally designed in 1903 by Manchester-based architect Henry Lord and is built of brick and terracotta with Lord's design cleverly arranged around a series of spaces surrounding a main gym. The Lads' Club is a scintillating mixture of very high-quality architecture, remarkable social history and strong local community use. It was opened on 30 January 1904 by Lord Baden-Powell, founder of the scout movement. Among former members are actor Albert Finney and Alan Clarke, the lead singer of 1960s pop group The Hollies. It has since become a shrine to Manchester band The Smiths fans from all over the world after it was used for the sleeve of their album *The Queen Is Dead*.

The building itself retains most of its original features despite the building being in continuous use for over 100 years. The club is also part of the New Barracks estate with Coronation Street at the heart of the area, which was originally built around 1900 on the site of an early nineteenth-century army barracks. It later gave its name to the world-famous soap opera written by Salford author Tony Warren. The Salford Lads' Club stands at one end of Coronation Street. The New Barracks estate was Salford's first local authority housing scheme and was notable for its housing quality and community provision, which also included St Ignatius Church. The estate was designed following a competition in 1899 won by Henry Lord. Both the club and the church were built on corporation land; the club by brewers J. G. and W. G. Groves and the church by Lord Egerton of Tatton. It was another local architect, Alfred Darbyshire, who designed St Ignatius Church. A Salford Council report commented 'that the new Barracks Estate has maintained much of its original architectural appearance and character, and remains a clearly legible planned model estate dating from the early years of the twentieth century. Its special interest lies in its importance in the social history of Salford's first public housing scheme and an early example of town planning, built by locally significant architects.' As part of a nationwide hunt to find the most iconic buildings in the country in 2007, the Lads' Club was third. A report by English Heritage also described the building as being the 'most complete example of this rare form of social provision to survive in England'.

The Groves family have continued their involvement with the club during the past 115 years. The club was part of the wider movement of lads' clubs set up by local companies and philanthropists such as the Groves between 1886 and 1910 in many industrialised cities, and in particular in the North West of England. The aim of these clubs was to provide positive alternatives to the teenage street gangs of the time with sports, arts, cultural and educational activities. Salford Lads' Club was one of the few to include a work bureau, finding employment for lads aged thirteen and upwards. It remains open to this day.

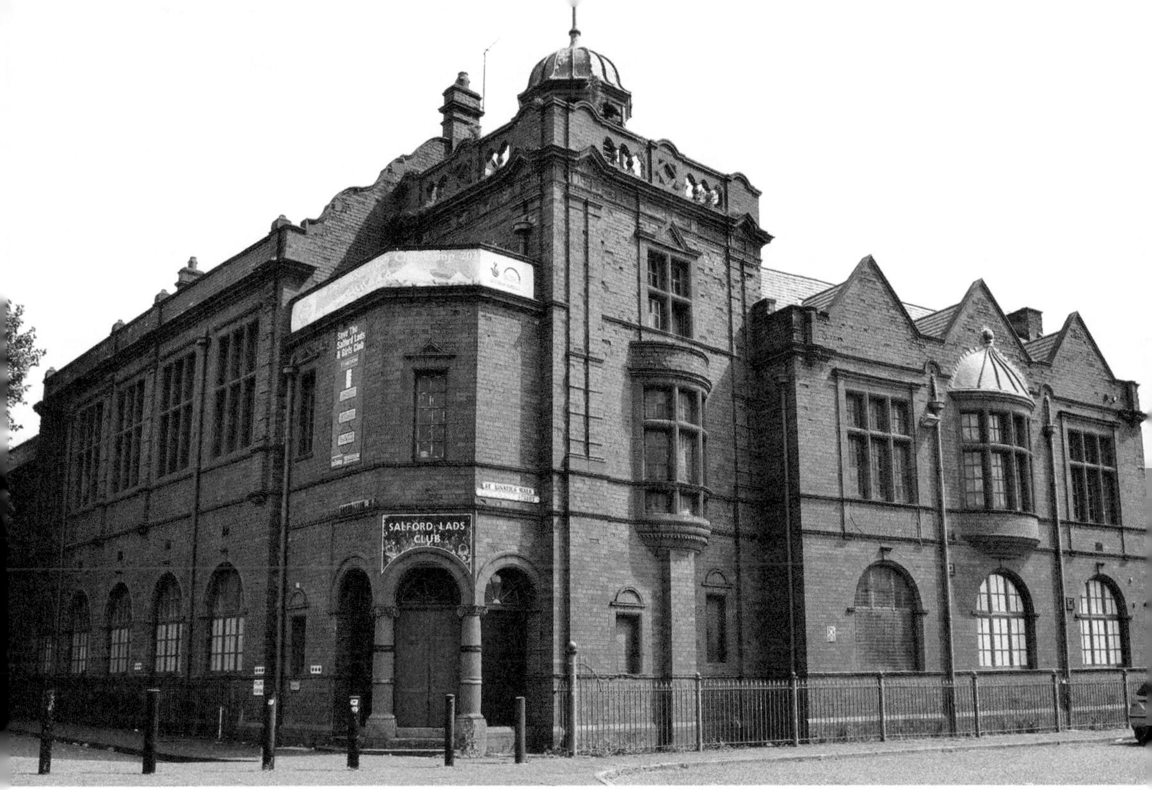

Above: Salford Lads' Club, in use for over 100 years. (© Ben Abel)

Right: The Salford Lads' Club, an important part of Salford's social heritage. (© Ben Abel)

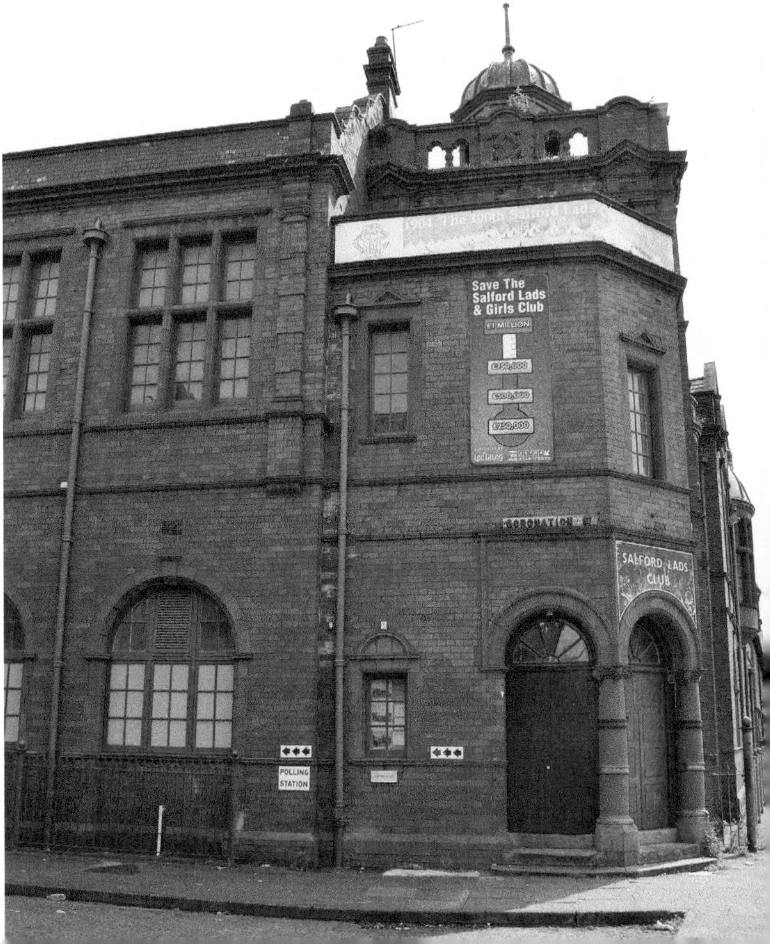

38. Halton Bank School, Broad Street

Halton Bank School was built in 1906 and designed by John Woodhouse (1847–1929). It occupies an awkwardly shaped site on Bolton Road. The building is an intriguing mix of yellow terracotta and red brick. The terracotta is used to emphasise the windows and for keystones.

It was the eighteenth council school to be opened in the city of Salford, with the foundation stone of the building being laid by the mayor, Alderman Isidor Frankenburg. The irregular Welsh slate roof is quite distinctive with pointed Gothic gables and occasional cupolas. The building is characterised by its large,

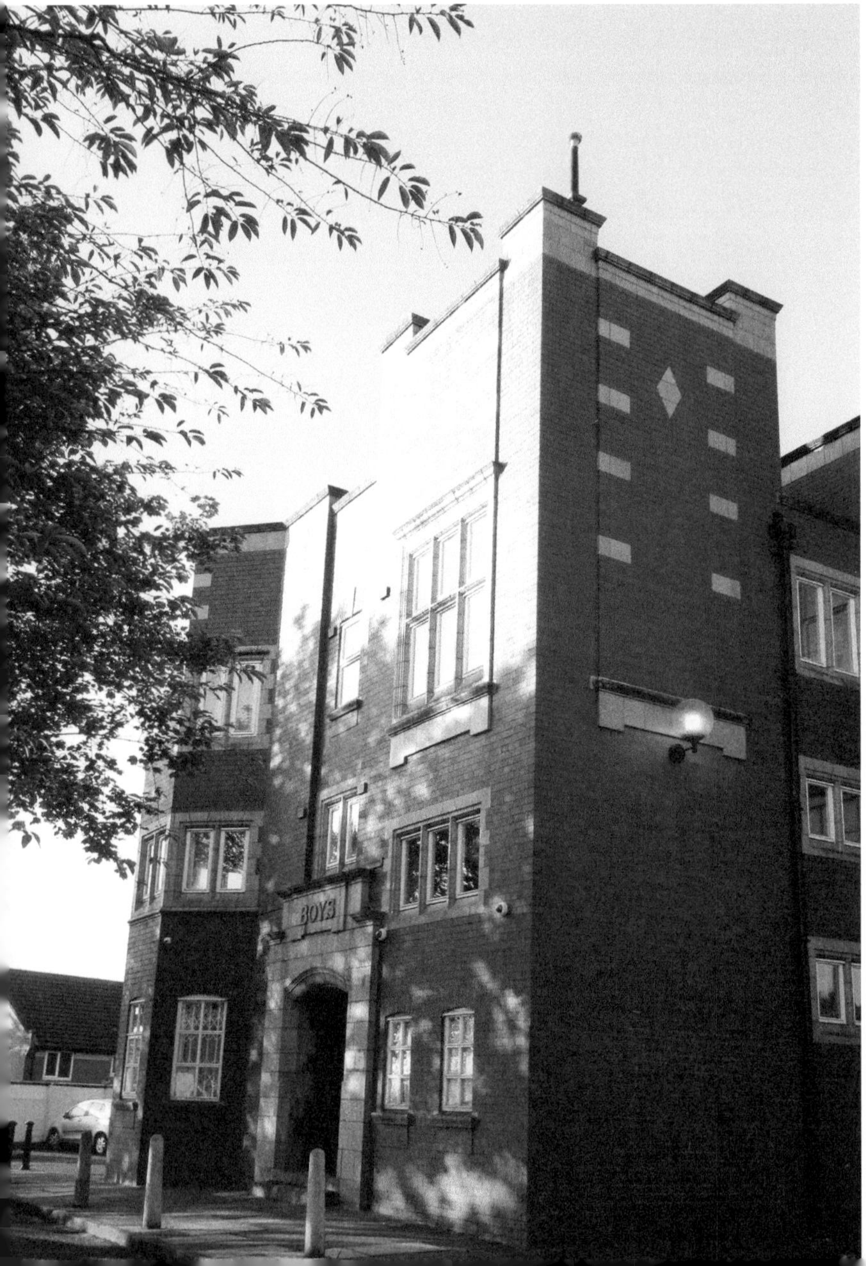

The former Halton Bank School in Pendleton – now apartments. (© Carole O'Reilly)

regular fenestration. There were separate entrances for boys and girls, each with a terracotta porch; the infants and junior sections were divided from each other by gates. The building is currently apartments.

39. Lamb Hotel, Eccles

This building dates back to 1862 but was rebuilt and opened in 1906. The hotel was designed by Mr Newton of Hartley, Hacking & Co. for Joseph Holts Brewery. The pub is notable for the quality of its interior décor and is built in the baroque style. It is a classic pub (or 'gin palace') of the early years of the twentieth century and is made of red brick and terracotta with tall chimneys.

The building is on the Campaign for Real Ale's National Inventory of Historic Pub Interiors. Of particular note is the billiard room, which maintains the original table by Burroughes and Watts, bell pushes and raised seats.

A narrow oriel window overlooks the main entrance on whose gable the year 1906 is carved. The vault is located to the right side of the entrance while the left side opens into a lobby and gives access to the lounges and the billiard room. The pub boasts art nouveau tiling, wood panelling and Jacobean staircase and door surrounds. The bar features the etched and curved glass bar windows that are very characteristic of Holt's pubs of this vintage. It continues to be a popular meeting place for locals.

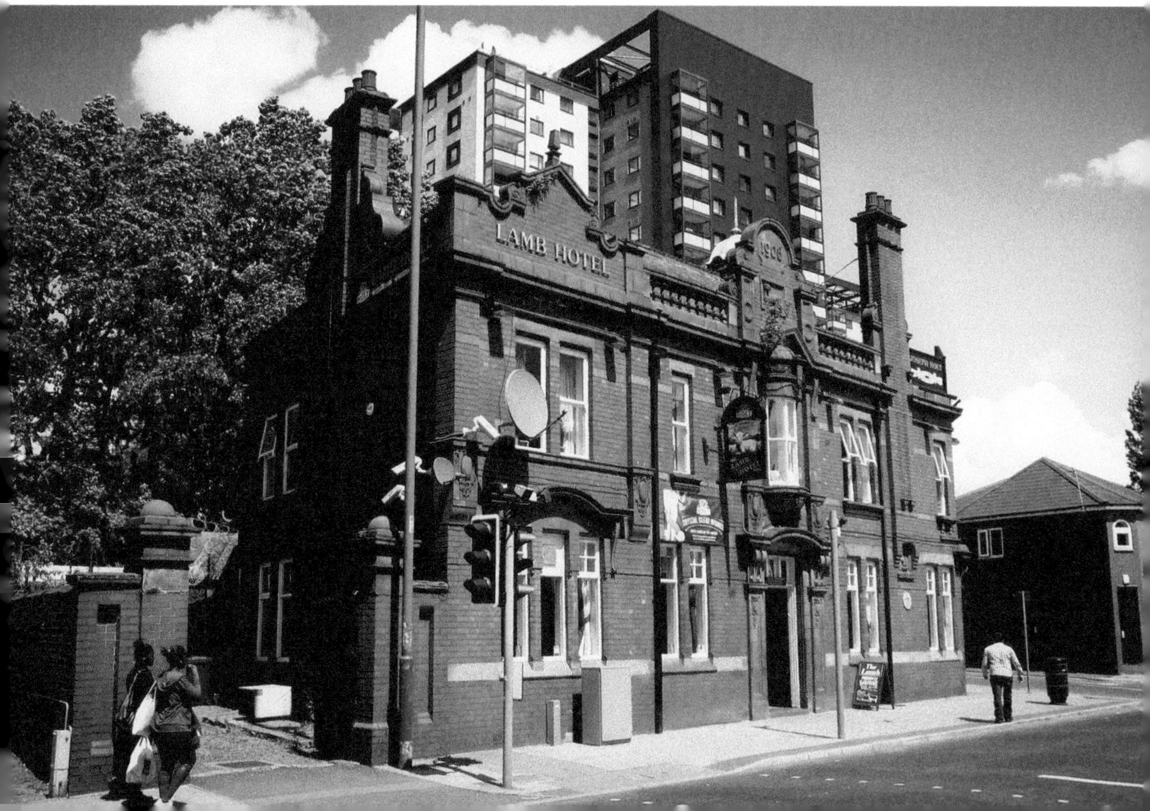

The Lamb Hotel, built in baroque style, dating from 1906. (© https://tigergrowl.wordpress.com)

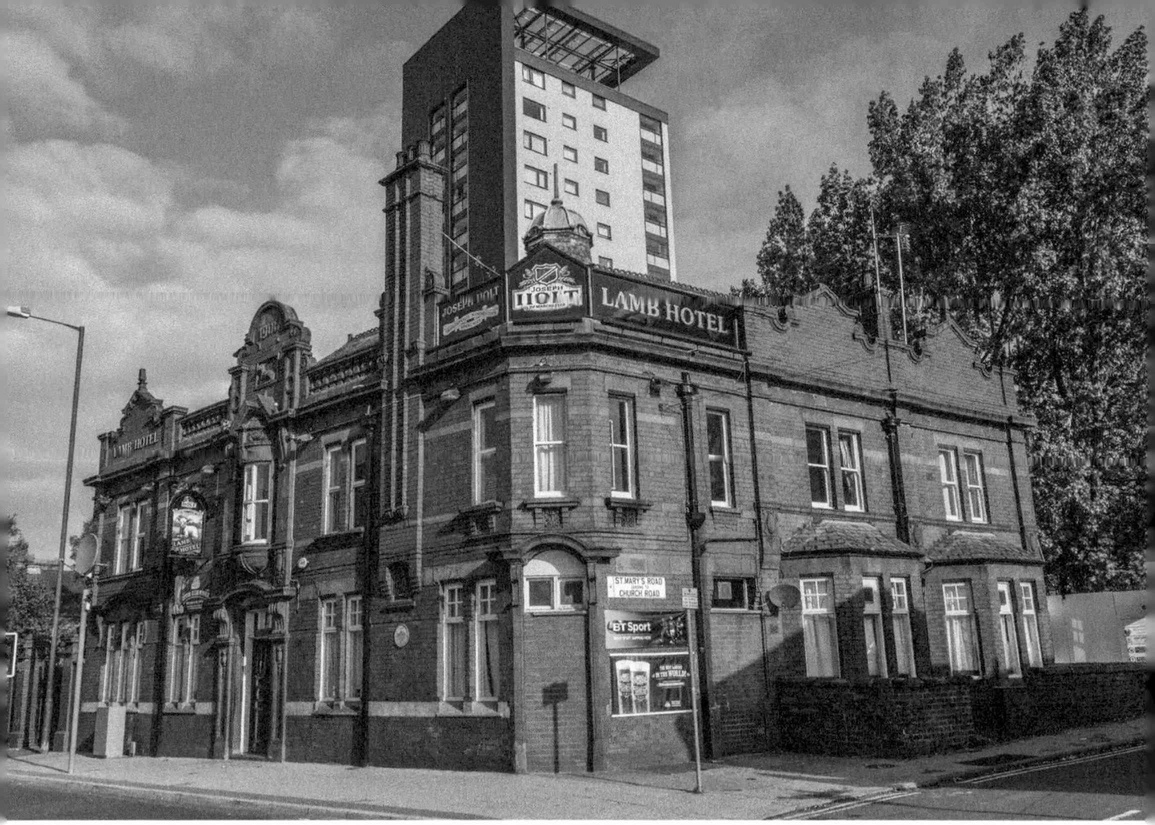

The Lamb Hotel also has a fine interior to equal its external appearance. (© https://tigergrowl.wordpress.com)

40. Eccles Central Library

This is a Carnegie library, funds for which were donated by Andrew Carnegie. The building was designed by Edward Potts in 1907. The building has two storeys, but single-storey additions were made in 1971. Potts was born in Bury but practised in Oldham. He designed an innovative method of fireproofing mills by using concrete flooring. He moved to Eccles in 1891 and served as a Liberal member of Eccles Council from 1902 to 1905.

The building occupies the centre of a small square. The library is a varied design, being made of brick and stone with terracotta and including rich carving. The roof is of stone slate. The interiors are of much interest with art nouveau glass carved with writers' names, a tunnel-vaulted ceiling and a bright reading room. Portrait medallions of various writers hang on the walls.

An octagonal belvedere is an unusual feature surrounded by a balustrade and crowned by a domed roof. The belvedere sits on top of a large two-storey bay with ornate carving on its panels and fan-lighted windows on the first floor.

Semicircular curved arches shelter the tripartite windows. Pairs of first-floor windows are separated by Ionic columns. Many of the building's panels contain rich carvings of scrolls and coats of arms. Taken as a whole, it is an atypical building but with much to interest the eye.

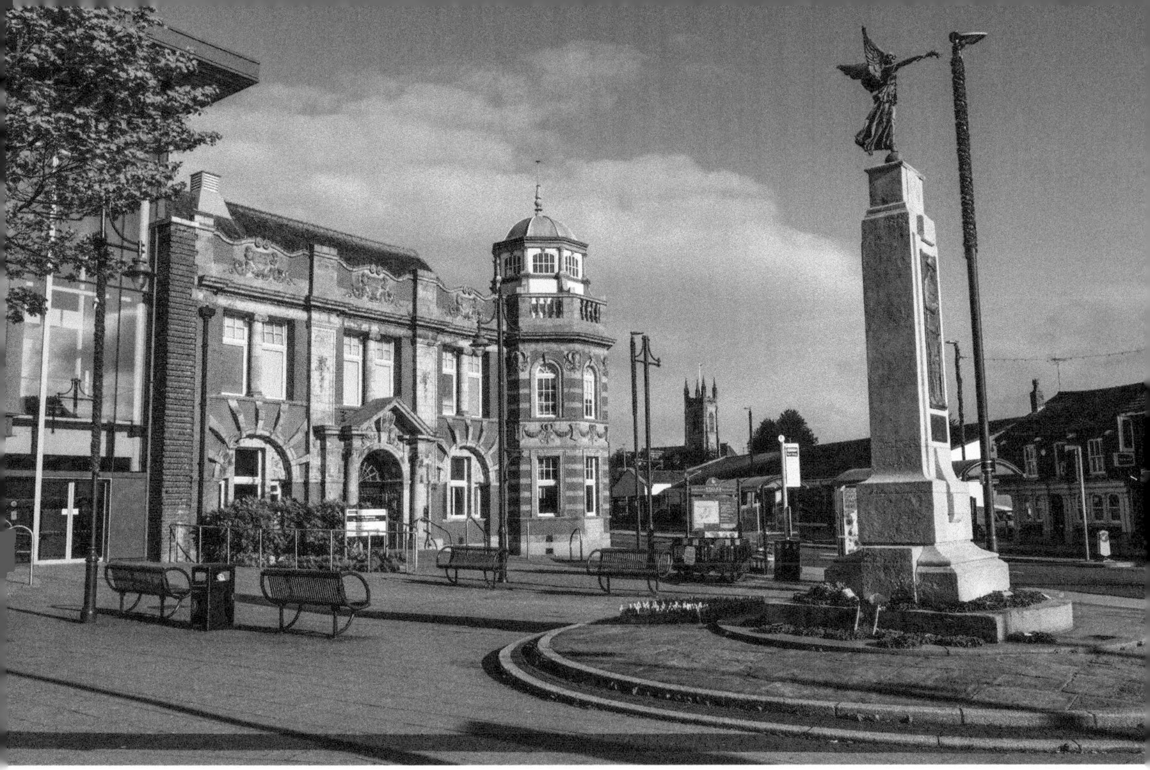

Above: The Eccles library is one of many donated by philanthropist Andrew Carnegie.

Below: The octagonal belvedere is an unusual addition to this building, designed by Edward Potts in 1907.

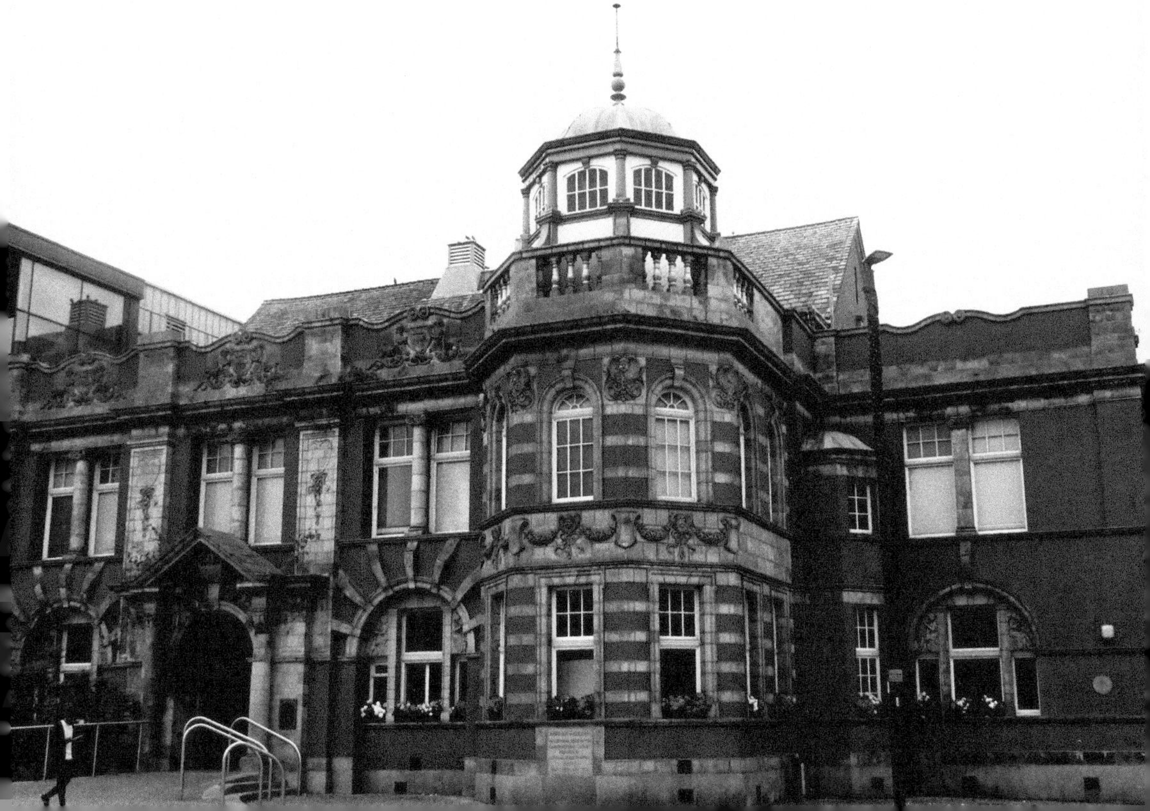

41. Salford Cinema, Chapel Street

Originally a Scottish Presbyterian church, the first building here was built in 1846 and had a tall spire, eventually taken down and fully remodelled as a cinema. This cinema on Chapel Street opened in November 1912 and was an immediate success. It was owned by Matthew Raymond who had previously built the Arcadia cinema on Blackfriars Road. The building was described in the Salford Reporter as 'a credit and an ornament to Chapel Street' and 'the handsomest picture palace in the Borough'. It is a building of elegance and designed as a showpiece with its baroque swags and garlands with its magnificent corner dome which was held up on columns and all cast in orange terracotta. It was incredibly popular and in 1913, a five-piece orchestra was introduced, adding to its attraction and increasing popularity. The cinema eventually changed its name in 1938 to the Rex but after the war with multiple slum clearance in the area, its long-term viability was affected. The last film to be shown here was *Blue Murder at St Trinians* in 1958 and the building was to lie empty for nine years. In 1967 it was reopened as a bingo hall. In 1985 it was taken over and used as a chapel called the Victory Chapel. It has been the New Harvest multicultural church for over two decades. The former Salford cinema is one of the finest Edwardian cinema buildings that remain in the country.

Below left: Salford Cinema, which opened in 1912 – a handsome building even to this day. (© Tony Reeves)

Below right: A magnificent corner dome, which is held up on columns and all cast in orange terracotta. (© Tony Reeves)

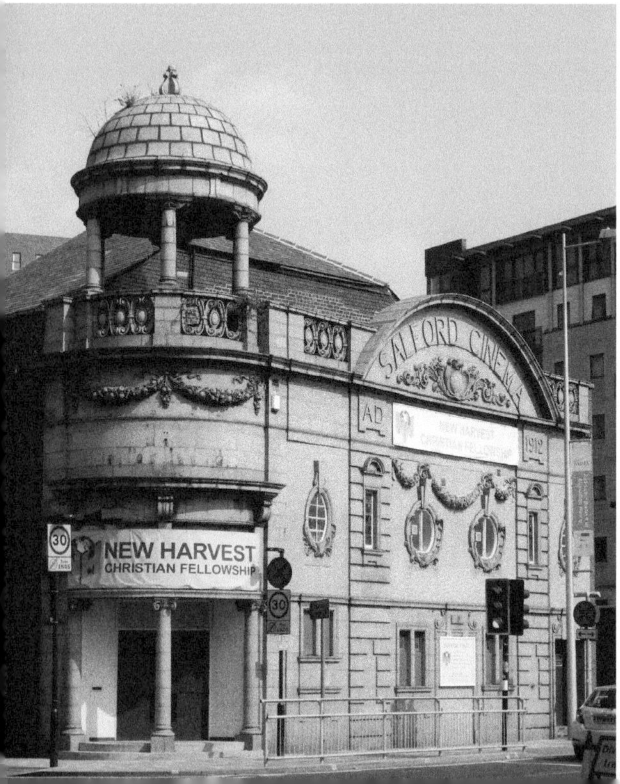

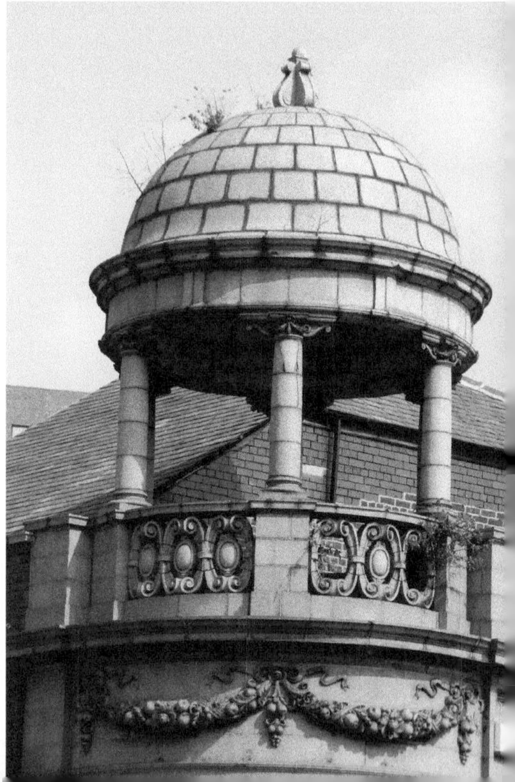

42. Adelphi and Centenary Buildings, Salford University

The large white building on the corner of Adelphi Street and Peru Street in Salford was part of Salford University's Adelphi Campus and was once home to the School of Media, Music & Performance but is now empty. In April 2011, the university campus plan stated that, 'Many of the existing University buildings look old and do not represent an image of an innovative, modern and quality learning environment. Older buildings generally exhibit poor thermal performance which results in high energy consumption,' and concluded that the Adelphi Building was a 'liability'. The university's long-term development plan was to dispose of a number of its outlying buildings, such as the Adelphi, and focus on the Peel Park Campus and the MediaCity Campus.

In the middle of the nineteenth century, the site was occupied by a reservoir, associated with the nearby Adelphi Dye Works. By 1909, it had been replaced by a timber yard. The building that exists today was opened in 1915. It was originally a chemical factory built for Griffiths Hughes, a company who made products such as Rennies, Radox, Kruschen Salts and Trugel. The company produced medicine products, housing a drug warehouse until the 1930s when Griffiths Hughes sold the building to a copper works company. The building was then purchased by the university in 1962 and it became the Salford Royal College of Advanced Technology and in the late 1980s was renamed the Adelphi Building. It eventually closed in 2016 and currently sits empty.

In contrast, the Centenary Building is a much more contemporary structure. It was designed by architects Hodder Associates and built between 1994 and 1995

The Adelphi building, once home to the School of Media, Music & Performance.

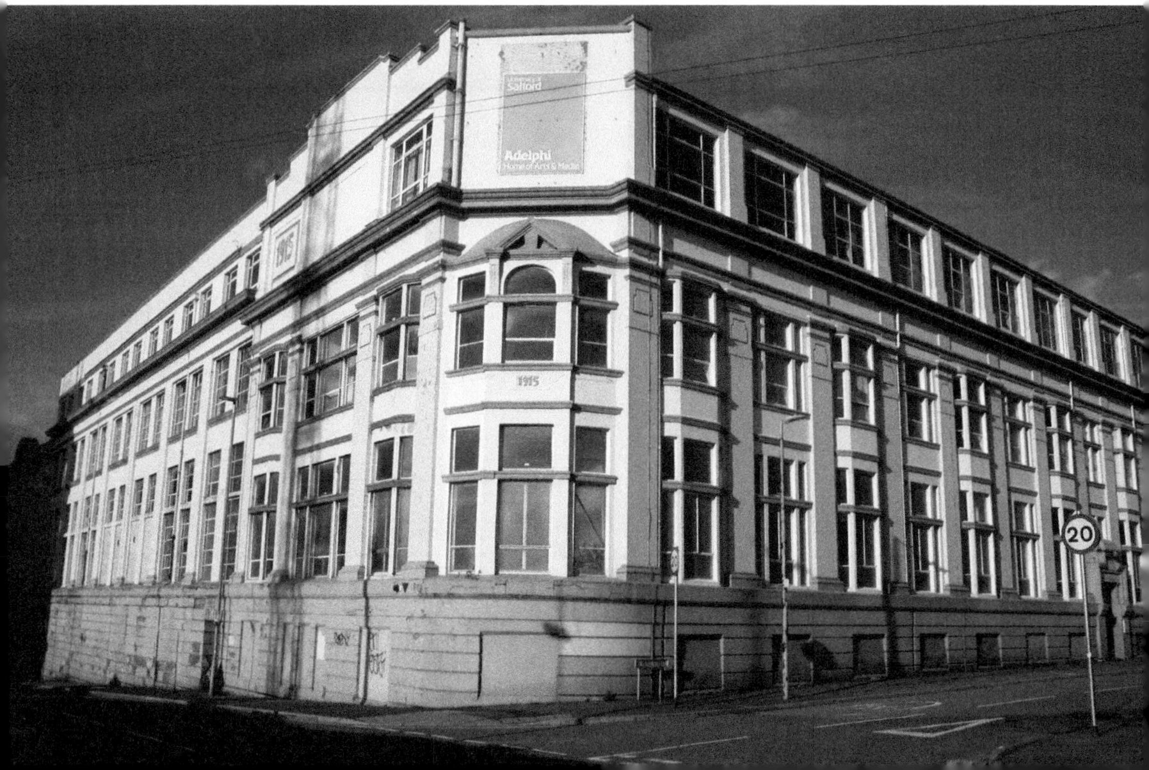

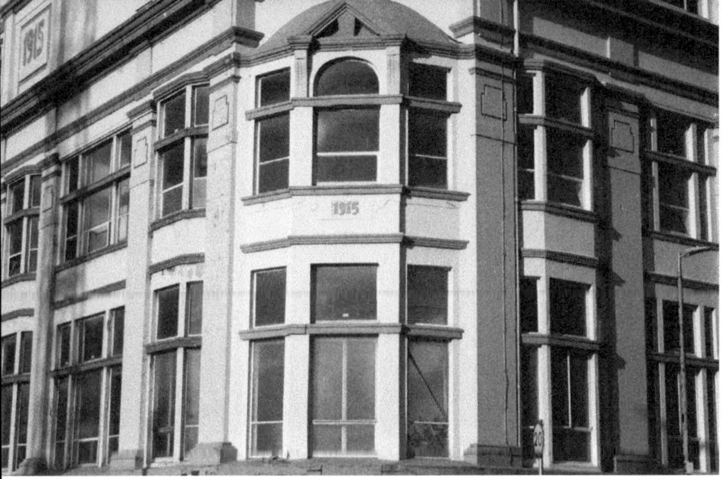

The Adelphi building, built in 1915.

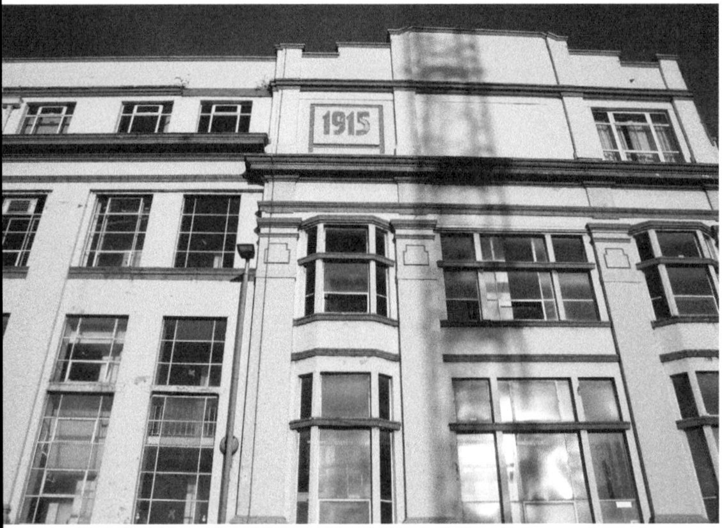

Left: The building is currently empty.

Below: The Centenary Building, completed in 1995 and a recipient of the first Stirling Prize in 1996.

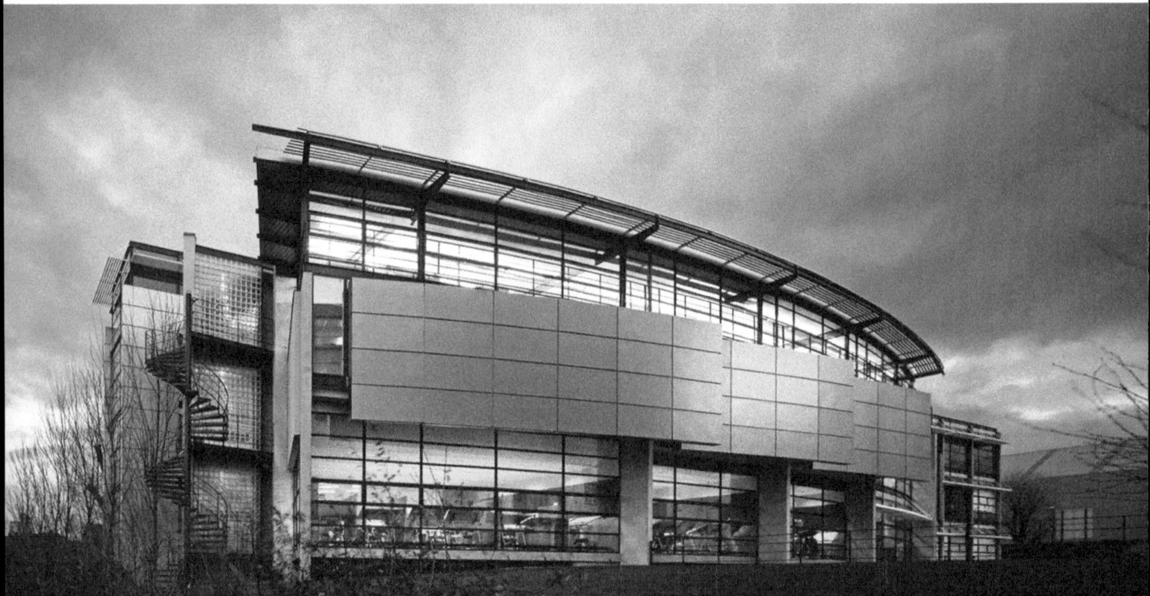

and was the recipient of the first Stirling Prize in 1996. The jury described it as, 'despite being built quickly and cheaply – the team had to be on site in just twelve weeks after appointment – the building is a dynamic, modern and sophisticated exercise in steel, glass and concrete. They have bowed out the main facade to create a wide studio and lecture theatre space with indirect daylighting; breaking the "internal street" with galleries and bridges, and exposing rooms to this central space to give an air of purpose and animation.'

43. Dock Office, Salford Quays

Opened in 1925, this building was designed by Harry Fairhurst & Sons. It is in simple and restrained art deco style and built in concrete. The Fairhursts were a powerhouse of architects and designed many of the public and commercial buildings in Manchester such as the Christie Hospital and the Rylands Building on Market Street (Debenhams). The building's plan is in the shape of a letter 'E'.

The unusual entrance gateway, also of concrete, has the engraved words 'Manchester Docks' along with two motifs of a ship's keel jutting out from the

The Dock Office on Salford Quays, built in an art deco style.

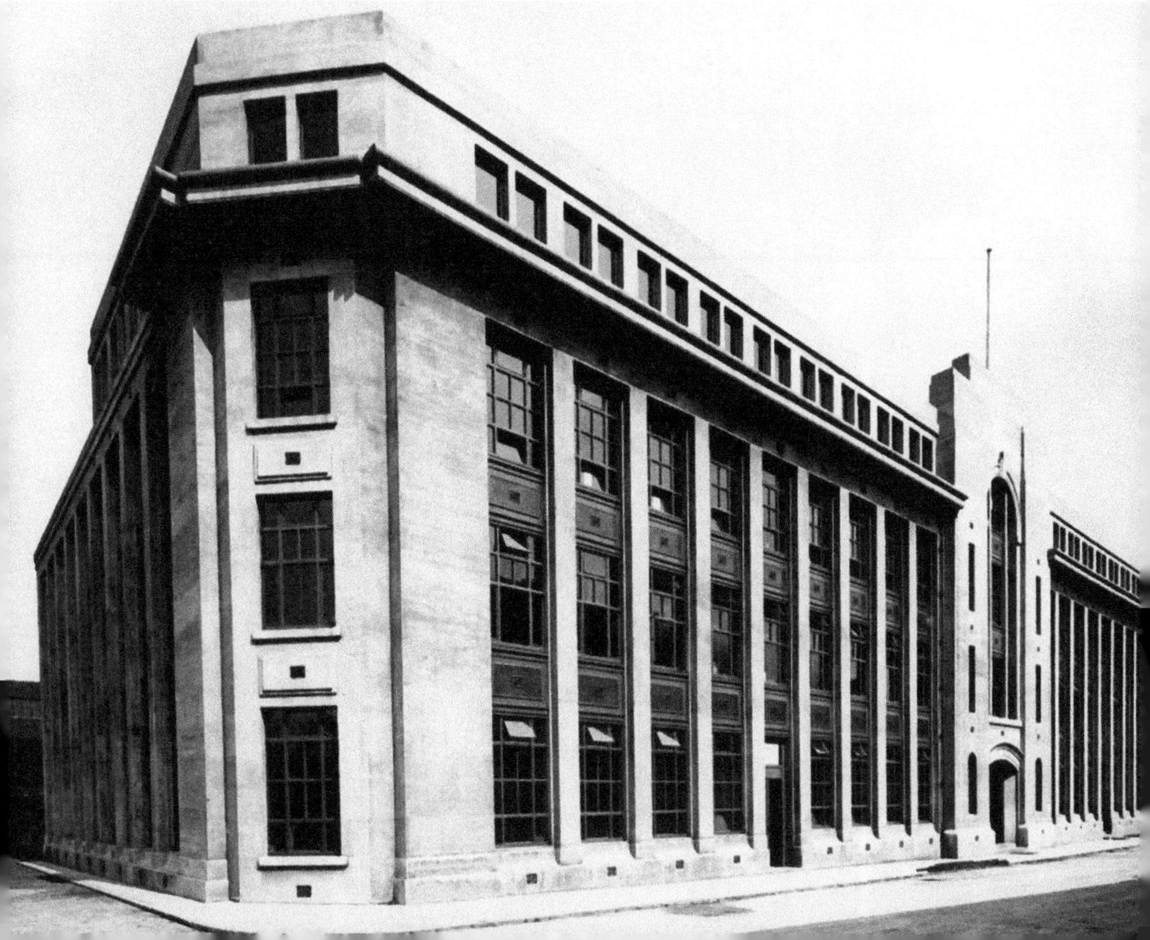

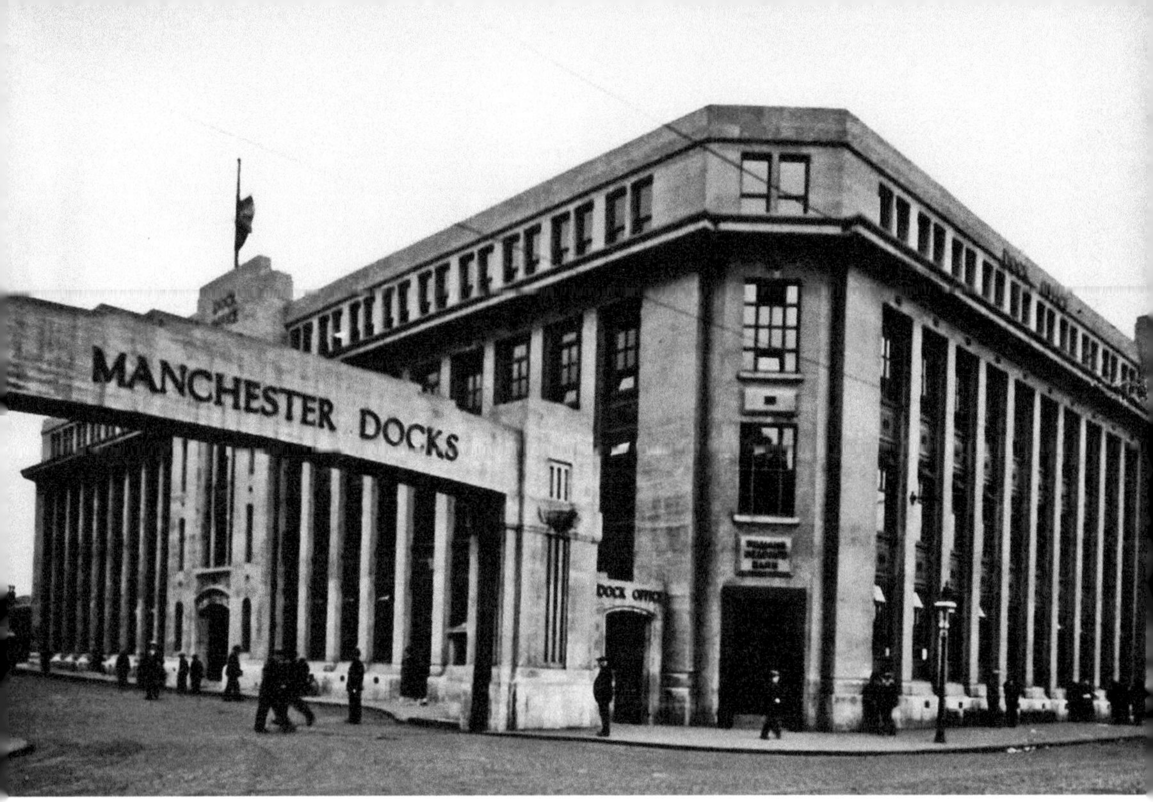

Above: The Dock Office in its prime.

Below: The Dock Office, Manchester Docks and the main entrance to the docks.

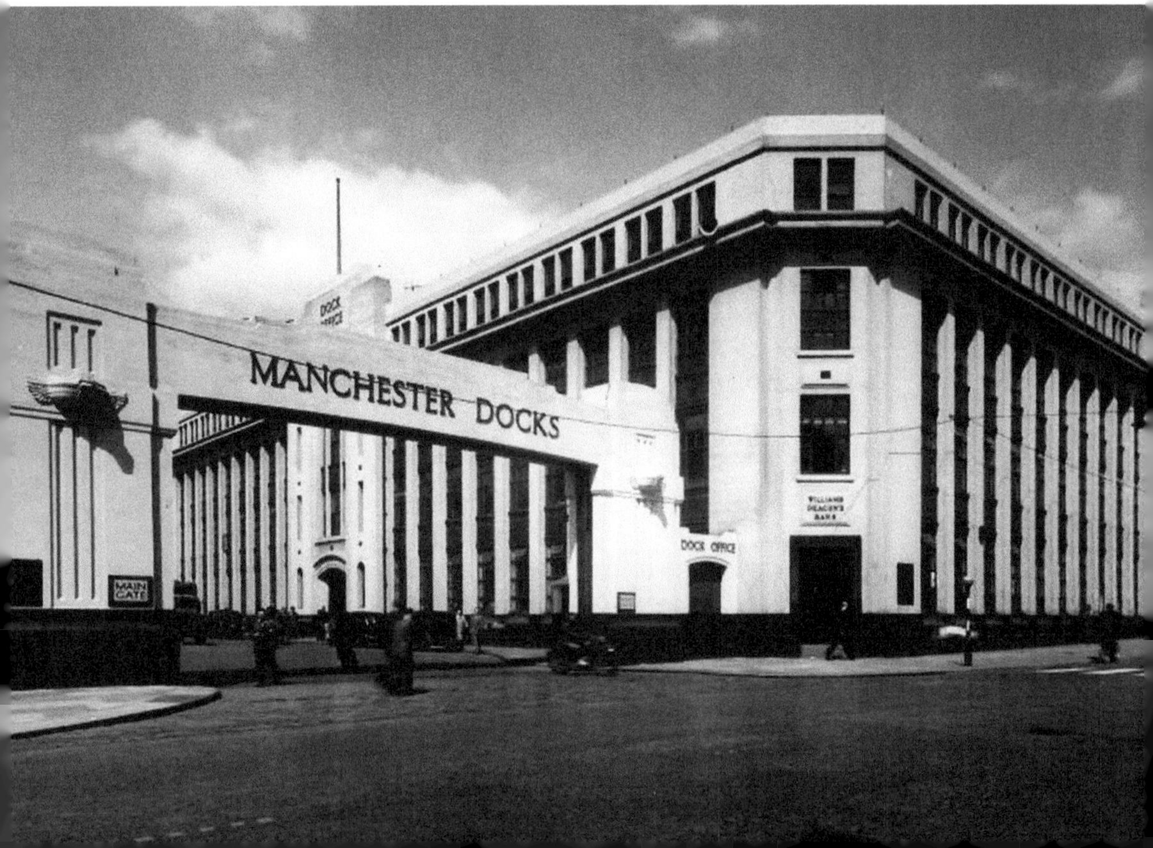

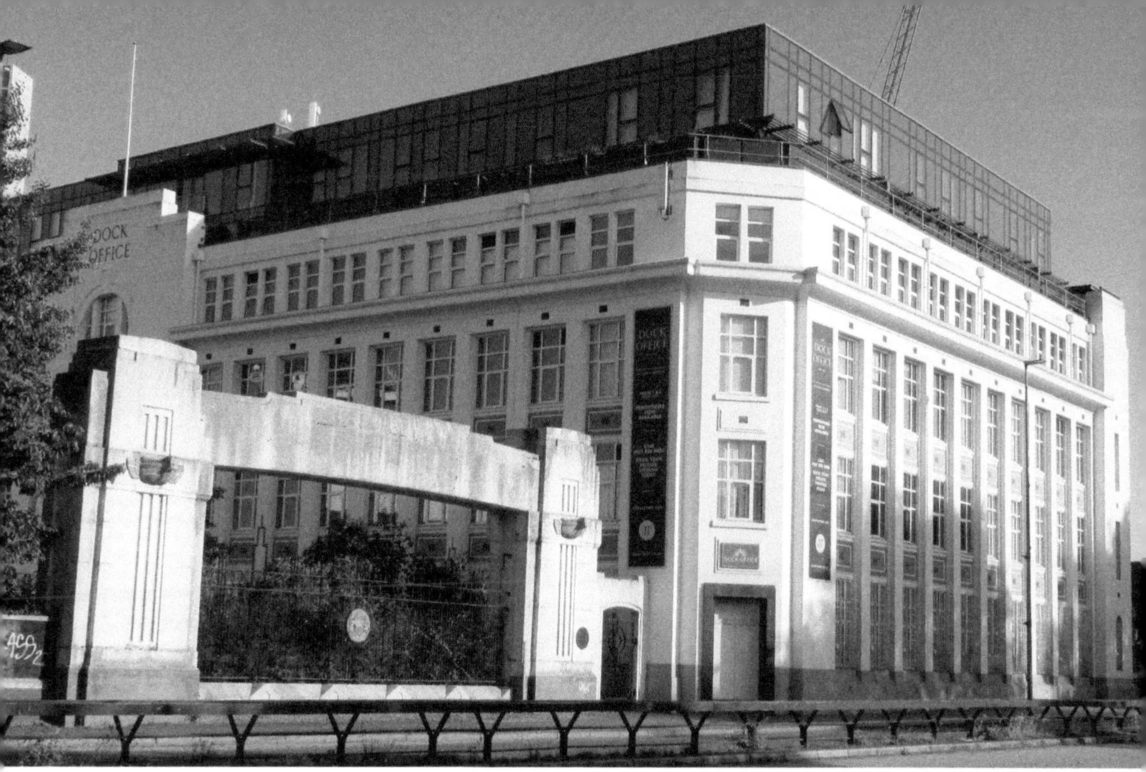

Above: Now apartments, but retaining the character of the former Docks Offices. (© Carole O'Reilly)

Below: Beautifully restored and a popular place to live. (© Carole O'Reilly)

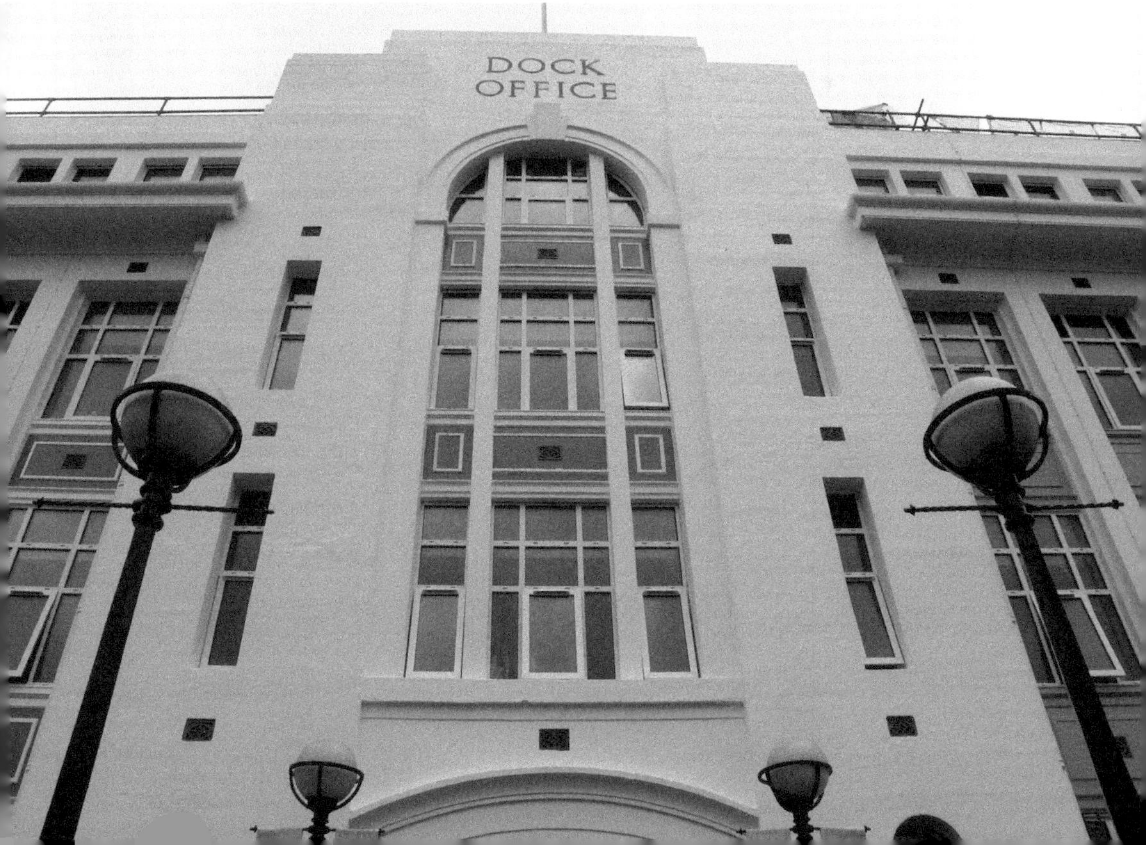

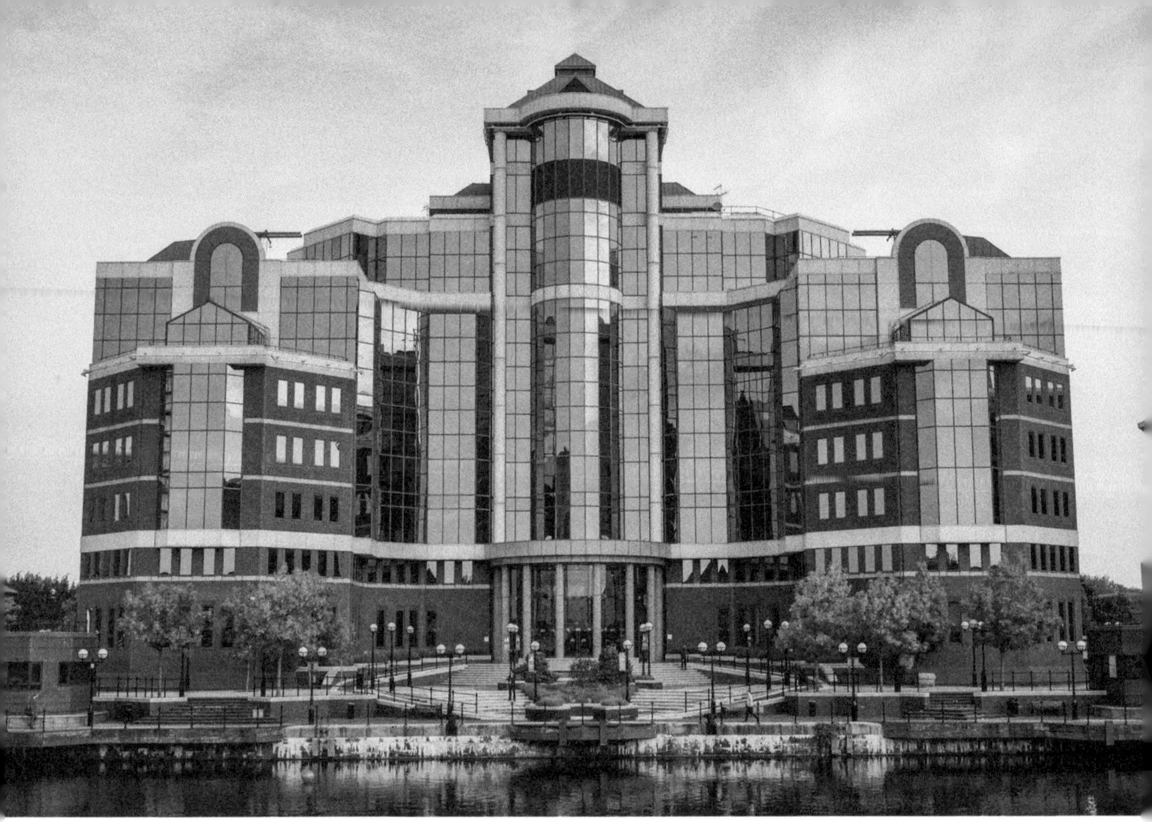

The Victoria is one of a number of office blocks built in the 1990s on the site of Salford Docks. It is one of the more eye-catching sites in the area. (© Steven Robertson)

stonework. The purpose of the gateway was to act as the main entrance to the docks. On the right-hand side of the gateway is a plaque that commemorates the opening of the Manchester Ship Canal by Queen Victoria in 1894.

The building was one of the first in the Salford Quays area to be refurbished and is currently used as an apartment building. Many new buildings have been added as part of ongoing regeneration of the area and include the Victoria and many other office blocks.

44. Higher Crumpsall and Higher Broughton Synagogue

This classical building dates from 1928 and is an interesting example of a place of worship for the local Jewish community. The corner stone was laid in October 1928 and the synagogue opened in 1929. It was designed by Pendleton and Dickinson. The building is faced with white ashlar and is composed of pink brick and it has a hipped roof of Welsh slate. It features three domes, one main and two ancillary, all of which are crowned with a lion's head.

Higher Crumpsall and Higher Broughton Synagogue joined this one in 1969. The building underlines the importance of the local Jewish community to Salford. The synagogue is located close to the border with the city of Manchester.

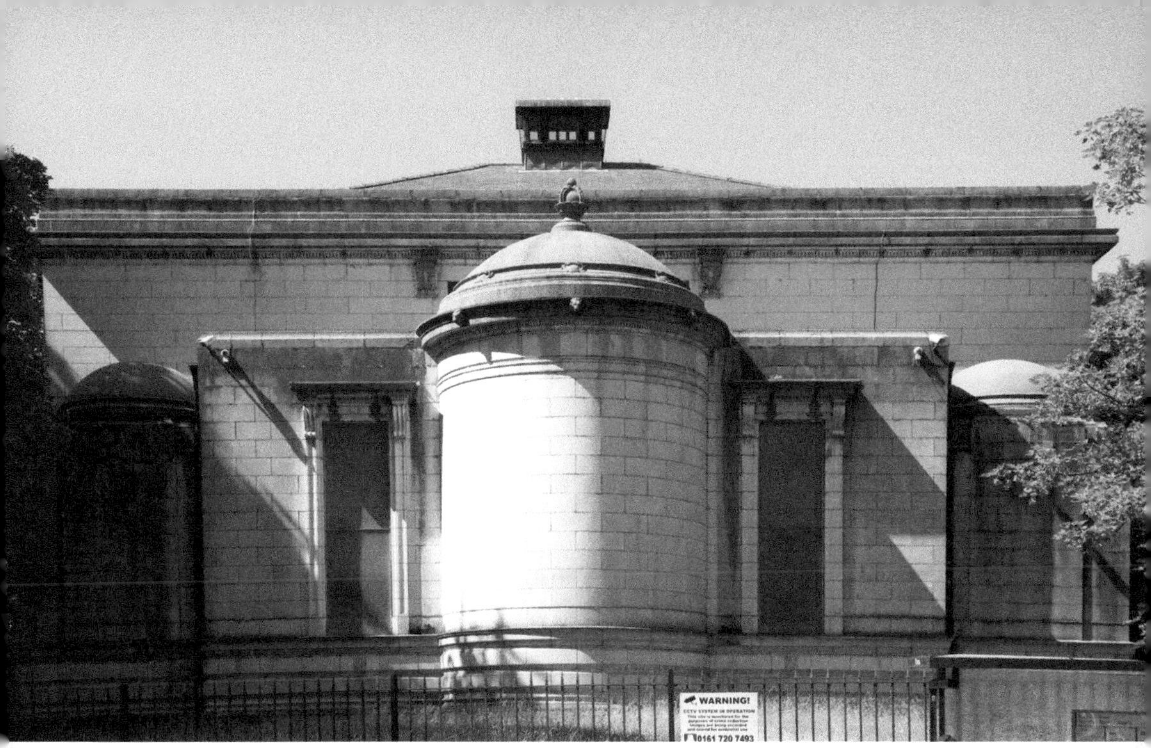

Higher Crumpsall and Higher Broughton Synagogue.

The interior is especially noteworthy with original oak seating, stained glass and marble Bimah (a platform that holds the reading material). The ladies' gallery is cantilevered, offering a clear view of the interior, and the building seats 900 people. A wooden memorial with gold lettering commemorates those members of the community who died in the Second World War.

In 2006, the building received a grant of £130,000 from English Heritage and the Heritage Lottery Fund for repairs and restoration. The synagogue was particularly renowned for the quality of its sung services.

In late 2017, it was announced that, due to demographic changes in the local Jewish population, the synagogue had been sold to the Haredi community for use as a yeshiva (school for studying Jewish texts). It was suggested that the more affluent members had moved away to be replaced by a more Orthodox form of Jewry and that the congregation had dwindled as a result. The scale of repair required to the building was felt to be too daunting to be fully realised.

45. Hemsley House, Salford Masonic Hall, Chapel Street

Hemsley House was built on Salford Crescent in the 1920s on the site of two Georgian houses. Much of the land along the Crescent was donated by Sir Humphrey Booth to the trustees of the Booth Charity (named after his grandfather). Ninety-nine-year leases were created as a result, with restrictions on what type and style of building could be constructed.

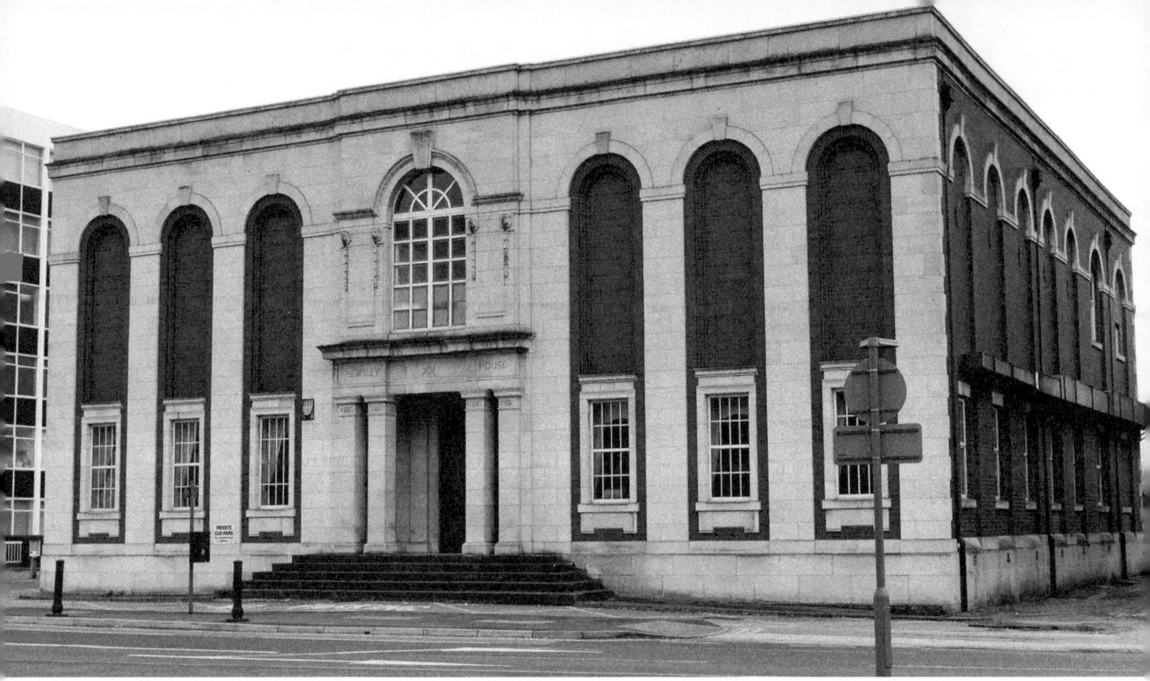

Hemsley House, Salford Masonic Hall, built in the 1920s. (© https://tigergrowl.wordpress.com)

The building is mostly of red brick with ashlared limestone facing. The simple classical style is designed to fit in with the Georgian style, which predominated on the Crescent. The upper storey of the building is tall and blind and very plain to echo the enclosed world of the Freemasons. This storey housed the main meeting hall of the lodge. The other rooms are used for Chapter meetings and for storing the Masonic regalia. A plain, arched window is situated above the main entrance. Four pilasters support the pediment, which is engraved with the name of the building and the Masonic symbol. Salford Masons are part of the Provincial Grand Lodge of East Lancashire (dating from 1826), which consists of sixteen lodges in total.

The building currently offers a variety of function rooms to rent to the general public and is part of the Crescent Conservation Area.

46. The Racecourse Hotel, Littleton Road

The Racecourse Hotel was built to serve patrons of the nearby Manchester Racecourse (despite being in Salford) at Castle Irwell. It also provided overnight accommodation for the jockeys. Fred Done (of Betfred) began his trade at the racecourse and the site was among the first to provide corporate hospitality boxes. The grandstand alone could seat over 1,000 people. The name Castle Irwell came not from an actual castle but from a former castellated building on the site, the home of the Fitzgerald family, MPs and owners of Pendleton Colliery. Racing began on the site in 1902.

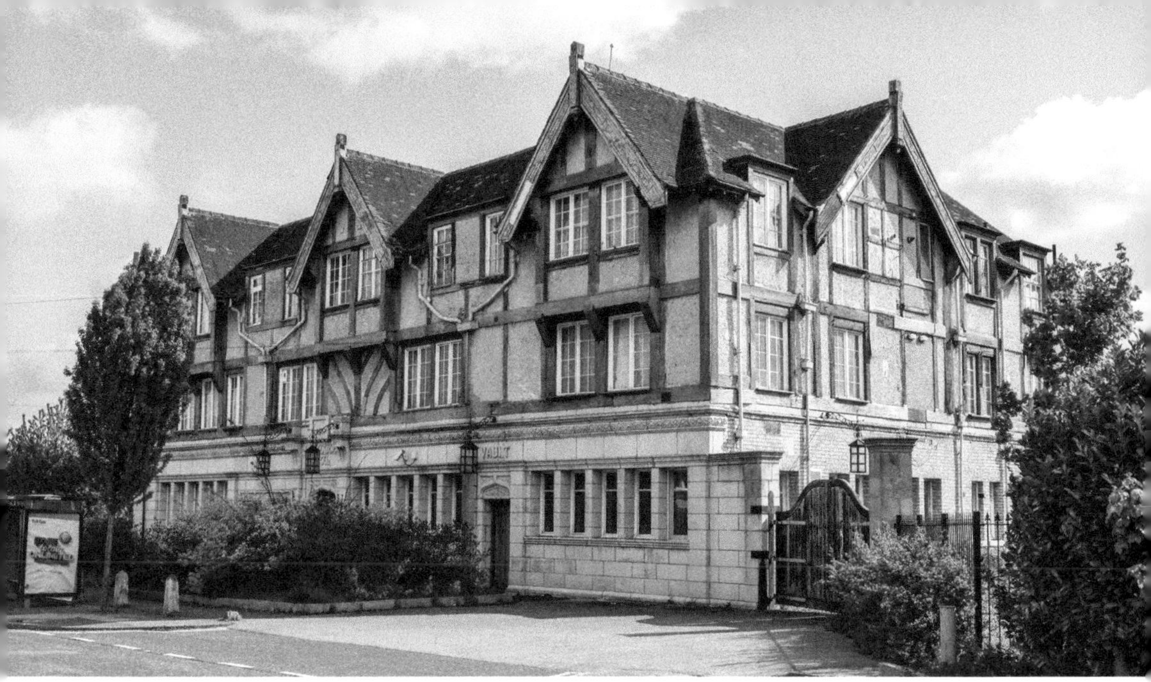

The Racecourse Hotel on Littleton Road has undergone a number of renovations after serving generations who have passed through its doors since it opened in 1930. (© Steven Robertson)

The size of the interior of the bar is a testament to the popularity of horseracing since it first opened in 1930. It was part of the Salford brewery company of Groves and Withnall. The building is characterised by its timber frame, wood-panelled interiors and the extensive use of leaded windows. It has a large cellar area and even offered a jockey's room. The racecourse itself closed in 1963 and the site was sold to Salford University. The pub shut in 2013 when its owners Oakwell Brewery of Barnsley went into liquidation. It was reopened by Sam Smiths of Tadcaster in December 2015.

47. Barton Aerodrome, Eccles

One of the more unusual building locations is at City Airport, often known locally as 'Barton Aerodrome'. This opened in 1930 as the first municipal airport in the country to be licensed by the Air Ministry. Its Grade II listed control tower is the oldest known to be in continuous use since it was built in 1932. In addition, the original hangar and the terminal building are also listed – Grade II. The aerodrome has a significant local history.

In the autumn of 1928, the works were commenced on a new municipal aerodrome to replace the temporary one at Manchester (Wythenshawe) Aerodrome. Works were completed by 1930 along with the first passenger charter flight from here. Up until 1933, it was operated by Northern Air Lines who had Avro 504s and other aircraft for training as well as club and charter flights. A number of scheduled services operated to London and Birmingham, but were subsidised by councils in Manchester, Birmingham and Liverpool.

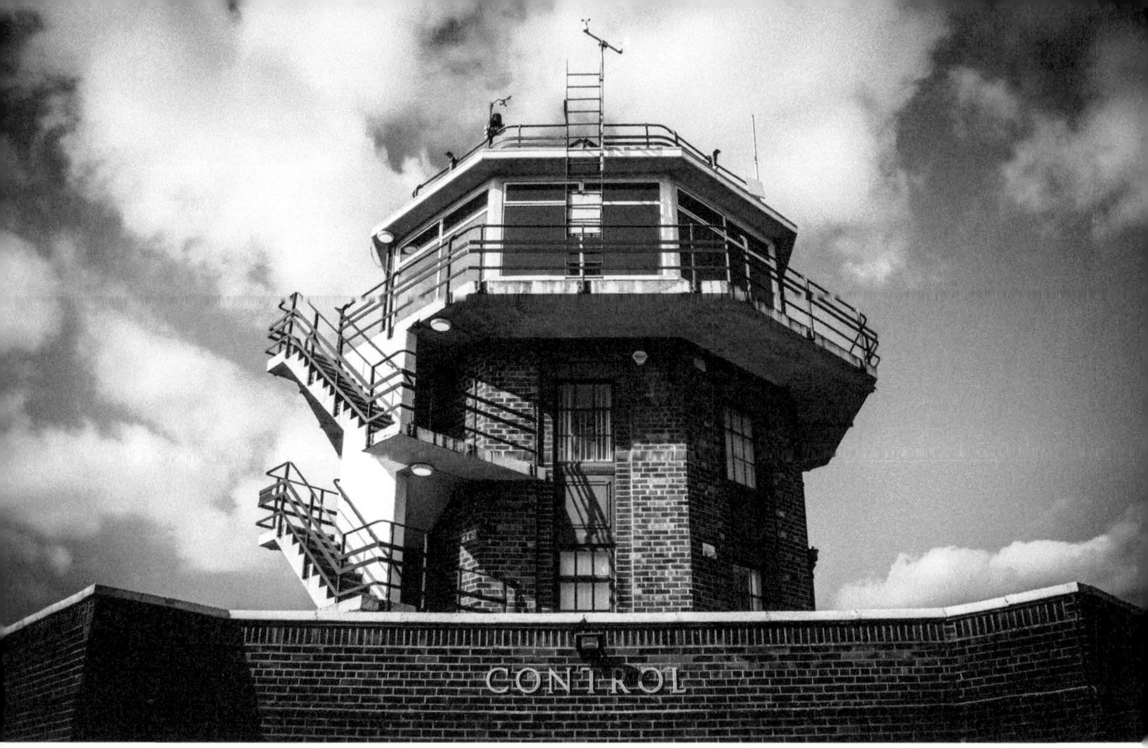

City Airport Barton Aerodrome. (© Ben Goodwin)

The airport was to expand with its new control tower and wireless station and Barton was the first municipal airport to be able to communicate with aircraft in flight and give bearings to pilots direct from the airfield. Further routes were introduced including Blackpool and the Isle of Man in 1935 but by 1938 all schedules were transferred to the newly completed larger Ringway airport. Barton also had a role to play during the Second World War and was used for military aircraft repairs and assembly.

After the war, the aerodrome was used primarily by Lancashire Aero Club and the Manchester University Air Squadron, flying Tiger Moths and Chipmunk trainers along with the No.2 Reserve Flying School. Ownership was to change with the sale from Manchester City Council to Manchester Ship Canal Developments in 2003 with the intention to develop the nearby area. Refurbishments of the control tower and the Pemberton hangar were carried out and by 2011 the clubhouse was refurbished and relaunched as the Airfield Lodge. The aerodrome has changed little since its opening, and is considered a good example of the airfields of the 1930s with its listed buildings of note. A regular location for filming, the control tower often features in dramas and films.

48. Swinton Civic Centre, Swinton

The Civic Centre (originally named Swinton and Pendlebury Town Hall) was built in 1937 on the former site of the Guardians of the Poor Industrial Training

School. The building was designed by Percy Thomas and Ernest Prestwich for £80,000, following a national design competition and was awarded the RIBA Gold medal in 1938. This accolade reflects the modernity of the design and the features of the landscape.

The building itself was set 90 feet back from the pavement to create the illusion of space. A low stone kerb was placed between the site and the pavement instead of a wall or railings in order to give the impression of space and ease of access. The building was originally intended to be complemented by the addition of a local library, clinics, a police headquarters and a girls' secondary school.

Most of the exterior of the building was kept plain, with the ornamentation on the central tower and main entrance. The tower itself stands at 125 feet and has four clocks on each of its faces. Each clock was neon-lit at night. The tower is crowned by a balcony at the top, which is reached by 160 interior steps.

Each department of local government inside the building was designed to be self-contained and the building allowed for future extensions to be easily added. The focus of the interior design was to maximise the workers' efficiency. These rooms were kept plain and well lit. Those for the public and for council members were more decorative, particularly the council chamber which made use of synthetic marble columns. The ceiling was decorated with shields representing prominent local families such as the Langleys of Agecroft. It was specially treated with sprayable asbestos to improve the acoustics.

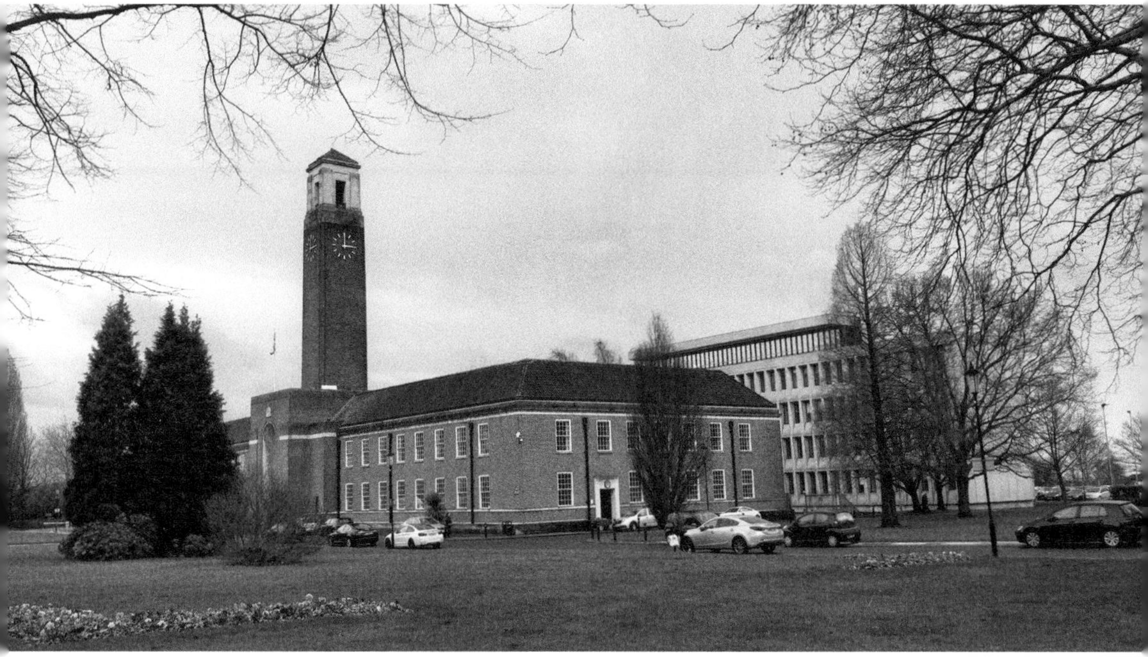

Swinton Civic Centre with its central clock tower.

49. Salford Precinct, Hankinson Way

This distinctive building opened in 1972. It was the result of a large-scale redevelopment of this area of Pendleton dating from the early 1950s, which had demolished 6,000 terraced houses over a 300-acre site. The original proposal was to include a hotel, offices and apartments on the site and it was described in the press as 'the finest in Europe'. The new Salford Market opened in 1970 and this was followed by the precinct itself in 1971.

A political scandal, which resulted in the jailing of the councillor in charge of the redevelopment, impacted on the plans for this amenity; the numbers of shops was reduced from 260 to ninety-five and the hotel was never constructed.

A central twenty-five-storey tower block (Briar Hill Court) contains 136 apartments and the exterior red lettering and arrow state 'Salford Shopping City'. The tower is surrounded by a low two-storey, brutalist concrete structure composed of six separate blocks, with the shops on the ground floor and offices

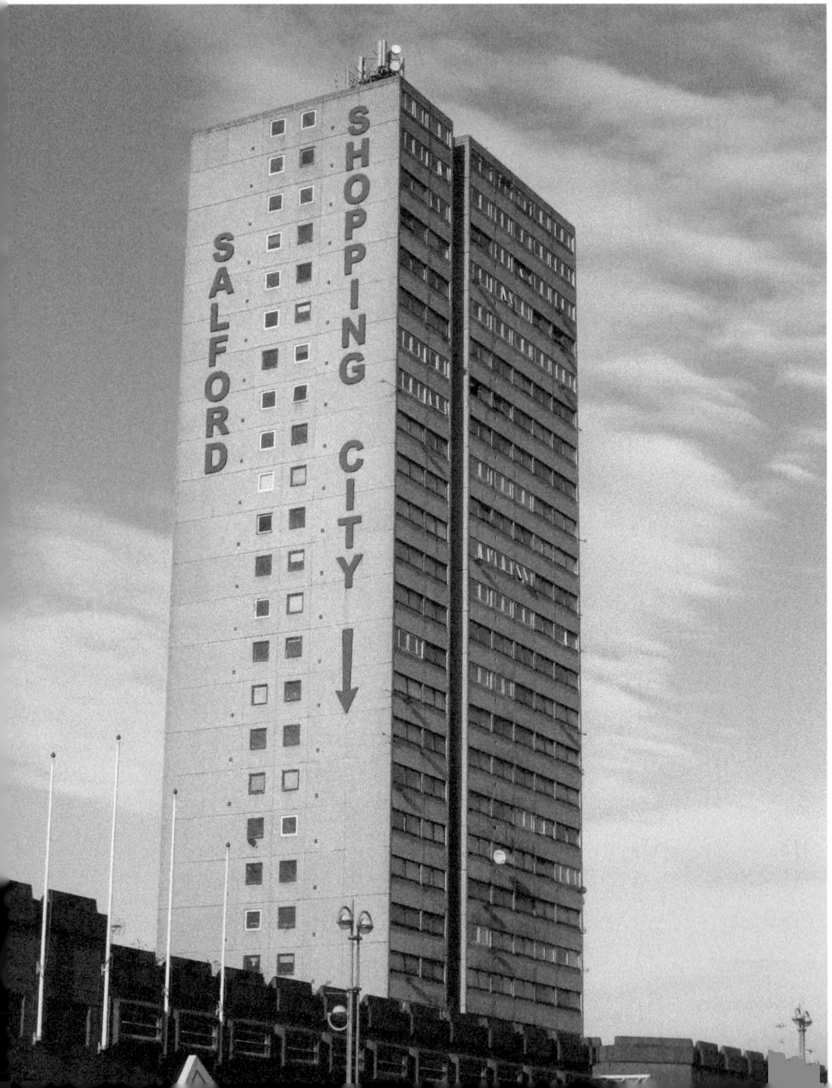

Salford Shopping City tower block. (© Richard Rogerson)

above. The concrete contains high-alumina cement, which makes it strong and fast to manufacture. The first-floor parapets are castellated and have small, regularly spaced horizontal windows. The tower complements nearby social housing developed by Salford Council and designed by the Architectural Research Unit of Edinburgh University in 1965.

The precinct was renamed Salford Shopping City in 1991. In 2000, Salford Council sold the building to a private investor. The market has been much reduced and many of the anchor tenants of the precinct such as Marks and Spencer have left. The opening of a new Tesco in 2012 adjacent to the centre was controversial and contributed to the further decline of the shopping centre.

50. The Lowry Theatre and MediaCity complex, Salford Quays

The Lowry is one of Salford's most iconic buildings and is named after the great early twentieth-century painter L. S. Lowry, best known for his paintings of industrial scenes in the North West. It was opened in October 2000 by Queen Elizabeth II. The new theatre was part of a major regeneration scheme led by Salford City Council from 1988 when the site was identified as having potential for leisure, culture and tourism. The flagship of the development was to be the creation of a performing arts centre.

Architects James Stirling Michael Wilford Associates were selected after a design competition with funding secured to progress the project in 1996 and the Lowry

The Lowry Theatre and its iconic award-winning design. (© Tony Shertila)

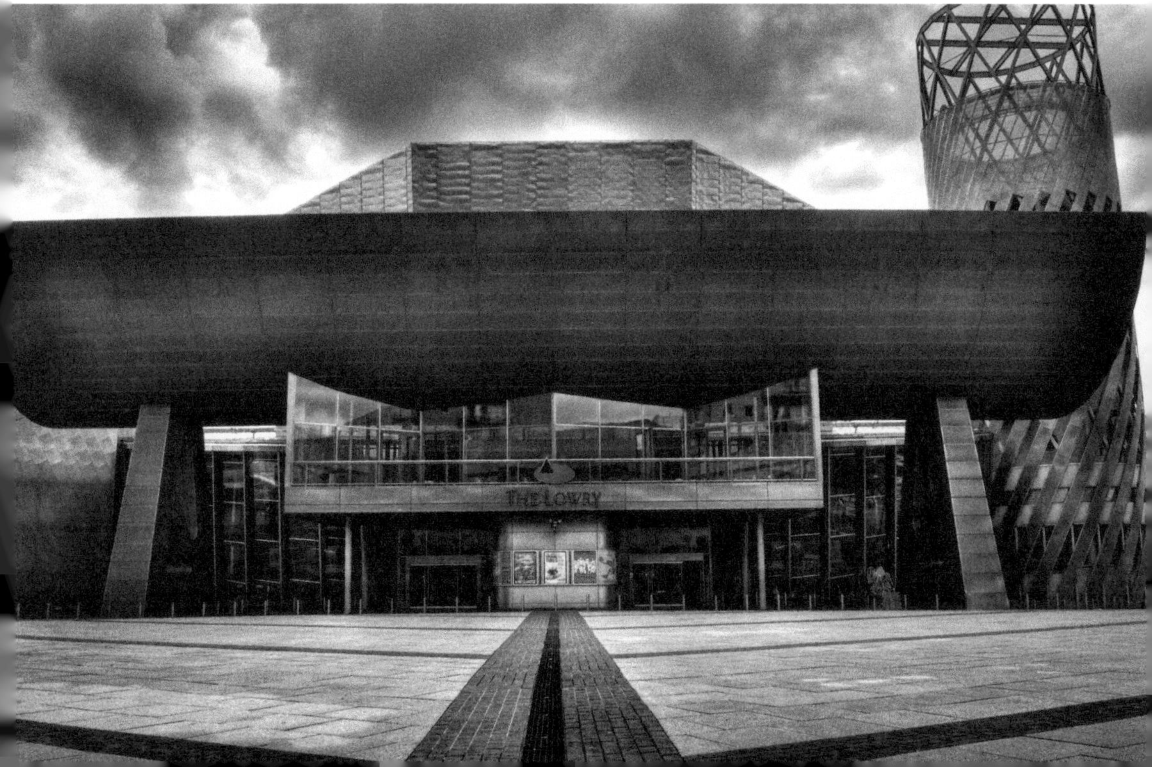

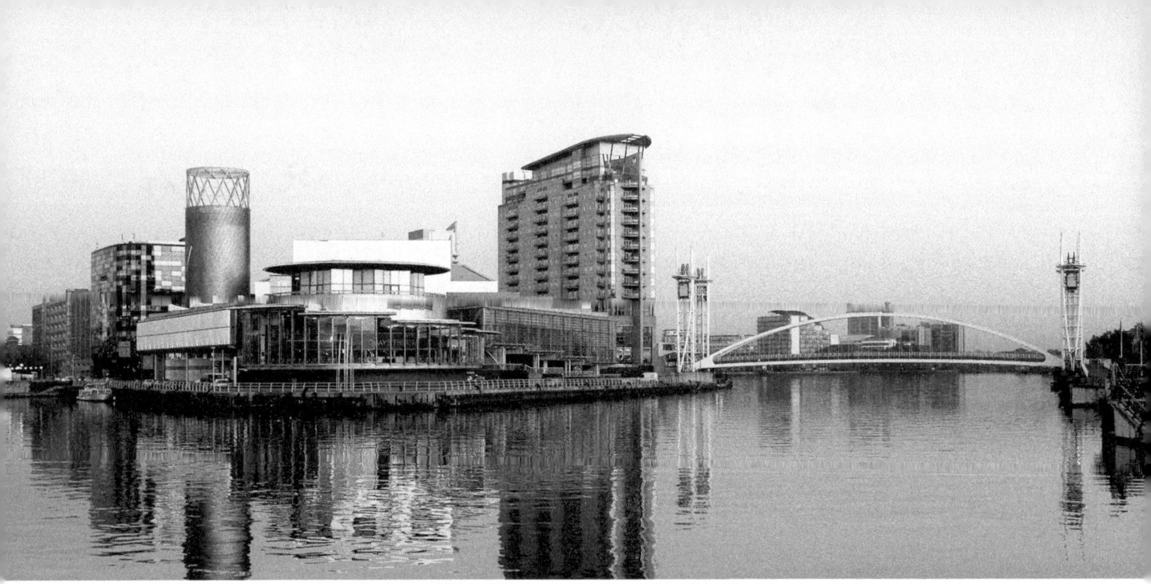

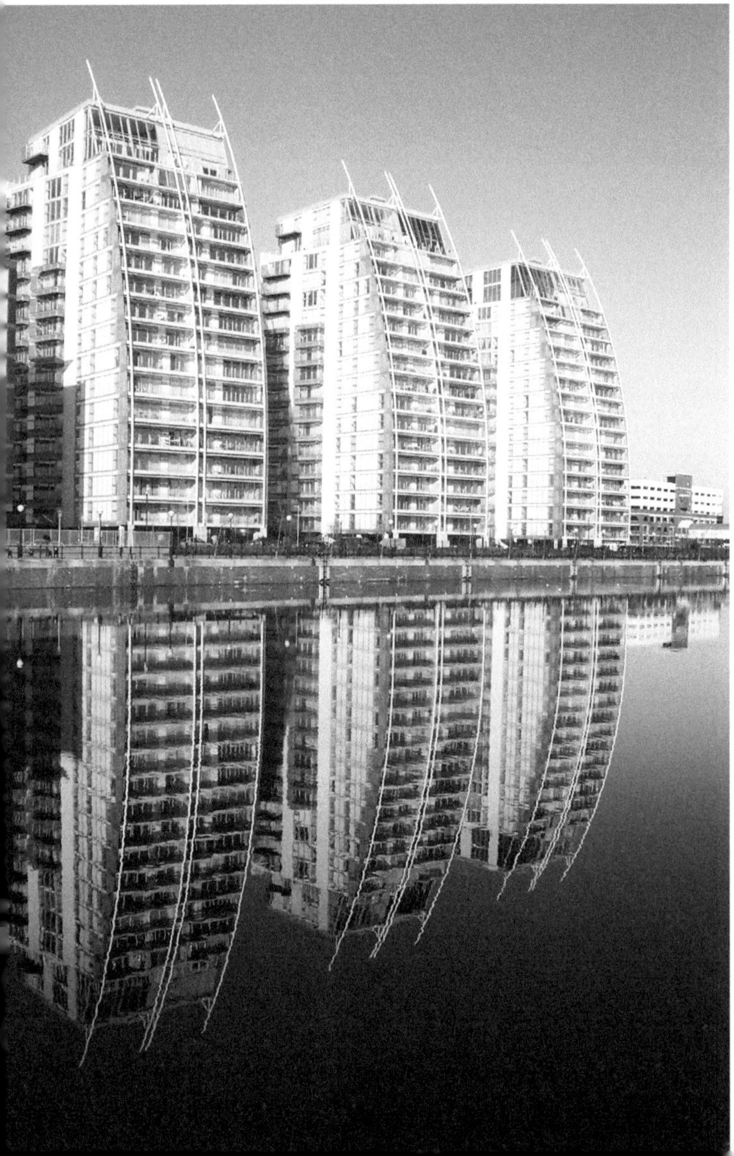

Above: The Lowry Theatre, Salford Quays.

Left: The NV Buildings were designed by Broadway Malyan and completed between 2004 and 2005. The development consists of three eighteen-storey residential towers, each 180 feet (55 m) in height. Costing £36 million, they stand in a line overlooking Huron Basin from the waterside of Pier 9 (North Wharf). Their curved frontages are designed to represent sails. At night, the buildings are illuminated by green lights atop curved poles, and green floodlights to either side. The Type 3 apartment in the NV Buildings won gold for 'Best Apartment' in 2004 What House? awards.

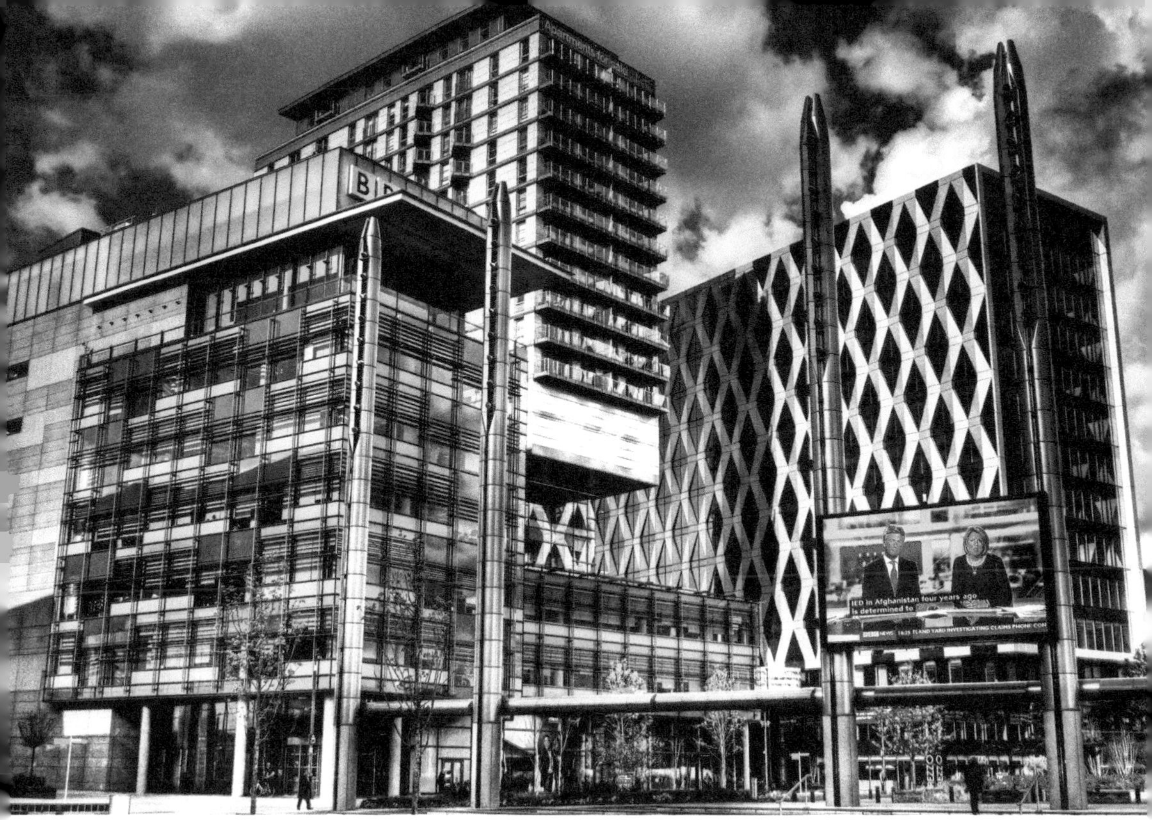

Above: MediaCity, Salford Quays. (© Gary Forrest)

Below: MediaCity BBC Studios. (© Steven Robertson)

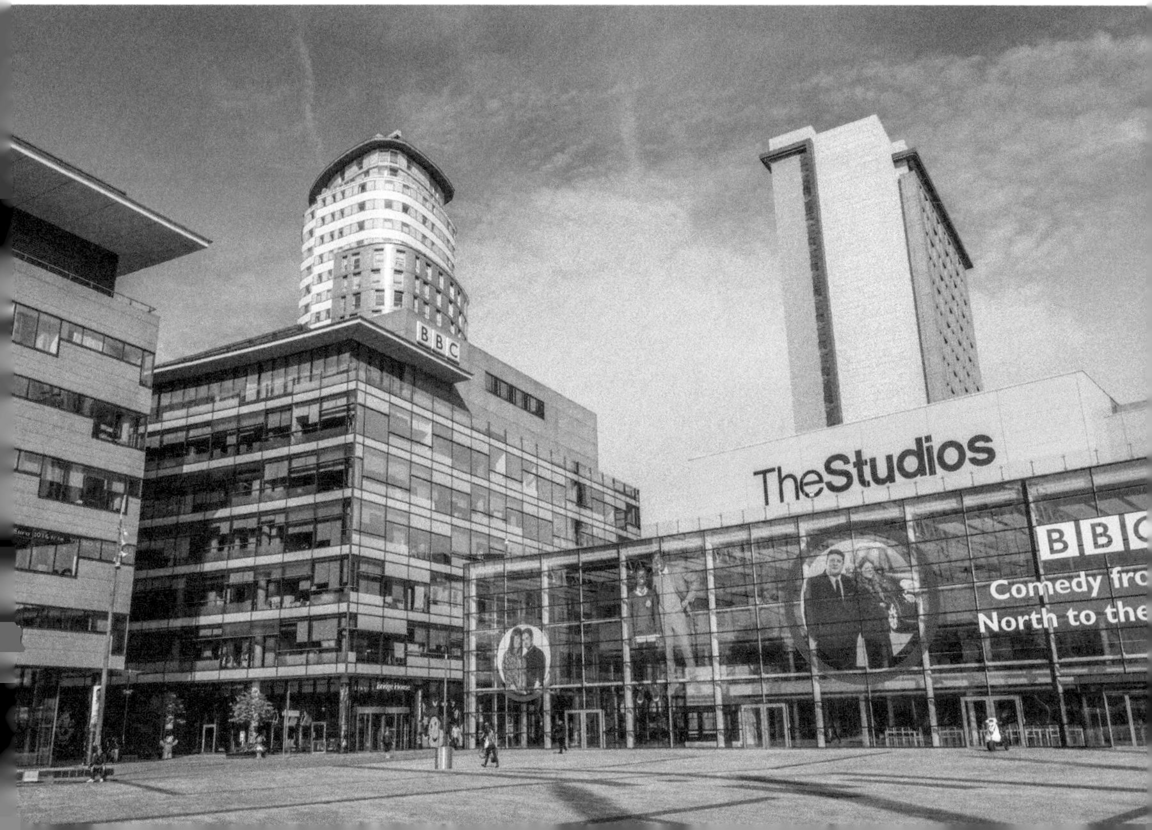

Trust became responsible for the overall project, which now included The Lowry Centre, the plaza, a footbridge, a retail outlet shopping mall and Digital World Centre. The project was completed in 1999 at a total cost of £106 million, with over £21 million from the National Lottery. By 2010 and 2011, it was Greater Manchester's most visited tourist attraction.

This important complex now includes 400 works in oil, pastel and watercolours from all periods of his career, having been collected by Salford Museum and Art Gallery from the 1930s.

MediaCityUK is a large 200-acre mixed-used development by the Manchester Ship Canal and was developed by Peel Media and is tenanted primarily by media organisations and the University of Salford. The land it now occupies was previously part of the port of Manchester and Manchester Docks.

The principal tenant at MediaCity is the BBC, who indicated their intentions to decentralise from London in 2004. Salford Quays was the preferred site and work began in 2007.They are now based in Quay House and several other buildings on the site. ITV Granada eventually moved here in 2013 too.

The architecture of the development has been criticised over the years, and in particular by the editor of *Building Design* magazine, Ellis Woodman, who described it as 'a crazed accumulation of development in which every aimlessly gesticulating building sports at least three different cladding treatments. The overriding sense is one of extreme anxiety on the part of the architect. Quite how the BBC has stooped this low is hard to fathom'. The development was awarded the Carbuncle Cup by *Building Design* for the worst new building in 2011.

Bibliography

Ching, F. A., *Visual Dictionary of Architecture* (New York: John Wiley and Sons, 1997)

City of Salford, Cultural Services Dept, *Salford: A City and Its Past* (1975)

Cooper, Glynis, *Salford – An Illustrated History* (Breedon Books Publishing, 2005)

Darlington, A. & N., *St. Paul's Church, Kersal Moor: Churchyard Trail* (2011)

De Figueiredo, Peter, *Victorian Manchester & Salford* (Ryburn Publishing, 1988)

Fleming, J., H. Honour & N. Pevsner, *Penguin Dictionary of Architecture and Landscape Architecture* (London: Penguin Books, 1991)

Flynn, Tony, *The History of Eccles Cinemas and Theatres* (Swinton: Neil Richardson, 1986)

Gray, Edward, *Salford: Britain in Old Photographs* (Alan Sutton Publishing Ltd, 1995)

Gray, Ted, *Greetings from Old Salford* (Printwise Publications Ltd, 1991)

Greenall, R. L., *The Making of Victorian Salford* (Carnegie Publishing Ltd, 2000)

Hartwell, C., M. Hyde & N. Pevsner, *Lancashire: Manchester and the South-East. The Buildings of England* (New Haven and London: Yale University Press, 2010)

Hayes, Cliff, *Salford: Yesterday and Today* (Memories Publication)

Hindle, Paul, *Salford Through Time* (Amberley Publishing, 2014)

Manchester Evening News, *Salford Past* (Heart Publications, 2007)

Pevsner, N., *South Lancashire: The Buildings of England* (London: Penguin Books, 1993)

Acknowledgements

Carole O'Reilly would like to thank Paul, her co-author, for his enthusiasm for all things architectural and Salford Local History Library for being a great repository of local information.

Paul Rabbitts would like to thank his co-author Carole for initiating this book, which has opened his eyes to the wonderful architecture, buildings and history of Salford. As ever, with writing such a book, an appreciation of such fine existing buildings is tinged with sadness for all those that have been lost, not only in Salford, but across the country.

The Manchester & Salford Savings Bank – one of many buildings that could have been included in *Salford in 50 Buildings*, but a wonderful legacy of architecture and design. (© Tony Reeves)

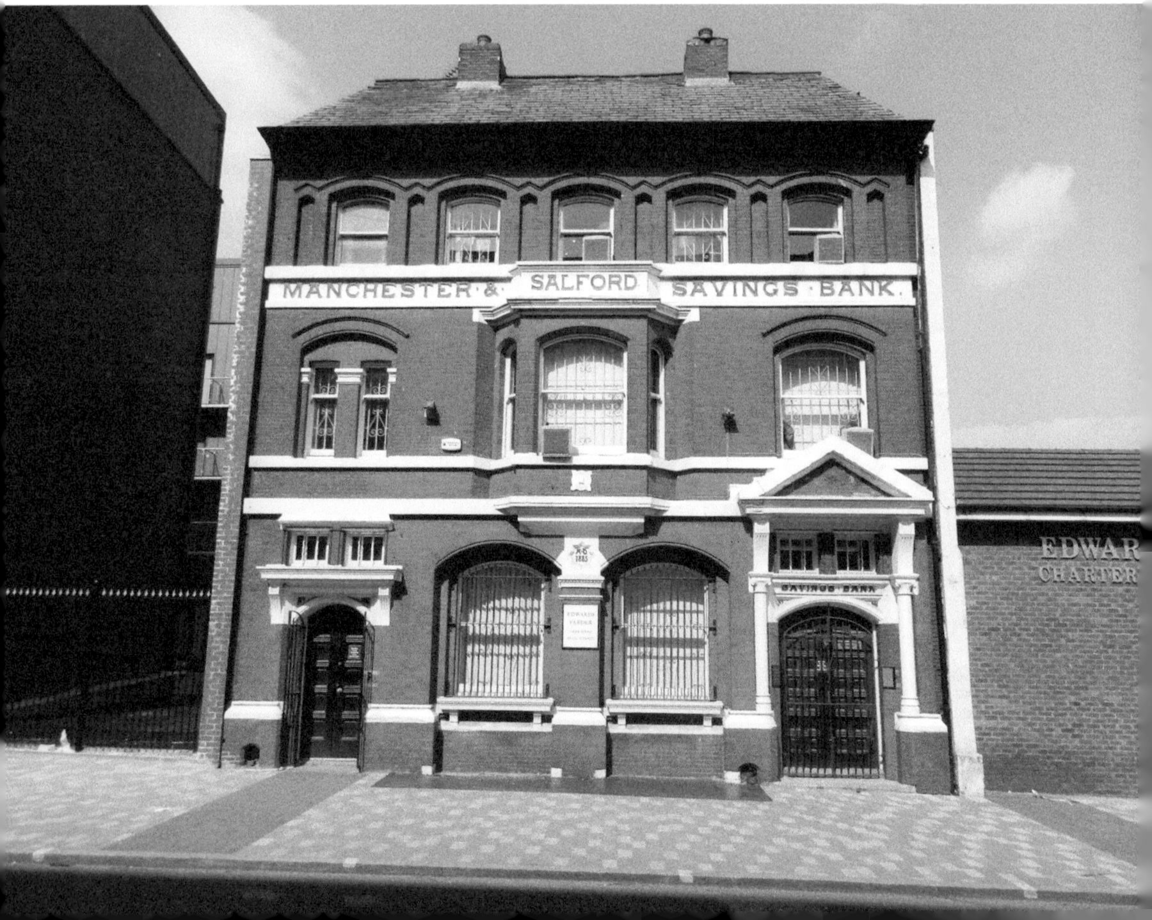

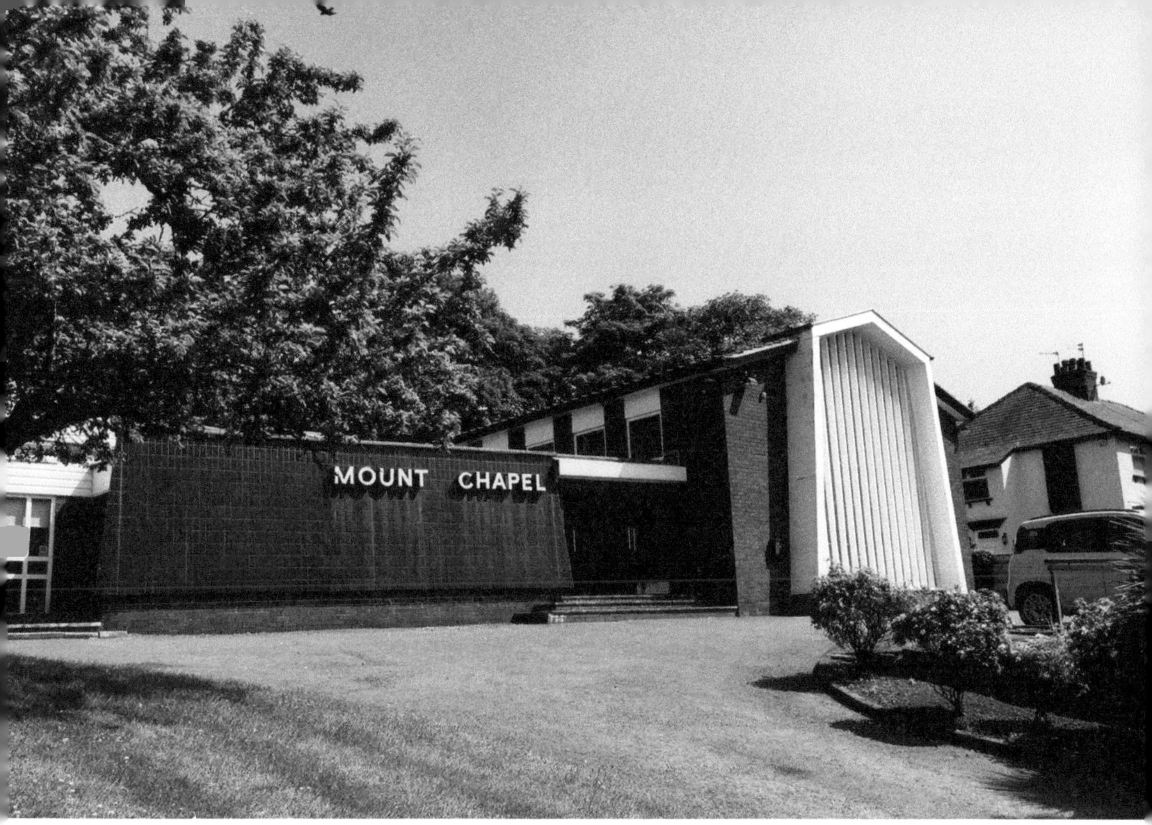

Mount Chapel, Eccles Road, another building that could have been included, showcasing the diversity of architecture in Salford. (© Carole O'Reilly)

About the Authors

Dr Carole O' Reilly is Senior Lecturer in Media and Cultural Studies at the University of Salford. She obtained her MA in Art and Architectural History from the University of Leeds and was awarded a PhD in History from Manchester Metropolitan University. Her research focuses on urban heritage and history. She has published in journals such as *Landscape History* and *Urban History* and her first book, *The Greening of the City: Urban Parks and Public Leisure 1840–1939*, was published in 2019.

Paul Rabbitts is currently Head of Parks for Watford Borough Council but is a prolific author on local history, ranging from public parks to the Victorian bandstand. He has co-authored *Manchester in 50 Buildings* and *Watford in 50 Buildings*, and is the sole author for the following books in the 50 Buildings series: Leighton Buzzard, Luton, and Windsor and Eton. He is a Fellow of the Royal Society of Arts as well as a Fellow of the Landscape Institute.